THE MECCA UPRISING

THE MECCA UPRISING

An Insider's Account of Salafism and Insurrection in Saudi Arabia

Nasir al-Huzaimi
Edited and translated by David Commins

I.B.TAURIS
LONDON · NEW YORK · OXFORD · NEW DELHI · SYDNEY

I.B. TAURIS
Bloomsbury Publishing Plc
50 Bedford Square, London, WC1B 3DP, UK
1385 Broadway, New York, NY 10018, USA

BLOOMSBURY, I.B. TAURIS and the I.B. Tauris logo are trademarks of
Bloomsbury Publishing Plc

First published in Great Britain 2021

Copyright © Arab Network for Research and Publishing, 2021
English translation © David Commins 2021

Originally published in Arabic as *Ayyam ma'a Juhaiman* by the Arab Network
for Research and Publishing

David Commins has asserted his right under the Copyright, Designs and
Patents Act, 1988, to be identified as Translator of this work.

For legal purposes the Acknowledgments on p. vi constitute an extension
of this copyright page.

Cover design: ianrossdesigner.com
Cover image © API/Gamma-Rapho/Getty Images

All rights reserved. No part of this publication may be reproduced or
transmitted in any form or by any means, electronic or mechanical,
including photocopying, recording, or any information storage or retrieval
system, without prior permission in writing from the publishers.

Bloomsbury Publishing Plc does not have any control over, or responsibility for, any
third-party websites referred to or in this book. All internet addresses given in this
book were correct at the time of going to press. The author and publisher regret any
inconvenience caused if addresses have changed or sites have ceased to exist, but can
accept no responsibility for any such changes.

A catalogue record for this book is available from the British Library.

A catalog record for this book is available from the Library of Congress.

ISBN: HB: 978-0-7556-0010-6
PB: 978-0-7556-0011-3
ePDF: 978-0-7556-0214-8
eBook: 978-0-7556-0215-5

Typeset by Newgen KnowledgeWorks Pvt. Ltd., Chennai, India
Printed and bound in Great Britain

To find out more about our authors and books visit www.bloomsbury.com
and sign up for our newsletters.

CONTENTS

Acknowledgments	vi
Notes on the Arabic and English Editions	vii
INTRODUCTION TO THE ENGLISH EDITION	1
THE MEMOIR	65
Memories of Childhood	65
My First Acquaintance with Islamic Movements	71
Islamic Movements in Riyadh	72
The Salafis in Mecca	75
Historical Roots of the Salafi Group	82
In Medina	84
Back to Riyadh	92
The Invasion of the Grand Mosque	100
Juhaiman's Ideas	104
Appendix I The Dreaming Nation: The Role of the Dream in Sanctifying Salafi Islamic Discourse, by Nasir al-Huzaimi	119
Appendix II The Grand Mosque Sermon	125
Appendix III "Juhaiman's Sin:" Nasir al-Huzaimi: This Is My Story with the Expected Mahdi	135
Appendix IV Interview with Nasir al-Huzaimi, by Badr al-Rashid	143
Notes	153
Further Reading and Works Cited	179
Glossary	189
Index	191

ACKNOWLEDGMENTS

It is a pleasure to acknowledge the assistance I have received from friends and colleagues in the course of developing and completing this work. The idea of translating Nasir al-Huzaimi's memoir came about during a visit to Riyadh in January 2011, when my good friend from graduate school days, Professor Abdulrahman al-Shamlan, introduced me to Nasir. His memoir offering unique eyewitness testimony of the men behind the 1979 Mecca uprising had just come out and he was interested in having it translated into English. The idea lay dormant until I received a sabbatical leave from Dickinson College in 2015. I very much appreciate Provost Neil Weissman and the Dickinson Faculty Personnel Committee for approving the proposal to dedicate the sabbatical leave to completing a draft translation.

At Dickinson College, I owe special thanks to Magda Siekert for lending her Arabic expertise to untangling some knotty passages; I could always count on Madeline Brown to deliver superb administrative support; Gregory Kaliss and Evan Young provided valuable feedback on annotations; and Steve Weinberger offered suggestions for improving the introduction.

The path to publishing the translation with I.B. Tauris/Bloomsbury began with Joanna Godfrey's insight that an introduction setting the memoir in historical context would make it more legible to an English-language readership. The next step was obtaining translation rights from the Arab Network for Research and Publishing in Beirut. I am grateful to Lama Zein for setting that in motion. Three anonymous reviewers offered thorough and perceptive criticisms of the translation that did much to improve it. At I.B. Tauris/Bloomsbury, Sophie Rudland, Olivia Dellow, and Yasmin Garcha gave the manuscript their careful, professional attention and deftly steered it through production.

I owe Professor Shamlan more than I can express for reviewing and editing multiple drafts. The exchange of working drafts would have taken much longer were it not for Najat Bukhari expediting matters for a couple of old friends who never got the hang of the latest technology. From beginning to end, my wife Susan Lindt has been a steady sounding board and loving companion. Finally, I am most grateful that Nasir entrusted me with the translation. I hope that I have done it justice. Responsibility for shortcomings and mistakes in the translation, annotations, and introduction falls on me.

NOTES ON THE ARABIC AND ENGLISH EDITIONS

The Arabic edition of Nasir al-Huzaimi's memoir, *Days with Juhaiman*, has five parts: (1) The Memoir; (2) Appendix I: The Dreaming Nation: The Role of the Dream in Sanctifying Salafi Islamic Discourse, by Nasir al-Huzaimi; (3) Appendix II: The Grand Mosque Sermon, Published in *al-Riyadh* Newspaper, January 17, 1980; (4) Appendix III: "Juhaiman's Sin:" Nasir al-Huzaimi: This Is My Story with the Expected Mahdi, Published in the Electronic Edition of *al-Majallah* Magazine, November 21, 2009; and (5) Appendix IV: Interview with Nasir al-Huzaimi, by Badr al-Rashid. The English edition contains an additional section about the author's childhood in Iraq.

Part 1 of the Arabic edition, The Memoir, is divided into five sections: (1) Beginnings; (2) In Mecca; (3) In Medina; (4) Return to Riyadh; (5) Millenarian Rule in Juhaiman's Thought.

For the English edition, I have divided the Memoir into nine sections and added subsections to guide the reader.

The Arabic edition mentions dozens of classical authors and texts that are moved to endnotes in the English edition. The Arabic edition also includes numerous footnotes indicated as "Footnote in al-Huzaimi."

Text in parentheses is part of the Arabic edition. Text in brackets is the translator's interpolation.

The English edition rearranges some of the text from pages 16 through 21 in the Arabic edition for the sake of narrative continuity.

INTRODUCTION TO THE ENGLISH EDITION

What Was the Mecca Uprising?

On the morning of November 20, 1979, a band of around three hundred armed men[1] from an obscure religious movement called the Salafi Group[2] stunned the world by seizing the Grand Mosque in Mecca, the spiritual axis of Islam. In the Muslim lunar calendar, it was an auspicious date for their action: the first day of a new century. The group's charismatic leader, Juhaiman al-Utaibi, had been preaching that recent events in Saudi Arabia—the rise of corrupt rulers and the spread of foreign influence—augured the coming of the Muslim savior, called the Mahdi. In the past year, group members had been telling one another about having dreams where they saw the Mahdi in the form of a fellow member. Firmly believing that the Mahdi was among their number, they stormed the Grand Mosque, expecting to partake in apocalyptic events foretold in tales from the Prophet. The millenarians fended off Saudi security forces for two weeks before surrendering. A month later, the Saudi government carried out public beheadings of sixty-three captured insurgents, including Juhaiman.

The Mecca uprising is considered a turning point in Saudi Arabia's contemporary history. In the 1960s and 1970s, the kingdom was starting to open up to Western influences, then abruptly reversed course in response to the events of November 1979.[3] The rulers felt the uprising meant they had to reaffirm their commitment to upholding Islam, so they took steps to curtail Western influence, imposing stricter censorship on liberal writers, enforcing puritanical restrictions on women's dress, and cracking down on interactions between unrelated men and women. They also increased funding for religious institutions and gave free rein to conservative voices in the media. At the same time the government promoted an ultraconservative religious climate inside the country it spread its homegrown puritanical doctrine to Muslim societies and Muslim communities in Western countries.

Nasir al-Huzaimi's Memoir

Many details about the Mecca uprising and its background remained unknown to the outside world until the early 2000s, when former members of the Salafi

Group began publishing accounts of their experiences and giving interviews to Western researchers, making it possible to trace the religious ideas that inspired the uprising and the Salafi Group's path to insurrection. The author of this memoir, Nasir al-Huzaimi, was one of the most helpful informants for the new studies.[4]

Huzaimi grew up in southern Iraq and moved to Saudi Arabia where he joined the Salafi Group in 1976. For two years, he spent much of his time in Juhaiman's company before drifting away from the group in the wake of a government crackdown. He did not participate in the uprising, but he was arrested in a government sweep of Salafi Group members and spent six years in prison. In 2011, he published his memoir, *Days with Juhaiman*, offering the most detailed picture we have of the Salafi Group and Juhaiman.

Huzaimi takes the reader deep into the puritanical subculture that incubated the uprising. Salafi Group members were so preoccupied with exact imitation of the Prophet that they debated whether they could peddle wristwatches with a logo in the shape of a cross. The world of religious activism comes into focus as well, revealing competition and cooperation between followers of various transnational Islamic movements. And most notably, the forceful, magnetic personality of Juhaiman emerges as the catalyst that set his faction on the path to seizing the Grand Mosque as part of a divine plan to purge the world of injustice and tyranny.

Historical and Cultural Contexts

Huzaimi's memoir assumes an audience familiar with Islamic beliefs and practices, the Muslim heritage of religious learning, the political and religious history of Saudi Arabia, and Islamic movements of the 1970s. The purpose of the introduction is to provide background on these topics for the general Western reader and to indicate how the Salafi Group, Juhaiman, and the Mecca uprising fit into patterns in the history of Muslim societies and Saudi Arabia.

Major Events of 1979

The Mecca uprising erupted and unfolded against a backdrop of regional crisis: the Iranian Revolution and the seizing of American hostages in Tehran; a Shiite rebellion in the eastern region of Saudi Arabia; anti-American riots across the Muslim world; and the Soviet Union's invasion of Afghanistan. From November 4 to December 24, 1979, one shock after another jolted the region.

> November 4: Protestors stormed the US embassy in Tehran and captured sixty-six Americans, setting off the "hostage crisis" that crippled the presidency of Jimmy Carter and ruptured diplomatic relations between Iran and the United States.
> November 20: Juhaiman led the seizure of the Grand Mosque in Mecca.

November 26–30: Five days of protests by Shiite demonstrators in Saudi Arabia's oil-rich Eastern Province deepened the atmosphere of crisis in the country.
December 24: Soviet forces invaded Afghanistan to prop up a faltering Marxist regime, aggravating the insecure mood in Saudi Arabia and alarming the United States.

The Iranian Revolution

The Iranian Revolution of 1978–9 transformed the country from a secular, pro-Western monarchy into a religious, anti-Western republic.[5] Iran's embrace of Western culture dated to the rule of Reza Shah (r. 1925–1941). When he came to power, the country was weak, divided, and dominated by foreign powers. Reza Shah built up the armed forces, expanded the reach of the national government, and initiated industrialization of the economy. He believed that for Iran to join the ranks of strong powers, it was necessary to abandon its Islamic past. Consequently, he took steps to diminish the influence of clerics and to promote Western habits and manners, most notably in banning the veil.

Reza Shah was forced to abdicate in August 1941 by invading British and Soviet forces. London and Moscow were allies in the war against Nazi Germany and were determined to turn Iran into a corridor for Britain to transport supplies to the Soviet Union. The foreign occupiers replaced Reza Shah with his young son, Muhammad Reza Shah, who would occupy the throne until the revolution. The new shah relaxed the ban on the veil but continued to promote secular, Western culture at the expense of religion. In foreign relations, he abandoned his father's neutrality and aligned with the United States in the Cold War. Iran became a major recipient of US economic and military assistance. When oil prices surged in the mid-1970s, the shah spent billions of dollars on American weapons to consolidate Iran's place as a major regional power.

The pivotal event in Iran's turn to the West was the oil nationalization crisis of 1951 to 1953. The crisis began when Prime Minister Muhammad Musaddeq signed a parliamentary bill to nationalize the British-owned Anglo-Iranian Oil Company. The British government retaliated with an embargo on Iranian oil and solicited American assistance to overthrow the prime minister. Under President Dwight Eisenhower, the CIA engineered a military coup d'état against Musaddeq in August 1953. In the next eight years, the United States gave Iran $1 billion in economic and military assistance and trained Iran's intelligence and security agency, the SAVAK, which became the instrument for the shah's harsh repression of dissent.

By the 1970s, many Iranians blamed the United States for propping up a brutal, corrupt government that squandered oil wealth on military purchases rather than spreading the national treasure more fairly. Furthermore, a huge culture gap yawned between a Westernized elite and pious Iranians. In December 1977, Muhammad Reza Shah invited US President Jimmy Carter to Iran. At a state dinner, Carter applauded the shah's leadership for making Iran "an island of stability in one of the more troubled areas of the world."[6] Days after Carter's visit, a protest against the government for slandering an exiled religious dissident, Ayatollah Ruhollah

Khomeini, was violently crushed. There had been episodic protests in the early 1960s, but the January 1978 demonstration snowballed and reached a crescendo in massive protests in December 1978–January 1979. The shah fled the country on January 16. Two weeks later, Ayatollah Khomeini returned from a fourteen-year exile. He commanded an extensive network of revolutionary clerics ready to wage a merciless struggle against liberal, socialist, and radical political organizations contending to lead the new Iran.

The Egyptian-Israeli Peace Treaty

While Iranian revolutionaries carried out bloody purges of monarchists in early 1979, the United States was seeking to stabilize the Arab-Israeli conflict, shepherding the final stages of peace talks between Egypt and Israel.[7] On March 26, they signed a peace treaty, ending thirty years of belligerency. The treaty was the outcome of Egyptian President Anwar al-Sadat's dramatic offer to visit Israel without preconditions in November 1977. When bilateral negotiations got bogged down, President Jimmy Carter invited Sadat and Israeli Prime Minister Menachem Begin to the United States to keep alive hopes for a peace treaty. Carter's mediation resulted in the Camp David Accords of September 1978.

According to the Camp David Accords, an Egyptian-Israeli agreement was to be negotiated at the same time the parties were to create a framework for autonomy for Palestinians who had been under Israeli military occupation in the West Bank and Gaza since the Arab-Israeli war of June 1967. Prime Minister Begin, however, was committed to keeping the Palestinian territories and he was able to press Sadat to sign a peace treaty and postpone Palestinian autonomy. The peace treaty crowned Sadat's diplomatic endeavor to bring Egypt into the American orbit, which resulted in Washington providing billions of dollars in economic and military assistance. For Israel, the treaty removed the largest Arab military power from the ranks of its foes. Egypt, however, paid a price for failing to deliver autonomy to the Palestinians: all but two Arab governments severed diplomatic relations with Cairo. For the United States, the peace treaty represented a breakthrough after decades of diplomacy and a positive achievement to balance the fall of its ally in Iran. The peace treaty was reviled by Islamic groups in Egypt and the rest of the Arab world. Indeed, two years later, Egyptian religious militants opposed to peace with Israel assassinated Sadat.[8]

American Hostages in Iran

One of the remarkable features of the Iranian Revolution is that it was achieved through mass nonviolent civilian protest. The aftermath, however, was extremely violent, in no small part because of Ayatollah Khomeini's vindictive campaign against high-ranking royal officials and ordinary Iranians "guilty" of enjoying a "corrupt" Western lifestyle. Revolutionary propaganda portrayed the United States as a brutal imperialist power, "the great Satan" that dominated global politics through puppet rulers, such as the former shah, and that oppressed the weak and the poor, such as the Iranian masses.

At first, the United States maintained diplomatic relations with the Islamic Republic, if only to keep Iran out of the Soviet sphere of influence. Inside the revolutionary government, how to deal with Washington became a point of intense disagreement. Pragmatists headed by the prime minister wished to preserve normal relations with the United States. Radicals feared the United States would replay the 1953 script of CIA intervention to remove the revolutionary government and restore monarchy. It was in order to preempt a potential American counterrevolution that militant students stormed the US embassy on November 4, 1979, and seized hostages. When Iranians cited the 1953 CIA coup as the reason for taking hostages, few Americans knew what they were talking about, failing to recognize that it was an unforgettable event in Iranian historical memory. The hostage-taking was a success for the radicals: the pragmatic prime minister resigned, diplomatic relations with Washington were severed, and the anti-Western mood grew stronger during the fourteen-month standoff with the United States over the hostages. At the regional level, the hostage crisis intensified the mood of crisis and fear of the Iranian Revolution's destabilizing effects.

Seizure of the Grand Mosque

Sixteen days after the American embassy fell in Tehran, Juhaiman's band seized control of the Grand Mosque.[9] The incident began at 5:00 a.m. The prayer leader was preparing to pronounce the dawn prayer on the first day of the fifteenth century in the Muslim calendar. Juhaiman shoved him out of the way to announce the arrival of the Mahdi, "the rightly-guided one" foretold in prophecies, who would lead the forces of good against the forces of evil in an apocalyptical war to restore justice and wipe out tyranny. A rebel preacher then began a sermon calling on the thousands of worshippers to pledge allegiance to the Mahdi. In the meantime, the militants chained shut all entrances to the mosque and took up defensive positions in the upper stories and minarets. The militants took some worshippers hostage and allowed the rest to escape through windows overlooking the streets surrounding the mosque.

The attack came as a total surprise to the Saudi authorities. For several weeks, Juhaiman's followers had eluded detection as they stockpiled arms, ammunition, and food supplies in the basement storerooms of the Grand Mosque. Key members of the ruling family were out of the country. Some were attending an Arab summit in Tunisia focused on formulating a response to the Egyptian-Israeli peace treaty. Others were on holiday. The first hasty counterattack by Saudi security forces on November 22 was a complete failure. Militant riflemen showered gunfire on troops crossing the broad pavement surrounding the mosque, forcing them to retreat.

Regional Reverberations

In the first days of the uprising, there was tremendous confusion over the identity of the attackers. Saudi and American officials thought the Iranians might be responsible; Ayatollah Khomeini hinted that the United States was to blame. Rumors of an American role spread throughout the Muslim world. On November

21, Pakistani demonstrators attacked and set fire to the US embassy in Islamabad, resulting in the deaths of two American guards and two Pakistani employees. Anti-American disturbances flared in Libya, Turkey, India, and Bangladesh as well.[10]

Second Assault by Security Forces

Security forces mounted a second, better planned assault on November 24 and 25. Troops shielded by armored vehicles were able to pierce the blocked gates and drive the militants into the mosque's extensive warren of underground chambers. At that point, the authorities secured the area around the mosque and the courtyard, but how they would uproot the militants hiding in the dark underground cells remained a puzzle.

Shiite Uprising

The atmosphere of crisis deepened when Saudi Arabia's Shiite minority rose up against the government.[11] For decades, Shiites had endured religious and economic discrimination. Saudi schools taught that Shiites followed heretical teachings. During the oil boom years, the government neglected their districts while showering nearby cities with expensive development projects. In the 1960s and 1970s, clandestine dissident groups formed through contacts with Shiite networks that spanned the Gulf region. Iran's revolutionary government stirred up antigovernment sentiment among Shiites suffering under Sunni rule throughout the Gulf region and a feeling of solidarity with Iran spread among dissidents.

On November 26, several thousand Shiites in the Eastern Province defied a ban on public observance by marching in a religious procession to celebrate Ashura, a Shiite holy day that commemorates the martyrdom of the Prophet's grandson Husain. Already shaken by the ongoing siege in Mecca, the authorities used force to suppress a march two days later, when protestors chanted antigovernment slogans and support for the Iranian Revolution. Around thirty protestors were killed in confrontations with security forces in the next few days.

The Final Assault in the Grand Mosque

To solve the problem of how to end the uprising, the Saudis decided to seek the assistance of French special forces. Three advisers arrived in Saudi Arabia on November 29 to plan the final assault.[12] They thought it would be possible to disable the militants by injecting a potent type of tear gas into the basement chambers. The tactic worked well enough to allow Saudi forces to make an initial push past the first line of defense, but the gas did not have as severe an effect as anticipated. Nevertheless, attacking troops succeeded in finally cornering the remaining militants, including Juhaiman, who surrendered on December 4. According to official Saudi sources, the fighting took the lives of 127 government troops, 117 militants, and 26 hostages.[13]

The Soviet Invasion of Afghanistan

Not long after Saudi authorities restored stability in Mecca and the Eastern Province (a second wave of protest would erupt in 1980), the region got another shock. On December 24, the Soviet Union sent military forces into Afghanistan in order to consolidate the position of the Marxist government that had come to power the year before. While Moscow viewed the intervention as a way to rescue the Marxist government in Kabul, Washington saw it as a provocation that demanded a response. The United States, Saudi Arabia, and Pakistan formed a common strategy to support the anti-communist Afghan insurgency. The three governments cooperated to fund and arm Afghan resistance in order to destabilize the Marxist government and sap Soviet resources.[14]

For the Saudi government, the Afghan cause was a convenient way to demonstrate solidarity with fellow Muslims and to distract religious activists from domestic issues. American, Saudi, and Pakistani efforts converged in Peshawar, Pakistan's major city along the western border with Afghanistan. Peshawar became the headquarters for pan-Islamic relief organizations providing humanitarian assistance to Afghan refugees. It also became the staging ground for Muslim volunteers from the Middle East, Central Asia, and Pakistan to wage jihad against Soviet forces in Afghanistan. Members of Islamic movements exchanged ideas about the plight of Muslims in places other than Afghanistan, such as Palestine and Kashmir. Among the volunteers was a young Saudi named Osama bin Laden. It was in Peshawar that he established al-Qaeda to coordinate resources and personnel for the Afghan struggle, nearly a decade before he rose the banner of "global jihad" against the United States and its allies.

After the Soviet withdrawal in 1989, Afghan militias waged a bloody struggle for power. In 1996, Pakistan threw its support behind a newly formed group that became known as the Taliban. The Taliban were able to conquer most of the country. It then took the fateful decision to allow Osama bin Laden, and al-Qaeda, to settle in Afghanistan, where they planned the September 2001 attack on the United States. In response to the attacks, the United States and its allies invaded Afghanistan to overthrow the Taliban and to destroy al-Qaeda. Both groups, however, survived the invasion by finding refuge in Pakistan. The Soviet invasion of Afghanistan, then, had a part in the genesis of al-Qaeda and the Taliban, thanks in part to the US–Saudi–Pakistani alliance against the Soviet-backed Afghan government.

Executions

On January 9, 1980, the Saudi government carried out death sentences against sixty-three men for their part in the Mecca uprising. The prisoners were dispatched in small groups to eight different cities where the executions took place in public squares. In Mecca, Juhaiman was the first to be beheaded. Most of the condemned were Saudis, but they also included men from Egypt, Kuwait, Yemen, Iraq, and Sudan.

Islamic Scriptures

The Prophet Muhammad

Muhammad is the prophet of Islam. In Muslim belief, he did not have divine qualities—divinity resides in God alone—yet he is considered the model for Muslims to follow.[15] He lived in the western region of Arabia called Hijaz—born in Mecca around 570 and died in Medina in 632. According to Muslim tradition, he began receiving divine revelations when he was around 40 years old. For the first twelve years of his prophecy, he preached to fellow Meccans and visitors to the town, which contained a sanctuary called the *Kaabah* that held idols belonging to the region's clans and tribes. Some Meccans became believers in his message, but the town's leaders rejected it and persecuted his followers. Muhammad negotiated a pact with leaders of a town some 280 miles away that made it possible for him and his growing community of believers to resettle there. The town was called Yathrib, but over time, it became known as Medina.[16]

The emigration to Medina is called the *hijrah*. The believers formed an autonomous community with Muhammad as its leader. In Medina, he continued to receive and recite revelations as he had in Mecca, but now he possessed the authority to determine rules regulating relationships among the believers and to make crucial decisions on matters of diplomacy and war between the believers and others. The emigration to Medina, then, was the critical turning point in the career of the Prophet. When a Muslim calendar was later established, Year One was the year of the hijrah, hence the calendar is known as *hijri*. Conflict with the leaders of Mecca did not end. Rather, it entered a more intense phase of fighting that ended with Mecca's surrender in 630. Quranic revelations refer to the fighting as "striving in the way of God," in Arabic, *jihad fi sabil Allah*.[17]

Muhammad did not return to live in Mecca after its submission. Nevertheless, it is the primary holy city for Muslims because the Kaabah shrine is located there and because Muslims have a religious duty to perform a pilgrimage to Mecca once in their lifetime. Medina is the second holy city. It is the site of the first mosque, established by Muhammad, and his grave is located there. Visiting Medina is not a religious duty, but many Muslims go there to honor the Prophet, sometimes after completing the pilgrimage to Mecca.

The Quran

The word *qur'an* means recitation. One of the Quran's earliest verses mentions a mysterious figure who appeared to Muhammad on the horizon and ordered him to recite. Several passages use the term *qur'an* to refer to the set of revelations Muhammad was receiving. For example,

> These are the verses of revelation, of a recitation (*qur'an*) that makes things clear.[18]

By the Book that makes things clear, We (God) have made it a recitation (*qur'an*) in Arabic that you may be able to understand.[19]

According to Muslim belief, the Quran is God's word revealed to Muhammad; it is not Muhammad's invention. It is one of a series of revelations that God has sent down to a series of prophets: Abraham, Noah, Moses, Jesus, and others.

The Quran is divided into 114 chapters called *surahs*, and each chapter consists of verses. Some chapters are very brief, with five or six verses. Some chapters have more than two hundred verses. The Quran's contents include stories about earlier prophets, descriptions of events that occurred during Muhammad's prophecy, theological arguments with unbelievers of different sorts—polytheists, Christians, and Jews—descriptions of God, Judgment Day, the afterlife, guidance for worship and everyday life, and other topics.

Sunnah: The Prophetic Tradition

Because the Quran is the word of God, it is the most authoritative source for what Muslims are to believe and how they are to live, both as individuals and as a community. It is therefore the fundamental source for Islamic law even though it does not provide a systematic law code. It also does not provide a blueprint for the kind of political system Muslims should establish.

The Quran exhorts the believers to obey and follow the Prophet as a model for living according to God's will. The idea that the Prophet is a perfect model of correct belief and practice is the basis for making the Sunnah, the Prophetic Tradition, the second source for religion after the Quran. During the Prophet's lifetime, Muslims could turn to him to tell them the exact meaning of verses in the Quran and how to live according to them. They could also turn to him as a source of rules for issues not addressed in the Quran.

Hadiths[20]

Whereas Muslims collected the verses of the Quran and put them in a specific order to create a uniform text, they did not establish a standard collection of reports comprising the Prophetic Tradition. These reports about the Prophet's words and actions are called *hadiths*. In Huzaimi's memoir, hadiths play a significant role in two ways. First, Salafi Group members were preoccupied with molding their lives in accordance with rules contained in hadiths. Second, the Salafi Group challenged Saudi religious authorities because its members followed an independent approach to using hadiths to define correct rules for worship.

A hadith has two parts. One part is a text that reports the Prophet's words or actions. Another part is a chain of transmitters, that is, a list of people who heard and passed on the text. A hadith can be very short, consisting of a sentence; or a hadith can be long, consisting of two or three paragraphs. The essential feature is its source—the Prophet.[21]

Here is an example of a chain of transmitters and a short hadith:

Umayya b. Safwan heard his grandfather Abd Allah b. Safwan say: Hafsa informed me that she heard the Prophet say:
"Verily, an army will be heading for this House to raid it, until when they are in a desert of the earth, the one in the middle of them will be swallowed up, and the first of them will call to the last. Then they will be swallowed up, and no one will be left but the fugitive who will give information about them."
A man said: "I witness unto you that you have not lied about Hafsa, and I witness unto Hafsa that she has not lied about the Prophet."[22]

If the Quran tells believers they are to obey and follow the Prophet and if believers are determined to comply, then why should there be any debate over hadiths? The answer is that during the Prophet's lifetime, there was no attempt to record all of his words and actions. Western scholars believe that hadiths did not possess religious authority until about a century after the Prophet. After all, he was present and accessible to believers wishing to follow his example. When he died, the men and women who knew him became sources for reports about him. The men and women who knew him are called the Companions.

Twenty-five years after the Prophet's death, the Arabs had conquered Egypt, Syria, Iraq, and Iran. Many Companions settled in these lands and became authorities on reports about the Prophet for younger believers (known as Successors) and converts. They would memorize hadiths and then pass them down to the next generation. The chain of transmission is the list of believers who memorized and passed on the hadiths. There was no central religious authority to verify the hadiths. In fact, hadiths increased in number, in part because the supporters of different theological positions invented hadiths to reinforce their doctrines and in part because the supporters of different political factions invented hadiths to bolster their legitimacy.

Western scholars believe that in the late 700s and early 800s, Muslim religious specialists reached a consensus that affirmed the authority of the Sunnah as a source of law. But by that time, counterfeit hadiths outnumbered authentic hadiths. Specialists in hadiths began to develop ways to rate hadiths on a scale from authentic to counterfeit, with intermediate ratings to indicate ones that were probably authentic or counterfeit. How to rate a specific hadith, however, was never pinned down to one method. To bring a degree of order to the sprawling body of hadiths—some of them written down, some of them handed down orally—specialists developed methods and criteria for assessing and ranking them.

The inspection of hadiths to weed out the counterfeits resulted in two developments that have defined the ways that Muslims understand and act on the Sunnah down to the present. First, methods for assessing hadiths emphasized examining the chain of transmitters, that is, the men and women who passed them from one generation to the next. Hadith specialists evaluated the probity and memory of transmitters. They researched where and when they lived in order to verify that they could have heard a hadith from the transmitter they mention. They tried to determine whether transmitters passed along hadiths verbatim or in paraphrase, orally or in writing. The hadith specialists then compiled books that were lists of transmitters and details about their reliability.

The second development arising from the inspection of hadiths was the compilation of collections of hadiths that were deemed authentic. It is said that the compilers sifted through hundreds of thousands of hadiths and set aside the vast majority as unreliable. The gold standard for a hadith was one that had multiple chains of transmission. For Sunni Muslims, there are six canonical collections of hadiths. The collections are organized according to topic: prayer, fasting, contracts, revelation, and so on. The most highly regarded one is the collection of al-Bukhari. It contains around 7,300 hadiths. The other canonical collections are those of Muslim (4,000 hadiths), al-Nasa'i (5,200 hadiths), Abu Daud (4,800 hadiths), al-Tirmidhi (4,300 hadiths), and Ibn Majah (4,500 hadiths).[23]

The six collections stabilized a rough consensus on what counted as the Prophetic Tradition for Sunnis, but they did not establish a fixed, finite text comparable to the Quran. A hadith specialist might not apply the same standards as the compilers to establish a hadith's authenticity. Because hadiths are a major source for how believers are to worship and conduct daily life, disagreement on which ones are authentic can result in disagreement on how to pray or what a mosque should look like, which in fact caused friction between the Salafi Group and Saudi authorities.

Some Early Islamic History: Belief in the Mahdi and Attacks on Mecca

The 1979 uprising was not the first time that fighting raged at Islam's holy center. Nor was it the first time that ideas about the Mahdi played a part in attacks that violated the Grand Mosque's sanctity. Western historians trace the genesis of belief in the Mahdi to strife over claims to the right to lead Muslims during the early stages of their history. While the Mahdi is not mentioned in the Quran, the Sunnah includes hadiths predicting the Mahdi's advent.[24]

Early Civil Wars, 656 to 692

The first Muslim civil war of 656 to 661 refers to a contest for leadership commonly regarded as the origin of the division between Shiite and Sunni Muslims. The protagonists in the struggle were the Prophet's kinsman Ali and the governor of Syria Muawiya. After an inconclusive battle, a stalemate took hold that lasted until 661, when Ali fell to an assassin dispatched by the dissident Kharijite faction. The main body of Muslims then accepted Muawiya's claim to the caliphate with a seat of power in Damascus, marking the end of Medina's role as the Muslim capital. Ali's loyal backers never reconciled to their defeat and formulated the idea that rightful leadership belonged to Ali's descendants. This idea was the germ of Shiism.[25]

The second civil war grew out of widespread discontent with Muawiya's bid to pass the caliphate to his son Yazid and thereby establish a dynastic succession for his Umayyad clan.[26] After Muawiya's death in 680, three factions emerged to oppose Yazid's caliphate. One faction was led by a prominent and wealthy Medinan, Abd Allah ibn al-Zubair. The Kharijites were the second faction. A third faction represented Muslims loyal to Ali's son, Husain.

Husain made a bid for leadership that came to a tragic end. On his way from Medina to join supporters in Iraq, his small party was intercepted and decimated by Yazid's troops. The massacre at a place called Kerbala became cast as a sacred act of martyrdom that would become a pillar of Shiite ritual and belief. More immediately, Husain's followers prepared to launch a revolt against Yazid.

In the meantime, Ibn al-Zubair gathered supporters in Mecca and called for Yazid's overthrow. In 683, an army from Damascus set out for Mecca to quell the revolt. For two months, Umayyad forces kept Mecca under siege, during which the Kaabah was destroyed by fire. Ibn al-Zubair had it rebuilt, replacing the original wooden structure with stone. When reports of Yazid's death of natural causes in Damascus reached Mecca, the besieging forces withdrew.

A complicated struggle for power consumed Muslims for nearly ten years. In Syria, factions in the Umayyad clan vied for supremacy; in Iraq, a rising on behalf of Ali's descendants broke out; in Mecca, Ibn al-Zubair tried to gain recognition for his claim to the caliphate; and the Kharijites were able to take over eastern Arabia. The different factions issued religious propaganda to support their respective claims to rightful leadership. It was in the context of religious propaganda that different contenders for power invented hadiths about the Mahdi.[27]

The leader of Ali's supporters claimed to fight on behalf of a grandson of Ali's who did not take part in the conflict.[28] Ali's party circulated stories that would become part of numerous hadiths about the Mahdi. Thus, one hadith stated that a man from Medina would go to Mecca to receive the oath of allegiance from believers assembled in the Grand Mosque. This hadith does not refer to the Mahdi, but later interpreters of the hadith claimed the Mahdi was meant by the phrase "the man from Medina." Other details about the Mahdi emerged in hadiths from this period: he will have the same name as the Prophet; he will have a prominent nose and a broad forehead; God will give him success in one night. As the civil war continued, the other parties coined hadiths that bolstered their cause. A hadith about the earth swallowing an invading army in the desert alluded to the first Umayyad expedition sent to uproot the Meccan faction—when the invaders received word from Damascus that the caliph had died, they retreated.

Ultimately, the Umayyads regained control over Iraq and then sent an army against Ibn al-Zubair in Mecca. The attackers mounted a catapult on the heights overlooking the town to lob large stones against the defenders, causing damage both to the town and to the recently rebuilt Kaabah. Except for a brief truce to allow the two sides to perform the pilgrimage, the siege last six months. Ibn al-Zubair's allies slipped away and he was forced to retreat to the Grand Mosque with a small remnant of his original forces. He rejected a final call to surrender and died in battle in 692.[29]

Hadiths about the Mahdi continued to serve political ends after the civil war. Umayyad supporters put forth hadiths to demonstrate that the caliphs of Damascus were rightly guided rulers. The Abbasid clan that overthrew the Umayyads in 750 claimed that their caliph was the rightly guided Muslim ruler. Ali's supporters, taking clear shape in this era as a distinct Shiite religious group, advanced hadiths to deny Abbasid claims. One of their hadiths specifies that the Mahdi will be a descendant of the Prophet, a claim Ali's party could make because of his marriage to the Prophet's daughter: "The Mahdi will be from me, with a broad forehead and a prominent nose. He will fill the earth with equity and justice as it was filled with injustice and oppression and will rule seven years."[30]

Reports about the Mahdi, then, were tailored to support one political cause or another in early Islamic times. And yet, belief in the Mahdi never gained universal acceptance among Sunnis. Not a single hadith about the Mahdi was included in two of the authoritative collections of hadiths (Bukhari and Muslim); some theologians did not incorporate the Mahdi in their writings on belief about Judgment Day; and the prominent historian Ibn Khaldun expressed skepticism about belief in the Mahdi in his descriptions of Mahdist movements. Furthermore, not all Mahdi hadiths herald Judgment Day; some herald a new historical era of righteous leadership. Beyond the Sunni realm, there is a rich tradition of Mahdism in Shiism rooted in the belief that a descendant of Ali had gone into hiding and would return as the Mahdi to save the world. In both the Sunni and Shiite traditions, beliefs about the Mahdi figured in revolts against corrupt, impious rulers accused of joining forces with infidels.[31]

The Carmathians Attack Mecca and Seize the Black Stone

A later attack on Mecca was a much simpler affair.[32] In 930, a Shiite faction based in Bahrain and eastern Arabia raided the holy city. The faction is known as the Carmathians or Qaramita. They were part of a Shiite faction that split over the claim of one leader in that faction to be the Mahdi. The faction that supported the Mahdi went on to establish the Fatimid Caliphate and rule Egypt for two centuries (969–1171).

The Carmathians had centers of power in Iran, Iraq, and Arabia. In 928, their Arabian leader Abu Tahir al-Jannabi interpreted an astronomical event, the conjunction of Jupiter and Saturn, as a portent of the Mahdi's advent. He led a military campaign to seize Baghdad from the Abbasid caliph. After two years of fierce combat, the Abbasids forced him to retreat to Arabia. Then, in 930, the Carmathians attacked Mecca during the pilgrimage, massacred pilgrims and Mecca residents, and stole the Black Stone that is lodged in a corner of the Kaabah.

The following year, Abu Tahir's fortunes took a turn for the worse when he announced that a Persian adherent to the Carmathians was the Mahdi. The acclaimed Mahdi, however, turned out to be a Zoroastrian, the religion of pre-Islamic Iran. When he took steps to institute Zoroastrian worship, Abu Tahir had him murdered, less than three months after announcing he was the Mahdi. Abu Tahir had to admit that he had made an awful mistake, and he restored the

Carmathian regime. As for the Black Stone, the Abbasids paid a ransom to have it returned to Mecca in 951.

Overview of the Wahhabi Mission and the History of Saudi Arabia

The Wahhabi Mission

The Wahhabi mission is a religious purification movement that began in central Arabia with the preaching of a religious scholar named Muhammad ibn Abd al-Wahhab (1703–1792).[33] Many religious scholars in Arabia and beyond rejected his views and coined the term "Wahhabi" to discredit his preaching as nothing more than one man's misguided, ill-informed distortions of religious doctrine. Ibn Abd al-Wahhab and his followers insisted that they were simply Sunni Muslims seeking to restore the way of the Prophet. The use of the word "mission" to describe the movement refers to the Arabic word *da'wah*, which literally means "call" in the sense of calling someone to a religious belief.

Muhammad ibn Abd al-Wahhab came from a family in central Arabia known for its religious scholars. His grandfather, father, and brother were religious scholars. Like other religious scholars in central Arabia, they were in accord with the Sunni consensus on belief and law (in fact, his brother staunchly defended the Sunni consensus). He broke with that consensus based on his understanding of a central doctrine in Islamic theology: how to define belief. He maintained that belief was not merely a matter of affirming the Muslim testimony of faith: There is no god but God, and Muhammad is the messenger of God. To be a believer, one had to devote all worship and any action that implies worship to God. In Arabia and much of the Muslim world, seeking the intercession of holy men and the Shiite imams was a popular practice, but Ibn Abd al-Wahhab classified it as idolatry because it implied worship of mortal creatures. Therefore, those who performed it were unbelievers. Just as the Prophet waged war against the unbelievers of his time, true believers in Ibn Abd al-Wahhab's time had the duty to wage war against unbelievers. How he came to this view is not clear. He might have been influenced by teachers in the holy cities, or by experiences he had during a stay in Iraq, or, as claimed by one of his grandsons, he might have come to this view through inspiration. Whatever the source, he began preaching his doctrine in 1740. He then spent four years seeking followers, debating religious scholars, and suffering expulsion from two towns for his controversial preaching. In 1744, he found refuge with the Saud clan and they agreed to support his mission, founding an alliance that has endured to the present.

History of Saudi Arabia

The history of Saudi Arabia is commonly divided into three periods.[34] The first period, from 1744 to 1818, is the period of the first Saudi state. The second period, from 1824 to 1891, is the period of the second Saudi state. The third period, from

1902 to the present, is the period of the third Saudi state, today's Kingdom of Saudi Arabia.

The first capital of Saudi Arabia was an oasis settlement called Dir'iyyah, located near the present capital of Riyadh. In the early 1700s, Dir'iyyah and the other towns of central Arabia were not part of any large Muslim empire. They were small, independent emirates, each ruled by a local family. The Saud family became the rulers of Dir'iyyah in the early 1700s. Their rise to prominence began in the 1740s, when they launched a prolonged campaign of military conquest. By 1800, the Saudi–Wahhabi alliance conquered all of central Arabia and parts of the Gulf coast.

The first Saudi state made it possible for Muhammad ibn Abd al-Wahhab to eradicate the old religious establishment and create a new one based on his teachings, in the name of erasing idolatry. Wherever Saudi power took hold, religious judges, teachers, and preachers were required to affirm fidelity to Wahhabi doctrine. Religious figures who embraced the new dispensation fit right in; religious figures who refused either moved away or were silenced. The drive to ensure universal adherence meant the purge and suppression of Sufis, Shiites, and Sunnis who rejected Ibn Abd al-Wahhab's doctrine.[35] By the time he died in 1792, his mission held nearly complete sway in central Arabia. Leadership of the Wahhabi mission passed to his descendants, who became known as "the sheikh's family," or "Al al-Sheikh."

The first Saudi state reached the height of its power in the early 1800s when it wrested control of Mecca and Medina from the Ottoman Empire. The Ottoman sultan assigned the governor of Egypt, Muhammad Ali, the task of reconquering the holy cities. In 1811, he launched his military campaign against the Saudis, first expelling them from the holy cities, then invading central Arabia to crush the first Saudi state. In 1818, it appeared that both the Wahhabi mission and Saudi power were suppressed forever.

Muhammad Ali's forces evacuated central Arabia in 1821 due to the difficulties of supplying garrisons deep in the desert. Three years later, a Saudi emir was able to reestablish his clan's power. Because Muhammad Ali's army had demolished Dir'iyyah, the emir made nearby Riyadh the seat of power for the second Saudi state. In 1838, Muhammad Ali sent his forces back to central Arabia and installed a compliant member of the Saudi clan. This interlude lasted three years before Muhammad Ali withdrew his forces once and for all, allowing an independent Saudi emir to regain power. The next quarter century was a period of stability for the second Saudi state under Emir Faisal. Wahhabi clerics were able to perpetuate their domination of religious life in central Arabia, in part by sealing it off from the rest of the Muslim world, which they viewed as an abode of idolatry. The clerics did their utmost to discourage travel outside the Saudi realm because they felt that interacting with infidels might influence one's religious beliefs. The clerics also did their utmost to prevent outside religious scholars from spreading beliefs at odds with Wahhabi doctrine.

Emir Faisal's death in 1865 set off a scramble for power among his sons. The protracted struggle for succession turned into a civil war, with tribes and towns siding with one Saudi emir or another. As a result, the second Saudi state lost control over territory to the Rashid clan based in northern Arabia. In 1891, Riyadh fell to the Rashid clan and the Saud clan went into exile in Kuwait.

The third Saudi state began in 1902, when a young Saudi emir, Abd al-Aziz ibn Saud, usually referred to as Ibn Saud, seized Riyadh from the Rashid clan's governor. By the outbreak of the First World War, Ibn Saud had regained control over central Arabia and part of the Persian Gulf coast. After the war, he rounded out his conquests in northern Arabia, Hijaz, including the holy cities, and the borderlands with Yemen. In 1932, Ibn Saud proclaimed his realm the Kingdom of Saudi Arabia. He would rule until his death in 1953. Since then, the throne has been held by six of his sons: Saud (r. 1953–1964), Faisal (r. 1964–1975), Khalid (r. 1975–1982), Fahd (r. 1982–2005), Abd Allah (r. 2005–2015), and Salman (r. 2015–present).

Two Phases in the History of the Wahhabi Mission: Exclusion and Accommodation

Under the first and second Saudi states, Wahhabi clerics were able to sustain a regime of exclusion to safeguard the doctrinal purity of their realm.[36] Under the third Saudi state, Ibn Saud took steps that forced clerics to temper the application of their doctrine. One way to think about this change is to divide the Wahhabi mission's history into two phases. The first "exclusivist" phase lasted from the 1740s until the early 1900s. The second "accommodationist" phase began in the early 1900s and has lasted until the present.

Accommodation meant opening Saudi Arabia to outsiders, both Muslim and non-Muslim. Ibn Saud achieved military and political success because he was a master of pragmatic maneuvering in a dynamic strategic environment where Great Britain had been emerging as the major Western power in the Persian Gulf since the early 1800s. After the First World War, the British expanded their regional influence by gaining control over Jordan and Iraq. To steer relations with London, Ibn Saud relied on foreign Arab advisers.

Previous Saudi emirs had never entered formal agreements with non-Muslim powers, but Ibn Saud signed treaties with Great Britain that shored up his military and political position. The British provided him funds and weapons. In return, he promised to refrain from seeking to annex the small Persian Gulf sheikhdoms under London's protection: Kuwait, Bahrain, Qatar, the Trucial states (future United Arab Republic), and Oman. Ibn Saud also broke the taboo on non-Muslims entering the Saudi realm in 1933, when he signed an oil concession agreement with US companies granting permission to American surveyors to explore his realm for oil. Ibn Saud further tempered the exclusivist spirit by overruling clerics' objections to the introduction of technological innovations such as the radio.

From Ibn Saud's perspective, these arrangements were perfectly sensible. From the perspective of Wahhabi doctrine, however, they compromised the exclusion of infidels that had been considered necessary in order to maintain a domain of true belief and correct worship. Nevertheless, most Wahhabi clerics went along with Ibn Saud's pragmatism. With the chaos of the Saudi civil war fresh in their minds, a few compromises for the sake of stability seemed reasonable. Some clerics, however, upheld the original vision of the Wahhabi mission, and while they were not outspoken, they kept the vision alive.

In the 1910s and 1920s, exclusivist clerics had powerful allies in tribal warriors known as the Brethren, or *Ikhwan*.[37] The Ikhwan were former Bedouin who abandoned their nomadic ways, settled in agricultural colonies, and became ardent devotees of the Wahhabi mission. The Ikhwan spearheaded Ibn Saud's military campaigns, not for the sake of Saudi dynastic power but as a jihad against infidels. When the Ikhwan took their jihad across newly established international borders into Jordan and Iraq, they triggered a crisis for Ibn Saud with Great Britain, which was responsible for defending the newly formed countries. Ibn Saud ordered the Ikhwan to cease their raids, and in response, several prominent chieftains revolted. Ibn Saud's suppression of the revolt in 1929–30 was a definitive defeat for exclusivist Wahhabism, although it would remain a lingering force that resisted accommodation with the outside world. Its influence was expressed by keeping Saudis away from non-Muslim residents, restricted to expatriate compounds, and by confining foreign Muslim influence on religious life to the holy cities.

The Salafi Group embodied the old exclusivist mistrust of non-Muslim influences. As the son of an Ikhwan warrior, Juhaiman himself strongly identified with their militant religious ethos and he considered Ibn Saud's suppression of the Ikhwan a betrayal of true religion for the sake of appeasing a non-Muslim power (Great Britain).

Salafi

Salafi is an Arabic noun and adjective that refers to Sunni Muslims who claim to follow the ways of the Pious Ancestors, *al-salaf al-salih*. The Pious Ancestors are typically defined as the first three generations of Muslims. In later centuries, some Muslims came to believe that fellow Muslims had strayed from the way of the Prophet that the Pious Ancestors correctly followed. In calling for a return to the way of the Pious Ancestors (the Salaf), they were seeking to restore Islam in its original, pristine form.[38]

Who counts as a Salafi is an unsettled question. In the late 1800s, some thinkers and activists called for a return to the Pious Ancestors as models of enlightened application of general religious principles. This group is often referred to as Islamic modernists because they wanted to import modern science, technology, and political institutions from Europe. They believed that Islam was fully compatible with modernity when properly understood in terms of what they considered its true nature as a religion of reason and flexibility.[39]

A different kind of Salafi advocates for purification of belief and practices by embracing a literalist theology and by eliminating illegitimate religious innovations. The Arabic term for innovation is *bid'ah*.[40] Innovations in a general sense refer to beliefs and practices that were introduced after the Prophet. Innovations in accord with the Quran and the Prophetic Tradition were considered legitimate. They include developments that support the believers' understanding of the Quran and the Prophetic Tradition, for example, methodical study of Arabic and methods to assess hadiths. Illegitimate innovations include additions to or changes in worship. Salafis are particularly critical of worship that implies attributing God's power to creatures, such as seeking the intercession of holy men. In general, Muslims view innovations in food, clothing, and other everyday customs as permissible, but there were controversies over the introduction of coffee and tobacco in the 1500s and 1600s. Eliminating innovations in worship was a priority for the Wahhabi mission and provided a basis for cooperating with like-minded religious movements in other Muslim societies.

In the early 1900s, grassroots religious movements such as the Muslim Brotherhood embraced the notion of returning to the Pious Ancestors.[41] Such movements were not seeking to justify importing modern ways from the West or to purify religious beliefs and practices. Their goal was to strengthen Muslim societies to enable resistance against Western domination. These grassroots religious movements have three distinguishing features. One is an emphasis on Muslim solidarity. They believed that Muslims were weak because they were divided over issues they considered secondary. In their view, secondary issues included disagreements over the details of Islamic law and rivalries between Sufi brotherhoods. They also thought that Muslims should not quarrel over theological questions such as how to interpret verses of the Quran that describe God as possessing physical attributes. By contrast, Wahhabis regard theology as primary and essential. The grassroots revivalists advocated a "big tent" idea of Islam in order to eliminate divisions and strengthen Muslims against the West. A second distinguishing element is their belief that Islam has the answers to all questions for all realms of individual and collective life: politics, economy, health, education, and so forth. In other words, there is no reason to borrow anything from the West because Islam has all the answers. A popular slogan expressing that idea is "Islam is the solution." A third distinguishing element is their focus on creating organizations and programs to spread their influence. In this regard, they resemble modern social and political movements in the West, from which they adopted much of their structure.

Today's Salafis do not consider the modernists or the grassroots movements to be Salafis. They uphold literal interpretation of religious texts—the Quran and the Sunnah. They also uphold a view of theology that condemns other theological views as errant, if not heretical. Furthermore, they consider correct religious practice to entail not only worship and law but also personal manners, dress, and grooming. They are recognizable by their long beards and short robes.

Saudi Arabia's Wahhabi mission is in accord with Salafis on literal interpretation of religious texts and theology, but they part ways in their approaches to Islamic law. The Wahhabi mission follows the mainstream Sunni Muslim tradition of Islamic law, whereas Salafis reject that tradition's binding authority. Instead, they elevate the authority of hadiths in determining Islamic law. This disagreement over legal method was a source of strains between Saudi clerics and the Salafi Group and played a role in the Salafi Group's path from pious revivalists to religious dissidents.

Saudi Arabia in the 1960s and 1970s

The Salafi Group's goals resembled those of other modern Muslim religious purification movements in two fundamental respects. First, it sought to restore religious beliefs and practices to their pristine form. Second, it sought to eliminate Western cultural influence. In the eyes of the Salafi Group, the two goals were connected: The infiltration of Western culture into Muslim societies was to blame for the corruption of religion.

Some modern religious purification movements were devoted to social reform through preaching and refrained from political activity. Others, however, believed that Muslim rulers were responsible for permitting the introduction of Western culture. Therefore, preaching alone would not restore true Islam. Political activism was necessary to either persuade rulers to change course or to remove them from power. The Salafi Group began as a movement preaching reform and took a political turn that transformed it into a militant movement in the thrall of a violent apocalyptic vision.

Huzaimi's memoir makes clear that Juhaiman's apocalyptic shift sprang from a reading of Saudi history that showed society moving away from truth and good in the direction of falsehood and evil. He became convinced that recent historical events augured the End of Time and the advent of the Mahdi to restore virtue and justice. In secular terms, when the Salafi Group was active, from 1965 to 1979, Saudi Arabia was undergoing rapid urban growth and creeping Westernization. In the eyes of the pious, such changes meant the country was moving in the wrong direction.

Rapid Urban Growth

Juhaiman's generation lived through a period of jarring social change visible in the expansion of cities through migration from small towns and villages, and relocation of tribesmen from the desert. Even before the great oil boom of the mid-1970s, oil revenues played an important part in urban expansion. Between 1955 and the early 1970s, Riyadh's population grew from 80,000 to 300,000; Mecca and Medina's populations doubled, from 100,000 to 200,000 and from 50,000 to 100,000, respectively.[42]

The quadrupling of oil prices in 1973–4 led to a manic phase in urban expansion and change, as Riyadh's population more than doubled to reach one million in 1980. At the street level, new high-rise office buildings engulfed the old city. In the name of progress, bulldozers demolished old mansions and razed traditional markets, turning them into parking lots and making way for a new cityscape of shopping malls and sprawling residential neighborhoods. The number of motor vehicles increased tenfold in six years (1974–80), exposing residents to choking air pollution and resulting in gridlock on the country's underdeveloped urban road networks.[43] The installation of electrical, water, and sewage infrastructure did not keep pace with construction of new commercial and residential zones. Just getting supplies into the country was a monumental challenge because the volume of imports overwhelmed the capacity of ports to move goods. A former American diplomat recalls that Jeddah's port was a "massive mess. At one point, 220 ships were waiting to be off-loaded. The line went out over 30 miles outside the port."[44]

Rapid urbanization ruptured the lives of migrants who found themselves in strange new surroundings and of townsmen who found themselves swamped by migrants from villages and the desert. Compounding drastic changes in the fabric of city life was the influx of foreigners seeking lucrative contracts and wages. For centuries, the towns of central Arabia such as Riyadh seldom saw strangers except for merchants accompanying their wares in caravans. Consequently, townsmen were unaccustomed to interacting much with outsiders, whose numbers were few in any event.

By contrast, residents of towns along the Red Sea and Persian Gulf historically looked outward because of the essential role that maritime trade played in their economies. Foreign traders were a common sight and foreign merchants often established long-term residence in the ports. Likewise, for residents of the holy cities, Mecca and Medina, foreign visitors were part of everyday life. In fact, people of Mecca and Medina were economically dependent on what we might call a tourism sector based on the annual pilgrimage when Muslims from around the world would gather for the solemn ritual. Quite often, pilgrims would take up residence in a holy place for a period of devotion, study, and reflection. They were known as "sojourners," or temporary residents; some would settle permanently. Neighborhoods evolved as centers for Muslims from particular regions, such as Java and Bukhara. Public recognition of the merit of sojourning led to the creation of endowments to provide lodging. The foreign workers arriving in the thousands during the 1970s did not come for religious devotion but for livelihoods, and outside the holy cities, many were non-Muslims. In the early 1970s, immigrants comprised one-fifth of the residents in Mecca and Medina, and roughly one-quarter in Riyadh. A common result of urban expansion was a rise in street crime and the spread of vices such as prostitution and drugs, which Saudis blamed on the large number of strangers.

Much as Wahhabi clerics had always feared, frequent interaction with Westerners resulted in the spread of Western habits and tastes. According to one account written only months before the invasion of the Grand Mosque, in Jeddah, near the tomb of Eve (in Muslim belief), newsstands offered American magazines and Saudis gathered to watch movies in abandoned buildings.[45] In Juhaiman's eyes, movies and magazines were not merely unwelcome as alien imports; they were violations of Islamic law and, ultimately, portents of the Last Judgment. How does his rejection of Western influence fit in the larger patterns of the Middle East's history of encounter with Western culture?

Western Culture in the Middle East: Common Historical Patterns

Western cultural influences infiltrated much of the Middle East starting in the early 1800s in the Ottoman Empire, Egypt, and Iran. Military defeats at the hands of Western powers prompted rulers in all three lands to send educational missions to

Europe and to employ Western experts to introduce European military advances in weaponry and training. Western power became associated with Western ways, and knowledge of European languages became an avenue to advancement in military and civilian institutions. Over time, statesmen, military officers, and bureaucrats adopted Western habits: men tossed off robes to don frock coats, shaved beards and instead wore trimmed mustaches, and turned away from historical Ottoman, Arabic, and Persian literary traditions to immerse themselves in French, English, and German letters. By the late 1800s, Arab, Turkish, and Persian writers were experimenting with imported literary genres such as the novel and the play. Parallel to shifts in the life of the mind, cityscapes began to take on a Western aspect in architecture, broad boulevards, public squares, and monuments. The wealthy furnished their homes with European mirrors, tables, beds, and cabinets. And in the political realm there appeared movements for women's rights and representative political institutions.

The spread of Western culture did not go unopposed. Starting in the 1870s and 1880s, conservatives condemned the aping of Western ways and asserted the centrality of religion as the core of heritage and identity. How exactly to define religion, however, itself became a point of controversy between modernists convinced it was a set of principles that allowed for flexible adaptation and conservatives convinced it was a set of fixed rules from which deviation meant abandoning religion altogether. But even among conservatives, arguments raged over defining those fixed rules. Ardent secularists, many of them privately pious, religious modernists, and religious conservatives have coexisted and clashed throughout the Middle East to the present day. For the most part, people enjoy movies and television, team sports are popular, and few give men's suits and ties a second thought. Women's dress is another matter, although why Islamic or Western dress for women is so contentious is a complex question that has no simple answer. At the same time, education for girls and professional careers for women gained general acceptance.

Western Culture in Saudi Arabia: A Different Historical Background

Saudi Arabia is an exception to the general pattern in the Middle East for three reasons. First, its rulers never had to cope with defeat by a Western army, although during the mid-1800s, the British navy in the Persian Gulf did limit Saudi expansion. As a result, Saudi rulers did not begin to import Western advisers or send educational missions to the West until much later in history. Second, Saudi Arabia never came under colonial rule, a phase of history when populations in Iraq, Syria, Lebanon, Egypt, and Palestine came under Western sway. Third, Saudi Arabia's Wahhabi mission regarded outsiders as a threat to religion. Consequently, until the 1920s, foreign Muslims were unwelcome, and people were discouraged from traveling to foreign Muslim lands. Christians from the West were not allowed into the country until Saudi Arabia signed an oil concession with American companies in the 1930s, and even then, clerics objected to allowing Americans to roam the deserts searching for oil.

The political and social influence of Wahhabi clerics impeded but did not halt the infiltration of Western ways into Saudi society. Soccer became a popular sport in the late 1920s and 1930s, spread by pilgrims from Southeast Asia and foreign workers for the American oil company. Clerics wanted to ban the sport because men played in shorts that exposed their legs. In 1951, however, the minister of interior, a member of the royal family, overruled them and created a special bureau for the sport.[46]

As more Saudis interacted with foreign workers and traveled to the West, the clerics and the agents of Committees for Commanding Right and Forbidding Wrong[47] waged a rearguard action to stem Western ways. For example, agents of the Committees searched homes if they suspected them of possessing phonographs, which they opposed because they considered music prohibited. Clerics protested allowing a woman's voice to be broadcast over radio, but King Faisal overruled them.[48] They had more success preventing the spread of cinemas. Members of the royal family would screen films behind the walls of their palaces, but the clerics blocked an initiative to open special clubs to show movies. Saudis were able to evade the ban by using abandoned properties as clandestine cinemas.[49]

The most ominous clash between creeping Westernization and religious principles took place over King Faisal's decision to bring television to Saudi Arabia. Even though romantic scenes were cut from foreign films, the innovation infuriated some Saudis. In September 1965, a young prince led a small group of protestors to attack the Riyadh television station. Police thwarted the attack and chased the protestors to the prince's residence. A standoff ended only when a police officer shot and killed the prince.[50] Ten years later, a relative of that prince took revenge by assassinating King Faisal.

The Saudi Political Context in the 1960s and 1970s

In 1964, Faisal became the third king of Saudi Arabia, after his father Abd al-Aziz ibn Saud and his brother Saud. His father recognized Faisal's abilities early on by appointing him to represent the country's interests as part of a delegation to London. In fact, his visit in 1919, which lasted several months, was the first by a member of the ruling family. Faisal played important roles in his father's military conquests and served as governor of the Hijaz when Saudi forces conquered it in 1926. Given the international religious significance of Hijaz, the post required a high degree of political acumen, which Faisal demonstrated throughout his life. In 1930, he became the country's foreign minister. By the time Abd al-Aziz died in 1953, Faisal was a strong contender for the throne, but his father had designated his brother Saud to succeed him and Faisal to stand as the crown prince. Saud turned out to be a controversial ruler, in part because of spendthrift ways. The ruling family soon divided into factions backing either Saud or Faisal. A ten-year contest for power unfolded. In the early 1960s, Saud was briefly forced to hand over power to Faisal, but when he sought to retake the reins of power in 1964, he was forced to abdicate and went into exile. Faisal then ruled until 1975.

In the 1960s, Saudi Arabia engaged in an intense struggle for regional influence with Egyptian president Gamal Abd al-Nasir, who represented anti-Western, revolutionary Arab nationalism. Educated young Saudis admired the charismatic Nasir's efforts to rid the Arab world of Western imperialism and gravitated to Arab nationalism as the way to restore the position of the Arab world in global affairs. Consequently, the Egyptian president represented a threat not only to Saudi Arabia's regional position but to domestic stability as well. Faisal responded to the popularity of Arab nationalism by formulating a strategy of Islamic solidarity, using the kingdom's status as homeland of the holy cities to make it a leading voice in the Muslim world beyond the Arab sphere.

Faisal's reign coincided with two Arab-Israeli wars. In the June 1967 war, Israel seized territories from Egypt, Syria, and Jordan, including Arab East Jerusalem with its Muslim, Jewish, and Christian holy sites. The restoration of Arab control over East Jerusalem became an urgent political cause throughout the Arab and Muslim worlds. The war delivered a devastating blow to Nasir's standing in the Arab world. In its aftermath, he muted the revolutionary propaganda that had generated so much rancor among conservative rulers like Faisal. The Saudi king in turn shifted his foreign policy from confrontation with Nasir to encouraging Arab unity for the sake of supporting the Palestinian cause and recovering East Jerusalem.

During the October 1973 war, Faisal played a leading role in punishing the West for supporting Israel by joining an embargo on Arab oil exports and raising petroleum prices. The "oil price revolution" quadrupled prices in a matter of months, paving the way for enormous increases in spending on economic and social development in the kingdom. The windfall gave the government hitherto unimaginable opportunities to demonstrate the dynasty's commitment to improving its subjects' standard of living, but the country lacked the capacity to turn monetary wealth into tangible results in the short term. The late 1970s were years of inflation, traffic congestion, haphazard construction, and profiteering for a few. Nevertheless, with the threat of revolutionary Arab nationalism a receding memory, the ruling clan had good reason to feel more secure than it had in decades.

The promise of prosperity mattered little if at all to the Salafi Group, preoccupied with scouring hadiths for guidance on correct ways to worship and bent on immunizing themselves against the germs of Western culture. As far as Juhaiman was concerned, King Faisal's assassination in 1975 and the succession of his half-brother Khalid to the throne merely meant the replacement of one corrupt ruler by another. From the perspective of the ruling family, the Salafi Group did not register as a problem, and to the extent that it did, it was a problem for the official clergy.

The Salafi Group and Religious Authority

When the Salafi Group formed in 1965, it sought and received the approval of the Saudi religious establishment. By around 1976, members' adoption of unorthodox worship practices was straining the group's relationship with Saudi clerics. In August 1977, an attempt by the group's clerical supervisor to rein them in caused a split between dissidents and loyalists. Juhaiman became leader of the dissident faction, which gravitated to an apocalyptic vision putting it on the path to seizing the Grand Mosque. Details in the memoir give a complicated picture of exactly how the Salafi Group shifted from conformity to dissent. Analysis of that picture underscores the significance of religious authority in Muslim societies: How is it created and sustained? Under what circumstances is it challenged?

Religious Authority in Muslim Societies

Religious authority defines and regulates correct belief and practice. In Christianity, religious authority took on the shape of a formal institution, the church. Muslim societies did not establish a formal religious institution. Instead, they developed different kinds of informal religious authority. It could be based on feats of piety and personal charisma, as in the case of Sufi holy men. It could be based on descent from the Prophet, as in the case of Shiite Muslims' belief in a line of religious leaders descended from the Prophet's kinsman Ali. It could be based on scholastic mastery of religious texts undertaken by scholars known as "ulama," as in the case of the Sunni tradition, which Saudi Arabia follows.[51]

Sunni religious scholars define correct beliefs and practices according to their understanding of the Quran and the Sunnah. The scholars typically specialize in particular fields of religion, such as theology (dealing with belief) or law (dealing with practice). The Salafi Group was in accord with Saudi clerics on theology, that is, Muhammad ibn Abd al-Wahhab's restrictive definition of belief and unbelief. But on a few details of law, the group challenged the clerics. The basis for their challenge rested on two questions: How do believers know the correct legal rule on any particular issue? Who has the authority to determine legal rules?

Islamic Law

Shari'ah is the Arabic term rendered as "Islamic law" in English. Shariah denotes a path that God lays down for believers to guide them to reward in the afterlife. Shariah has rules for marriage, inheritance, contracts, and other aspects of social life that are covered by law in the Western sense. Shariah also has rules for how to perform ritual duties such as prayer, pilgrimage, fasting, and other aspects of worship that do not come under law in the Western sense.

Muslims believe in the duty to follow shariah and they look to the Quran and the Sunnah as the sources of specific legal rules, but they do not follow uniform methods for extracting legal rules from these sources. The use of different methods results in different legal rules for the same issue, for example, how to perform prayer. In order to prevent an anarchy of conflicting legal rules, beginning in the ninth century, the Sunni religious scholars developed a consensus on confining legal authority to four main legal traditions that are called *madhhab*s, or legal schools, in the sense of schools of thought.[52] How the Sunni consensus came about and how it has weakened in modern times are keys to understanding the Salafi Group's challenge to Saudi religious authority.

The Authority of the Four Sunni Legal Schools

Some matters in Islamic law are clear and obvious, for example, the duty to pray five times a day at prescribed times. Other matters, however, are not so obvious, for example, details about the wording of prayers. In early Islamic times, religious scholars debated how to arrive at rules for the "not so obvious" cases, and they developed technical methods and terminology that comprise Islamic legal theory. One point on which they agreed is that a legal rule that is not based on clear, unambiguous verses in the Quran or hadiths is a matter of conjecture. In other words, the experts on Islamic law acknowledged that many of the legal rules that they adopted were, in essence, matters of learned judgment, not divine edicts.

Such intellectual modesty seems like a shaky foundation for the authority of legal experts. The principle of consensus[53] helped shore up that foundation, even though the precise nature of consensus (whose consensus, to what degree of consensus) was a matter of some debate. One of the main areas of consensus among Sunni legal experts was restricting authority to determine Islamic law to four legal schools named for men who lived in the eighth and ninth centuries: Malik, al-Shafi'i, Abu Hanifah, and Ahmad ibn Hanbal; the names of the legal schools are Maliki, Shafi'i, Hanafi, and Hanbali. There had been other legal schools based on the teachings of other men and on regional traditions, but these eventually became extinct.

Sunni legal experts agreed on three additional points of consensus that bolstered the authority of the legal schools. First, the legal schools were equally valid. This meant that a spirit of pluralism prevailed between different interpretations of the law for the sake of stability and order. Second, ordinary Muslims were obliged to follow one of the four legal schools, essentially setting up a monopoly on religious law. Third, ordinary Muslims were obliged to respect the authority of the legal scholars.

The Authority of Legal Scholars

Legal scholars specialized in different fields of law, such as inheritance, contracts, marriage, and so on. Most legal scholars attained a degree of learning that qualified them to apply the rules of their respective legal schools according to each school's consensus. What happened when a case arose for which the legal school did not provide a rule? Such cases were the domain of the great legal experts. Only they possessed the learning necessary to discover rules for cases without precedent through the application of independent reasoning to relevant texts in the Quran and the Sunnah.

Independent reasoning to solve a difficult legal question is called *ijtihad*, a word that means exerting full effort.[54] There is no single list of the qualifications one must possess to undertake ijtihad, but they typically include thorough knowledge of the Quran and the Sunnah; the ability to interpret ambiguous Quranic verses and hadiths; knowing the methods for assessing the legal weight and implications of hadiths; the "rules of abrogation" whereby certain verses of the Quran and hadiths may cancel others; legal issues on which scholars have reached consensus; methods of analogical reasoning to derive rules for new cases; technical linguistic analysis of the Quran and the Sunnah; and technical proficiency in Arabic grammar and rhetoric. Because the legal experts were presumed to possess special insight into the meaning of the Quran and the Sunnah, ordinary believers were expected to look to them for guidance and instruction on the rules for worship and social relations, according to the saying, "Whoever follows a scholar meets God safely."[55]

Challenging the Authority of the Four Legal Schools in Modern Times

Challenges to the authority of the legal schools have come from two different movements. Traditionalist Muslims sought to revive an idealized conception of early Islam. Modernist Muslims called for flexible adaptation to modern conditions. The traditionalists included a movement that elevated the study of the hadiths and the role of hadiths in establishing the rules of Islamic law, as opposed to accepting the legal school consensus. This movement first emerged in Medina, India, and Yemen in the late 1700s and early 1800s among religious scholars who wished to restore an ancient tradition known as the Hadith Folk, or *Ahli Hadith*. Their rejection of the obligation to follow the legal schools stemmed from their conviction that the schools had placed reasoning above authoritative religious texts, namely the hadiths, with the result that Muslims were acting according to the speculative conclusions of legal scholars and not according to the divine revelation contained in the Quran and the Sunnah.[56]

The Salafi tendency that arose in the late 1800s in Arab countries endorsed the Hadith Folk's emphasis on hadiths. The Salafis also challenged the legal schools by observing that they developed long after the time of the Prophet. If Muslims were to return to the ways of the Pious Ancestors, that meant abandoning the legal schools. A related argument put forth by Salafis was that the power and dynamism of early Islam were based on Muslim unity. Divisions over religion weakened Muslims, and the legal schools were a cause of division.[57]

The modernists' challenge to the authority of the legal schools represented a response to the confrontation between Muslim societies and European imperialism. Muslim rulers, statesmen, and thinkers came to believe that their societies could repel European power only by borrowing what appeared to be the sources of that power: ways of organizing government institutions, new military and communications technologies, experimental sciences, education systems, and so on. Muslim rulers imported European law codes to regulate trade and they established "mixed courts" comprising European and Muslim judges to handle disputes between Muslim and Europeans. In these conditions, it seemed that the four legal schools were relics of a bygone historical age and therefore unsuited to modern times. Some religious thinkers agreed. They maintained that the foundations of Islamic law were general principles, such as safeguarding public welfare, that were applicable to the conditions of every era of history. As historical conditions changed, legal scholars were to revise legal rules by exercising independent reasoning, that is to say, ijtihad, and to reject the binding authority of the legal schools.[58] The Arabic term for abandoning the legal schools is *la madhhab*, which means, "no legal school."

Under assault by traditionalists and modernists, the defenders of the legal schools confronted a mood of skepticism that extended to the consensus on expert learning as a requirement to reach judgments in Islamic law. As a forerunner of the Hadith Folk wrote in the late 1700s, "To comprehend the Quran and Hadith does not require much learning, for the Prophet was sent to show the straight path to the unwise."[59] We will see that Juhaiman shared that view and contended that piety, literacy, and familiarity with the Quran and the Sunnah were sufficient qualifications for the believer to figure out legal rules.

The Wahhabi Mission and Religious Authority in Arabia

How does Saudi Arabia fit into the history of religious authority in Muslim societies? Before the rise of Saudi power in the 1700s, religious authority in central Arabia was in accord with the Sunni tradition. Religious scholars followed the Hanbali legal school and recognized the validity of the other legal schools. Ambitious religious pupils would travel to the holy cities, Damascus, Baghdad, and Cairo to study with distinguished scholars. Popular religious beliefs and practices in central Arabia mirrored those in neighboring Arab lands.

Then along came Muhamad ibn Abd al-Wahhab. His movement was a revolt against established religious authority because it tolerated worship practices that he considered idolatrous. At the same time, he maintained two important parts of the Sunni consensus on Islamic law: the authority of the four legal schools and the authority of legal scholars to decide legal questions.[60]

The first two Saudi states put in place a religious establishment enforcing Ibn Abd al-Wahhab's doctrine and excluding other religious ideas. Then under the third Saudi state, clerics accepted a degree of accommodation with the outside world. Accommodation included admitting foreign Muslims for the sake of consolidating Saudi control over the holy cities when they came under Saudi rule in the 1920s. Some of the foreign Muslims allowed in were supporters of the Hadith Folk and the No Legal School tendency. In essence, accommodation opened channels for challenges to the Sunni consensus on Islamic law upheld by Saudi clerics.

Wahhabi Clerics and Foreign Muslims in the Holy Cities

Throughout the history of Islam, caliphs and sultans burnished their prestige by acting as the protectors of the pilgrimage and guardians of the holy places, undertaking the repair and embellishment of shrines, funding religious education, and supporting charitable institutions.

Ibn Saud's conquest of the holy cities in 1924–5 presented him the opportunity to attain greater stature than ever before. No longer merely the ruler of remote, thinly populated central Arabia, he possessed the Muslim world's most valuable symbolic prizes. The challenge for Ibn Saud was how to implant Wahhabi religious authority in towns firmly tied to the rest of the Muslim world through the annual pilgrimage. For centuries, it was customary for pilgrims to remain in Mecca and Medina after the ceremonies as "sojourners" for a year or longer. Some sojourners from remote parts permanently settled, giving rise to colonies from Java and Bukhara, and putting a cosmopolitan stamp on the holy cities.[61] In addition, residents of the holy cities exhibited a spirit of toleration, within the confines of the Sunni consensus, that was fostered by the arrival and departure of religious scholars from all parts of the Muslim world.[62]

In addition to local sensibilities, Ibn Saud had to account for foreign opinion: Muslim leaders and colonial powers ruling over large Muslim populations (such as the British in India) were watching his moves. Attaining international approval required a prudent approach to instituting a Wahhabi religious regime.[63] Consequently, while he followed the Saudi custom of placing Wahhabi clerics in charge of religious institutions, he added a new wrinkle by enlisting foreign Muslims to work with them to gain the confidence of local and international audiences. Fortunately for Ibn Saud, Wahhabi clerics were eager to harness the prestige of the holy cities to their mission. But their reflexive mistrust of outsiders meant they were willing to cooperate only with like-minded foreign Muslims.[64]

Such like-minded foreign Muslims came from the Hadith Folk and Salafi revivalist currents that emerged in the Arab world and India in the late 1800s. They shared a number of the same ideas as the Wahhabi mission: the need to purify worship of illegitimate innovations, a view of religion as the foundation of Muslim society, and a desire to keep Western culture at bay. While they differed on the authority of the legal schools, the similarities were enough to chip away at the legacy of religious hostility between Wahhabis and foreign Muslims and to form a basis for cooperation.

Clerical Authority in Saudi Public Institutions

Saudi clerics proved to be adept at finding ways to take advantage of the dynasty's development of formal government institutions when oil revenues began to climb in the 1950s. The dominant religious personality at the time was Muhammad ibn Ibrahim Al al-Sheikh, a descendent of Wahhabism's founder. He was determined to preserve the Wahhabi mission's authority in religious affairs and did so by grafting it to modern bureaucratic institutions. Religious education moved from lesson circles held in mosques to classrooms in schools where pupils studied newly composed textbooks incorporating Wahhabi doctrine. The government created a college of Islamic law that became the foundation for the kingdom's religious universities. An office to review and approve all religious publications gave clerics powers of censorship. A government office to organize religious affairs centralized control over hiring staff for mosques (imams and preachers) and appointing administrators of endowments that funded religious institutions, stipends for religious pupils, and salaries for teachers and other personnel.[65]

Following Muhammad ibn Ibrahim's death in 1969, no single cleric possessed the stature to succeed him as head of the sprawling religious establishment. A collective leadership took shape under a new body, the Committee of Senior Clerics, to oversee religious education, religious law courts, and the holy places. For the first time, a cleric from outside the Al al-Sheikh clan rose to become the most influential religious figure: Abd al-Aziz ibn Baz, who happened to also be the Salafi Group's clerical supervisor.[66]

In the long run, accommodation by Wahhabi clerics to foreign Muslims spawned contradictory effects. Clerical authority became entrenched in government institutions that cemented the sway of Wahhabi doctrine over mosques, schools, and public morality. In addition, enlisting foreign Muslim revivalists to legitimize the Wahhabi mission outside Saudi Arabia gave rise to what some call the export of Wahhabism. At the same time, those same foreign Muslim revivalists imported the No Legal School tendency and the elevation of hadiths in determining Islamic law, creating the potential for dissent and controversy over religious matters.

The Hadith Institutes

In 1931, an Indian cleric residing in Medina established the Hadith Institute (*Dar al-Hadith*), which became an important site for the Hadith Folk to spread their ideas. The founder, Ahmad ibn Muhammad al-Dihlawi, was known for writing articles in Indian Muslim publications supporting Saudi annexation of the holy cities. He moved to Medina shortly after it fell to Saudi forces. Ibn Saud rewarded him by giving him permission to set up the Hadith Institute, an early token of foreign Muslim participation in developing Saudi religious institutions in the holy cities.[67]

Dihlawi followed in the footsteps of Indian scholars who had established private schools in the holy cities in the previous fifty years.[68] The Hadith Institute aspired to train highly accomplished scholars of hadiths in a ten-year course of study, with a curriculum combining courses in hadith subjects with a few "secular" subjects such as grammar and mathematics, but nothing that might be considered contrary to religion, such as logic, philosophy, and modern sciences. In 1932, Dihlawi set up a similar institution in Mecca, this time officially affiliated with the Hadith Folk movement. To head the institute, he designated another foreign Muslim: an Egyptian who also held the positions of prayer leader and preacher at the Grand Mosque.[69]

The Islamic University of Medina

The Hadith Institutes along with a Saudi school created in Mecca called the Scholastic Institute were precursors to a larger project to bring Saudi Arabia out of its religious isolation.[70] In 1961, King Saud proclaimed the establishment of the Islamic University of Medina. Part of the impetus for the new university was the need to compete for regional influence with Gamal Abd al-Nasir, the popular leader of Egypt. In the late 1950s, Nasir had risen to become the dominant figure in Arab politics by championing anti-imperialism, revolutionary secular Arab nationalism, and socialism. The Saudis felt threatened by Nasir's appeal, particularly for the young, educated generation at home. The Islamic University of Medina was part of a political strategy to counter Nasir's revolutionary Arab nationalism with a Saudi claim to religious leadership, not merely by creating an "Islamic" university but also by making it an international center for advanced religious education that reserved places for non-Saudi students and hired foreign Muslims to fill teaching and administrative positions, under the supervision of Saudi clerics.

The Medinan Hadith Institute became part of the Islamic University a few years after it opened, bolstering the ranks of foreign Muslim spokesmen for the Hadith Folk and the No Legal School tendency. Saudi Arabia's growing oil revenues in the mid-1970s funded university expansion, which brought more foreign Muslim students, thereby increasing opportunities for mixing between Saudi and foreign students, and exposing Saudis to foreign religious movements.

Nasir al-Din al-Albani

The Islamic University and the Hadith Institutes served as incubators and recruiting grounds for the Salafi Group. One Islamic University instructor in particular who inspired pupils to embrace the views of the Hadith Folk and the No Legal School tendency was Nasir al-Din al-Albani (1914–1999).[71] He was the most influential Salafi thinker of the late twentieth century. His unrivaled knowledge of hadiths made him a prestigious authority, a beacon of independent thinking, and an emblem of authenticity for Muslims seeking a sure guide to the ways of the Prophet and the Pious Ancestors.

When he was a young child, his family moved from Albania to Damascus (in Arabic, "Albani" means "Albanian.") He spent his formative years and most of his life in Syria before political conditions in the 1960s, the rise to power of the secular Arab nationalist Baath Party, forced him to relocate to Jordan. Albani's training in religious studies in Damascus was unusual in that he did not attend the lessons of established scholars. Instead, he took an independent approach through reading on his own and wound up embracing Salafi positions on the legal schools and hadiths. But he went further than other Salafis and made original claims about the reliability of canonical hadiths, which led him to adopt legal rules that were at odds with Saudi views.

The most common method for rating hadiths was to consider the credibility of men who passed them down from one generation to the next, or the chain of transmission. Albani adopted a more restrictive criterion for rating hadiths according to their mode of transmission, that is to say, how a reporter of a hadith learned about it. If he heard it directly from a trusted source, then Albani approved. If he only implied that he heard it directly from a trusted source, Albani might disqualify it. On such technical details hinged the justification for common religious practices. Clerics criticized him for downgrading nearly 1000 hadiths that Sunni scholars had long considered to be reliable.[72]

Albani's Brief Career in Saudi Arabia

Albani came to Saudi Arabia in 1961 to teach at the Islamic University of Medina. During his two years in Medina, students flocked to his lessons at the university and at the Hadith Institutes. His penchant for independent thinking, however, made him unpopular with Saudi clerics. Most notably, he published an essay where he claimed that nothing in the Quran or the Sunnah justified the requirement that women cover their faces. In a work on prayer, Albani stirred controversy by favoring minor changes in the ritual that diverged from Saudi practice, which was based on the Hanbali legal school. The differences may seem trivial—a matter of adding two words, changing the position of one's hands during prayer, and permitting worshippers to wear shoes during prayer—but they caused such turmoil that Albani's followers wound up praying in separate mosques.[73] Unwilling to tolerate a popular teacher dispensing unorthodox legal rules, the Saudis allowed his contract to lapse and he had to leave the country, but he had already made an impact on the religious scene in the holy cities.

Albani's former students obtained teaching positions at the Islamic University and the Hadith Institutes where they espoused the doctrines of the Hadith Folk and the No Legal School tendency. In the 1970s, his views were dominant among the university's faculty who taught courses on hadiths. According to a former follower,

> The hadith had become a virtual dictatorship. When in a sermon or a conference an *'alim* [religious scholar] cited a hadith, he could be interrupted at any moment by one of his students asking him: "Has that hadith been authenticated? Has al-Albani authenticated it?" That could hardly fail to reinforce the mistrust felt by the ulama belonging to the religious institution toward al-Albani.[74]

Albani's Influence on Huzaimi

Nasir al-Huzaimi first encountered Albani's writings when he was still living in Zubair. He heard that Albani was a Salafi but did not know exactly what that meant other than someone who tried to live according to the Sunnah. In Riyadh, Huzaimi found that the Islamic bookstores held few of Albani's writings, especially his work permitting women to uncover their faces. During his first visit to Mecca, he became a follower of the Salafi Group after attending a lesson led by one of Albani's pupils, Ali Mazrui, a teacher at Medina's Hadith Institute. Mazrui's method of citing passages in the Quran and hadiths rather than referring to classical legal authorities so impressed Huzaimi that he decided to enroll at the Hadith Institute, but without a diploma from a Saudi school, he had to wait for special permission. In the meantime, he attended the Haram Institute in Mecca, which had grown out of study circles held under the porticoes of the Grand Mosque. A short time later, Huzaimi met Albani during the pilgrimage and attended his lessons, after which he blindly followed Albani's legal opinions.

Albani's Influence on the Salafi Group

Salafi Group members highly valued their copies of Albani's works, considering them authoritative guides to religion. He also influenced their mistrust of the Saudi religious establishment, and he specifically warned them that their supervisor, Abd al-Aziz ibn Baz, was easily misled by others. As for the Saudi rulers, Albani did not consider them worthy of a believer's oath of allegiance according to Sunni doctrine, which requires caliphs to belong to the Prophet's tribe Quraish. Furthermore, Albani considered them to be corrupt and too close to Western powers, but he did not condemn them as unbelievers.[75]

Juhaiman's Criticism of Albani

Juhaiman commended Albani for inspiring Salafis in Kuwait and Syria to combat illegitimate innovations in worship, to rely exclusively on the Quran and the Sunnah for legal rules, and to toss out inauthentic hadiths. Nevertheless, Juhaiman found fault with Albani for failing to realize the political implications of his ideas about Muslim rulers, including the Saudis, whom he accused of trampling religion.

The Salafi Group and Saudi Clerics

The Salafi Group started in Medina, where Saudis mingled with Arab, African, and South Asian Muslims as teachers, administrators, and pupils at the Hadith Institute and the Islamic University of Medina. The Wahhabi clerics supervising religious education ensured conformity with their core theological doctrine by allowing teachers to only use books sanctioned by the Wahhabi tradition.[76] Foreign Muslim teachers in other courses were able to spread the No Legal School doctrine and the emphasis on hadiths in determining Islamic law. The hybrid religious climate mixing Saudi and foreign Muslim religious thinking accounts for the inherent ambivalence in the Salafi Group's relationship with Saudi clerics. The group not only fully embraced Wahhabi theology but also followed Albani's view on the legal schools and hadiths. The religious climate also reflected tensions in the Wahhabi mission itself between exclusion and accommodation. The group's inclusion of foreign Muslims and high regard for Albani tell us that its members did not want to go back to the isolation of earlier centuries. But their puritanical impulse and rejection of Western influences mirrored the exclusivist spirit that originally animated the Wahhabi mission.

Commanding Right and Forbidding Wrong

The puritanical impulse first brought notoriety to some of Albani's former students vehemently opposed to signs of Western influence, such as the display of human images in advertising. In 1965, they smashed a store window to destroy some female mannequins.[77] In the "breaking windows" incident, the young men were taking upon themselves the religious duty to command right and forbid wrong, which is based on verses in the Quran and several hadiths. Perhaps the most famous Quranic passage is 3:104: "Let there be one community of you calling to good and commanding right and forbidding wrong."⁷⁸

The duty to command right and forbid wrong has a long history of interpretation in Islamic law, with different views on how believers are to fulfil it. According to a famous hadith, "Whoever sees a wrong and is able to put it right with his hand, let him do so; if can't, then with his tongue; if he can't, then with his heart, which is the bare minimum of faith."⁷⁹ There are different views on whether the duty is an individual duty incumbent on all believers, similar to prayer and fasting, or a collective duty that is satisfied when one or more believers carry it out. If it is an individual duty, then any believer should forbid wrong as a matter of demonstrating belief. If it is a collective duty, then its performance may be delegated to a particular group of believers.⁸⁰ The latter view is expressed in a widespread saying that is suited to quelling moral vigilantism: "Putting things right with the hand is for the political authorities, with the tongue for scholars, and in the heart for the common people."⁸¹

In early Islamic times, the Abbasid caliphs of Baghdad enforced commanding right and forbidding wrong as a collective duty with the appointment of a public official called the *muhtasib*. This official oversaw markets to ensure fair commerce, inspected weights and measures, monitored public morality, and upheld rules for prayer and fasting.⁸² The first two Saudi states did not appoint public officials to oversee commanding right and forbidding wrong, although district governors monitored attendance at mosque prayers and punished men who skipped them.⁸³ The first official government body dedicated to the task was a committee established in 1926 in Mecca, shortly after the Saudi conquest of the holy city. The committee's duties included enforcement of attendance at prayer in the mosques, supervision of imams and muezzins to ensure compliance with Saudi standards, and policing public areas to enforce bans on alcohol, tobacco smoking, and mixing between men and women.⁸⁴

The committees underwent expansion along with the rest of the religious establishment in the 1950s. After Faisal became king in 1964, however, expansion came to a halt. To the dismay of the clerics, the king fostered a climate that tolerated Western customs, such as soccer, photography, cinema, and foreign publications. Rather than criticize Faisal, the clerics blamed Western intrusion on the influx of foreign workers that accompanied the rise in oil revenues.⁸⁵ In this context, the "breaking windows" incident implied that the religious establishment was falling short in fulfilling the duty to command right and forbid wrong and therefore individual believers had to "put things right with the hand." By approving the establishment of the Salafi Group that Commands Right and Forbids Wrong,⁸⁶ Saudi clerics tried to curb the vigilante spirit animating the restless young puritans and to reassert control over a duty reserved to government authorities.

The Salafi Canon

The Salafi Group's dedication to reviving the ways of the Pious Ancestors depended on learning those ways from writings that, according to Salafi scholars, contained all a believer needed to know. The approved set of writings were a very small subset of the rich intellectual legacy devoted to studying the Quran and the Sunnah that includes specialized subfields in Arabic grammar, rhetoric, and lexicography; legal theory and legal rules; theology; exegesis of the Quran; and methods for assessing hadiths and using them for legal rules.

Salafi scholars advocated restricting intellectual endeavor to a limited set of topics and scholars. In doing so, they constructed a canon, or a body of authoritative authors and works, that distinguished them from other Muslims. In simple terms, the Salafis claimed that believers could rely on only certain authors and works for authoritative knowledge of true belief and correct practice. Furthermore, they claimed that other authors and works were not worthwhile, and even dangerous to study. Finally, they claimed that only certain fields of study would help believers to understand the ways of the Pious Ancestors and that other fields posed the risk of exposure to ideas that could lead believers astray. By the 1960s, Saudi Arabia was playing a leading role in defining and advancing the Salafi canon in the Muslim world, particularly through the Islamic University of Medina.[87]

The Salafi Group further restricted the scholastic tradition to theology and hadiths, leaving out Islamic law and legal theory and replacing them with Albani's writings on how to use hadiths to derive legal rules. Huzaimi's description of the Salafis' personal book collections notes that only two members possessed legal works. Juhaiman's book collection contained the six canonical collections of hadiths; classical and modern commentaries on them; three classical works on exegesis of the Quran; theological works by Ibn Abd al-Wahhab, Ibn Taymiyyah, and Ibn a-Qayyim; and Albani's writings; he had no books on the legal schools. Religious students at the Islamic University might study other topics, but the Salafis considered them a waste of time and a source of religious error. When Huzaimi began to study a text on logic, members of the group persuaded him to give it up because the Pious Ancestors viewed logic as an illegitimate innovation, and therefore it was not to be included in the studies of someone following their way.

As scrupulous as Salafis were about excluding sources that might get in the way of accessing the earliest Muslim generations, they relied on scholars who lived centuries after the Pious Ancestors. For guidance about theology, Salafis read the works of fourteenth-century scholars Ibn Taymiyyah and Ibn al-Qayyim along with those of eighteenth-century scholar Muhammad ibn Abd al-Wahhab. For the hadiths, they studied the works of fifteenth-century Egyptian scholar Ibn Hajar al-Asqalani on technical terms and analytical method. Salafis may claim to dispense with the scholastic tradition, but in fact they depend on a selection of works embedded in that tradition.

Challenges to Clerical Authority

At several places in the memoir, Huzaimi describes incidents where the reader sees locations for challenges to Saudi religious authority, the mechanisms for exercising authority, and the issues on which it was challenged.

Challenging the Sunni Consensus on Teaching Islamic Law

Control over religious learning was an essential part of establishing and perpetuating the domination of Wahhabi doctrine. Shortly after the Saudi conquest of Mecca, Ibn Saud authorized the clerics to supervise lesson circles at the Grand Mosque. One of their first steps was to promote the Hanbali legal school, which previously had a minimal presence.[88] They also preserved the Sunni consensus on restricting Islamic law lessons to the Sunni legal schools and on excluding instruction about the extinct legal schools.

Huzaimi describes an incident illustrating how Saudi clerics enforced the obligation to follow the Sunni legal schools through their control over who could teach and what texts were permitted in lessons at the Grand Mosque. One of his teachers, a Pakistani sheikh from the Hadith Folk tendency, gave lessons on a legal treatise by Ibn Hazm (d. 1063), a famous eleventh-century scholar of Muslim Spain. Ibn Hazm's treatise was controversial because it rejected the obligation to follow the four legal schools and sharply criticized the Hanafi legal school. Furthermore, teaching Ibn Hazm's treatise violated the prohibition on teaching extinct legal schools, in this case, the Zahiri school, which had died out around 1400. Salafis were drawn to the Zahiri legal school because of its emphasis on literal interpretation of the Quran and the Sunnah.[89]

The memoir gives the impression that there was more to the incident than choosing texts for a syllabus. The Pakistani sheikh's circle of pupils gathered near a lesson circle led by a sheikh from the Hanafi legal school. The Pakistani sheikh would loudly recite passages from Ibn Hazm's book that harshly criticize the Hanafi school. To make matters worse, the sheikh made a vulgar pun when pronouncing the word "Hanafi" by changing the first consonant to pronounce the word for "effeminate." The Hanafi students complained to the sheikh in charge of teaching at the Grand Mosque, Muhammad ibn Subayyil, accusing the Pakistani of insulting the ulama and of teaching an extinct legal school. Ibn Subayyil summoned the sheikh and encouraged him to be courteous and to stop teaching Ibn Hazm's book, recommending that he teach an exegesis of the Quran approved by Wahhabis.[90] Huzaimi mentions a similar episode at the Grand Mosque when official clerics banned a Saudi sheikh from teaching because he had given lessons on the Zahiri tradition and criticized the custom of following the four legal schools.

Challenging the Qualifications of Teachers

Saudi clerics controlled who had permission to teach and what texts they could teach, but they confronted another problem from religious pupils demanding that clerics cite hadiths to support their views. Huzaimi describes the clerics as unprepared to respond because they were accustomed to having commoners passively accept their teachings without having to justify them. Salafi pupils broke an unspoken rule against arguing with clerics, posing questions about the sources for their views and the merit of hadiths they cited, as strong or weak. The clerics were not hadith experts, so their only response to such questions was to cite legal treatises.

Challenging Clerical Control over Islamic Law and Worship

The Salafis' rejection of the legal schools and their emphasis on hadiths resulted in their adoption of religious practices that defied Saudi insistence on conformity with Hanbali law on worship. Huzaimi traces tensions between the Salafi Group and Saudi clerics to an incident in 1976, when a leading member of the group, Ali Mazrui, broke with the customary position on when fasting begins each day during Ramadan. He asserted that the fast begins at the break of dawn whereas the customary position endorsed by Saudi clerics maintained that it begins earlier, with the call to the dawn prayer. Mazrui did not merely express his opinion to fellow Salafis. He declared it before an audience at the Grand Mosque. Mazrui's insistence on the right to undertake independent legal reasoning to arrive at a different position on the rules for fasting was an open challenge to clerical authority and the clerics responded by banning him from teaching and by putting the Salafis under surveillance.

The Salafi Group also defied clerical authority over two aspects of prayer: the call to prayer and wearing sandals at prayer. In the Prophet's lifetime, the custom began of designating a man to issue a call to prayer, in Arabic, *adhan*. The man who recites the adhan is a muezzin, typically a man with a loud voice (recalling that amplification is a modern invention) and a talent for reciting the adhan in a rhythmic cadence. The first muezzin is an honored figure of early Islam, Bilal, a freed slave of an Arab father and African mother. The wording in the call to prayer is fixed, although there is some variation between Sunnis and Shiites. The Salafis added a line to the dawn call to prayer. Because worshippers hear the call to prayer five times a day all their lives, variation in its wording is noticeable, disturbing, and controversial, as if someone added or subtracted words from the Christian Lord's Prayer.

The Salafi Group's position that worshippers may wear sandals at prayer contradicted the universal custom for Muslims to pray barefoot. Mosques frequently have a special place for worshippers to leave their sandals and shoes at the entrance to the prayer hall or courtyard. For someone to enter a place of worship with footwear is a desecration. Because the validity of prayer depends on its correct performance, the Saudi authorities censured the Salafis for wearing sandals at prayer because it renders their performance of the prayer invalid, which meant they were guilty of neglecting a religious duty.

Summary

Islamic law establishes rules for worship, morality, personal habits, and social relations. The Sunni tradition of law developed four main approaches, the legal schools, to authorize and limit legal rules. Saudi Arabia's Wahhabi mission conformed to the Sunni historical tradition by following the Hanbali legal school.

The Salafi Group, however, rejected the Sunni historical tradition of law in favor of the No Legal School tendency. In addition, Juhaiman rejected limiting the authority to issue legal rules to highly trained experts. Rejecting legal school authority opened the way to adopting unorthodox worship practices that produced friction with Saudi clerics and schism in the Salafi Group.

The Salafi Group and Islamic Movements

Tablighi Association: Established in the 1920s in India; calls on Muslims to regular observance of worship; organizes ordinary Muslims (not clerics) to go on group preaching tours; stays out of politics; maintains branches in many Muslim countries; large global membership; active in Saudi Arabia among Saudi nationals and foreign Muslims.

Ansar al-Sunnah: Established in the 1920s in Egypt; calls on Muslims to eliminate illegitimate innovations and to focus on studying hadiths; seeks return to correct religion through education and preaching in traditional settings of schools and mosques; stays out of politics; small membership in Egypt, Sudan, and Saudi Arabia; played a role in fostering the Hadith Institutes.

Muslim Brotherhood: Established in the 1920s in Egypt; calls on Muslims to regular observance of worship and infusing religious values in all aspects of life, including politics maintains branches in several Arab countries and Muslim diasporas; sizable global membership; active in Saudi Arabia among Saudi nationals and foreign Muslims; played a role in fostering educational development in Saudi Arabia blending modern political concerns with religious identity; divided between reform and revolutionary camps since the late 1960s.

Society of Muslims: Established in the 1970s as a Muslim Brotherhood splinter group; considers most Muslims to be unbelievers and calls on true believers to withdraw from society; doctrine is inherently political because it brands Muslim rulers unbelievers unworthy of loyalty or obedience; suppression by Egyptian government forced members into exile, including Saudi Arabia, where their doctrine of excommunication (takfir) became a point of controversy in the Salafi Group.

Introduction

There is a popular saying that if the Islamic State were to come about, the Tablighis would be the commoners, the Salafis would be the religious leaders, and the Muslim Brothers would be the political leaders.[91]

Huzaimi recounts interactions between the Salafi Group and other Islamic movements originating in the mid-1920s: Ansar al-Sunnah and the Muslim

Brotherhood in Egypt, and the Tablighi Association in India. All three established footholds in the holy cities soon after their annexation to the Saudi realm. The Islamic movements and the Salafi Group shared a commitment to reviving religion and combating secular and Western influences, but their different priorities and their desire for popularity made them competitors rather than allies. The Saudi religious establishment gave a boost to compliant movements with subsidies and jobs; movements that challenged the establishment risked repression.

Huzaimi's account of the Islamic movements provides a window into how they appeared to a pious young man committed to finding the right religious path. In addition, the Salafi Group's unique profile comes into focus through its interaction with other movements.

The Preaching Association: Tablighi Jama'at

The Preaching Association originated in British India at a time of rising communal tensions between Hindus and Muslims.[92] In 1926, Muhammad Ilyas Kandhalawi, a cleric educated at the reformist Deoband School, founded the Association to revive religious practice, especially among rural Muslims known for sharing beliefs and practices with Hindus and Christians. His activism was in some measure a response to a Hindu revivalist movement that was striving to "reconvert" rural Muslims to Hinduism, claiming that these Muslims were former Hindus. Tablighi's distinctive activity was the preaching tour. Members might commit to join a preaching tour for one day or weekend each month, or they might undertake forty-day tours in other countries. Tablighi had a broad view of religion that focused on reviving observance of Islam's five pillars rather than dwelling on illegitimate innovations and correct theology that preoccupy Salafis.

Tablighi's template for pious activism proved attractive in Saudi Arabia. Several Salafi Group members, including Juhaiman and other founders, had their first taste of religious activism with Tablighi's preaching tours, which may have inspired Juhaiman's own energetic preaching mission. Huzaimi relates that the Tablighi was known in Riyadh for preaching in poor neighborhoods. When the Salafi Group undertook preaching tours to villages near Mecca, it found that no matter where it went, Tablighi had already been there to preach and recruit. According to Huzaimi, Tablighi's success stemmed from members' gentle manners and avoidance of confrontation.

The Tablighi Association and the Salafi Group were similar in two ways. They eschewed political activism and they upheld the Prophet as the model for believers. The Tablighi, however, did not emphasize careful study of hadiths to distinguish between unreliable and authentic ones. The Salafis also faulted Tablighi because it did not teach correct theology, the duty to command right and forbid wrong, and the principle of loyalty to believers and disavowal of unbelievers. Consequently, the Salafis regarded Tablighi members as misguided but sincere Muslims whose activist disposition made them potential recruits.

Helpers of the Prophetic Tradition: Ansar al-Sunnah al-Muhammadiyyah

Ansar al-Sunnah al-Muhammadiyyah was created in Egypt in 1926.[93] The founder, Muhammad Hamid al-Fiqi (1892–1959), a graduate of the Azhar seminary in Cairo, was a preacher and prayer leader. He took his inspiration from Wahhabi proselytizing and set out to revive medieval theological works by Ibn Taymiyya and Ibn al-Qayyim by publishing them in modern editions.

Ansar al-Sunnah's purpose was to combat illegitimate innovations and modern intellectual currents making inroads among the growing number of Egyptians pursuing Western-style education. In the 1920s, the ideas of Darwin, Freud, and Marx were popular with the young educated set. Fiqi was a severe critic of the Muslim Brotherhood, blaming it for ignoring illegitimate innovations such as seeking the intercession of holy men.

Ansar al-Sunnah's agenda meshed with the Wahhabi mission's concerns about illegitimate innovations, theology,[94] and, to a lesser extent in Saudi Arabia during the 1920s, the adoption of Western customs. When the Saudis created committees to enforce the duty to command right and forbid wrong in Hijaz, they appointed a member of the Ansar al-Sunnah, Abd al-Zahir Abu al-Samh, to oversee them.[95] The Saudis recognized the group's theological kinship and worked with it to broaden educational outreach. Ansar members taught at the Hadith Institute in Mecca, served on the advisory board for the founding of the Islamic University of Medina, and taught at the university.[96] Huzaimi's account mentions an Egyptian resident at the Salafi Group's house in Medina whose father was a member of the Ansar who had immigrated to Saudi Arabia and settled in Medina.

Muslim Brotherhood: Jama'at al-Ikhwan al-Muslimin

The Muslim Brotherhood was founded in Egypt in 1928 by a young schoolteacher, Hasan al-Banna (1906–1949).[97] Banna came of age as Egypt was emerging from four decades of British rule (1882–1924) that accelerated the spread of Western cultural influence and deepened Western economic domination. He believed that for Egypt to undergo regeneration, Islam had to be reestablished as the foundation of social, economic, cultural, and political life.

The Muslim Brotherhood was the first grassroots movement in the Muslim world to harness religious revival to an organizational structure that enacted a wide-ranging activist agenda. Banna presided over a hierarchical structure that included a national consultative council, district councils, and local branches. Special committees handled finances, legal issues, and social welfare. The Brotherhood created separate sections for workers, students, and professionals.

The organization's branches undertook various activities to demonstrate the ways Islamic principles serve public welfare—operating health clinics, providing assistance to members in financial need, offering adult literacy classes, and hosting religious celebrations. Youths were organized into scouts who went on camping trips and performed public services such as street cleaning in poor neighborhoods. The Brotherhood also set up sports clubs for wrestling, boxing, and soccer.

Banna publicized the Brotherhood's mission and activities in a newspaper. This new model of religious activism thrived. By the mid-1940s membership reached 500,000, and branches surfaced in Jordan, Palestine, Syria, Lebanon, Yemen, and the Gulf.

Under Banna's direction, the Muslim Brotherhood established a section called the special apparatus to prepare members for jihad against Islam's enemies by providing rudimentary drills in arms. The militant emphasis found an outlet in the 1948 Palestine war. The Brotherhood joined a chorus of political groups that pressed the Egyptian government to dispatch the army to prevent the partition of Palestine into Arab and Jewish states approved by the United Nations in November 1947. When the Egyptian army intervened in May 1948, Muslim Brotherhood members joined volunteer units fighting for the Arab cause. By the end of the year, Israeli forces had prevailed and the Egyptian government agreed to a ceasefire and armistice talks, outraging the Brotherhood. In December 1948, a member of the special apparatus assassinated the Egyptian prime minister. Two months later, Egyptian security forces retaliated by gunning down Banna and the government banned his organization. How to respond to government repression divided the Brotherhood between moderates who renounced violence and radicals who embraced militancy.

The inspiration for the radicals came from the writings of Sayyid Qutb (1906–1966).[98] There was no hint in Qutb's early career that he would become the intellectual founder of radical Islamism. He worked for the Egyptian government in the Ministry of Education and carved out a place in the country's literary scene, primarily as an essayist. Religious themes appeared in his writings in the 1940s, notably in his influential *Social Justice in Islam*. He joined the Muslim Brotherhood in the early 1950s and quickly became a prominent voice in the movement. Qutb adopted a radical stance when the Egyptian government under Gamal Abd al-Nasir jailed hundreds of Muslim Brothers, including Qutb. He spent most of the last twelve years of his life in prison. The Egyptian government executed him in 1966 on charges of sedition.

During his prison years, Qutb came to believe that Arab societies had lapsed into a state of pre-Islamic spiritual ignorance, or *jahiliyyah*, and that Arab rulers posing as Muslims were actually apostates who must be fought and overthrown. He called on true Muslims to form a vanguard to revive Islam by reenacting the Prophet's original jihad against unbelievers. Some took that to mean waging armed struggle to overthrow Arab regimes, but other interpreters of his writings maintained that Qutb's discussions of jihad referred to moral and social struggle. In the 1970s, the militant interpretation divided the Muslim Brotherhood between followers of Banna seeking change through education and preaching on one side and followers of Qutb seeking change through armed struggle. Followers of the militant interpretation formed a number of radical splinter groups, such as the Society of Muslims.[99]

In the 1960s, Saudi Arabia became a haven for Muslim Brothers suffering political repression in Egypt and other Arab countries, largely because the Saudis and the Muslim Brothers rejected secular Arab nationalism and upheld a central role for religion in society and culture. Furthermore, Saudi Arabia's efforts to develop a modern education system were hampered by a scarcity of citizens qualified to contribute. Many Muslim Brothers were educational professionals and they were able to get a foothold in Saudi schools as teachers, administrators, and staff. The Saudi government never allowed the Brotherhood to set up an official branch, but members were able to spread the movement's ideas through schools, mosques, and religious activities. Its emphasis on contemporary affairs and activism proved attractive to young Saudis. Informal networks of Saudi supporters became influential voices in debates over Western cultural and political influence.[100]

In the memoir, the Muslim Brotherhood appears primarily as a competitor with other Islamic groups. Huzaimi describes the scene in Riyadh, where the Muslim Brotherhood's two factions and the Tablighi Association sent members to seek recruits at discussion groups led by imams at small neighborhood mosques. Members of the rival movements sometimes got into heated arguments at those meetings. Juhaiman felt that the Muslim Brotherhood poached members from the Salafi Group and the Tablighi Association by pretending to join and then participating in their activities. The Brotherhood had two assets in the contest for recruits. First, its writers produced a body of literature that refuted the popular secular leftist trends of the day—communism, socialism, Arab nationalism—and upheld the superiority of Islam to all worldly ideologies. The one Islamic bookstore in Riyadh in the mid-1970s stocked works by Muslim Brotherhood authors. Second, persecution by Arab nationalist regimes gave the Brotherhood a heroic reputation for having the courage to defy powerful rulers for the sake of religious convictions.

The Salafi Group and the Tablighi Association appealed to youths like Huzaimi who were more interested in the call to purify and revive religious practice than in politics. Nevertheless, the Salafis envied the Brotherhood's reputation for political courage and relished the opportunity to stand up to the Saudi authorities. When the government ordered the detention of Salafi dissenters at the end of 1977, members remaining at large felt they had achieved parity with the Muslim Brotherhood for enduring persecution. In the wake of the arrests, the Salafi Group attracted new members, including some from the Muslim Brotherhood.

There were substantial differences between the kinds of religious revivalism espoused by the Muslim Brotherhood and the Salafi Group, which adopted Nasir al-Din al-Albani's critical attitude toward the Egyptian movement. He thought that their emphasis on political activism reflected an obsession with power that distracted from the more important task to promote correct belief. He expressed his attitude toward political activity in the saying, "the good policy is to stay away from politics."[101] Purification of Muslim life through teaching and preaching required a patient, long-term approach. Pride in the vocation of religious learning may have played a part in Albani's critical stance toward the Brotherhood, which he accused of disrespecting religious scholars. For its part, the Brotherhood thought that the Salafi focus on "secondary" matters of doctrine needlessly divided and weakened Muslims. Its members boycotted Albani's lesson circles and its writers published rebuttals of his ideas.[102]

The Society of Muslims: Jama'at al-Muslimin

The Society of Muslims, better known as "Excommunication and Emigration,"[103] was a radical offshoot of the Muslim Brotherhood.[104] Its reputation for emphasizing excommunication made it a forerunner of the "takfiri" trend that would wreak havoc in Algeria's civil war during the 1990s and later became identified with the al-Qaeda offshoot, the Islamic State.[105]

In the Saudi context, excommunication doctrine has a controversial history. Muhammad ibn Abd al-Wahhab's strict definition of belief at least implied casting other Muslims as idolaters. His critics accused him of twisting the Sunni consensus on excommunication doctrine with the effect of turning Saudi military campaigns against fellow Muslims into jihads against infidels. The Wahhabi mission's foes resorted to name-calling, branding Ibn Abd al-Wahhab and his followers latter-day Kharijites, the early Islamic group whose rebellion against caliphs gave it a bad reputation. Ibn Abd al-Wahhab naturally rebutted the accusations and claimed his excommunication doctrine was in accord with the example of the Prophet. Later Wahhabi clerics tempered their position on excommunication; nevertheless, the reputation for hasty, unjustified excommunication of believers continued to haunt the Wahhabi mission.[106]

The Society of Muslims founder, Shukri Mustafa, was a former student of agricultural sciences who was arrested in 1965 for membership in the Muslim Brotherhood. During his six-year prison term, he embraced Sayyid Qutb's position that Egyptian government and society had lapsed into the pre-Islamic condition of spiritual ignorance and that true believers had to separate themselves from society, in imitation of the Prophet's emigration from Mecca to Medina.

Mustafa rejected the traditional Islamic idea that believers should tolerate unjust rulers for the sake of preventing anarchy. In addition, he was hostile toward the official clergy and referred to them as "pulpit parrots," opportunists who shaped their religious pronouncements to suit the interests of illegitimate rulers. Official clerics were therefore viewed as obstacles in the path of reviving religion and the Society of Muslim members avoided praying behind government-approved clerics.[107]

Mustafa was released from prison in 1971 as part of a general amnesty granted by Anwar Sadat, who became president of Egypt after Nasir died in 1970. Mustafa set about recruiting members, who undertook emigration to preserve their religious purity. Some relocated to remote parts of southern Egypt and others formed urban communes. Mustafa did not initially favor violent confrontation with the government. Instead, he sought to reform society through preaching and exhortation in a manner similar to the Salafi Group. In 1977, however, his attitude shifted in response to the arrests of some Society of Muslim members. His followers kidnapped a former government minister and announced they would set him free in exchange for the release of fellow members in detention. When the government rejected their demand, they executed their captive. The government moved to crush the movement with a wave of arrests. The Society of Muslims fought back and engaged in shootouts with security forces. Mustafa was caught in the crackdown, tried, and sentenced to death, carried out in 1978.

The Society of Muslims members who evaded the authorities migrated to the Gulf states, so the men Huzaimi encountered in Medina would have been fugitives. Shukri Mustafa's exiled followers tried to spread their doctrine of excommunicating Muslims and proclaiming the illegitimacy of Muslim rulers. Huzaimi relates that they had some success with Egyptian and Yemeni students at the Islamic University of Medina. While the Salafi Group's leadership rejected excommunication, members sympathized with the exiles and helped them find lodging and jobs. They thought they might be able to persuade them to give up the excommunication doctrine through dialogue.

As it turned out, three members of the Salafi Group embraced the excommunication doctrine and decided to emigrate to the desert to withdraw from society. Juhaiman worried that if the authorities heard that some members adopted the excommunication doctrine, they would use it as an excuse to persecute the Salafi Group for taking up the beliefs of the Kharijites. Huzaimi describes how Juhaiman took advantage of a visit to Medina by Nasir al-Din al-Albani to hold a meeting to uphold the correct positions on excommunication, legitimate rule, and the Kharijites. The meeting apparently achieved its purpose, and to drive home the point, members agreed to study a work by Ibn Taymiyyah that Salafis considered an authoritative text for defining belief, unbelief, and excommunication doctrine.

Conclusion

The foreign Islamic movements shared a commitment to one or another conception of religious revival—whether through regular performance of worship (Tablighi), rigorous attention to theology and ritual innovations (Ansar al-Sunnah), asserting a central public role for religious principles and social activism (Muslim Brotherhood), or drawing a sharp line between the pious and the rest (Society of Muslims). The Salafi Group was a unique blend of elements from various movements—Tablighi's missionary outreach, Ansar al-Sunnah's elevation of hadith study, and the Society of Muslims' rejection of society. In addition, the Salafi Group upheld the homegrown Wahhabi focus on theology and ritual. The Salafi Group might have kept a low profile as a minor religious tendency on the fringes of Saudi society had Juhaiman al-Utaibi not emerged as the leader of a dissident faction and turned the group into an apocalyptic sect preaching the Mahdi's advent. While other Islamic movements pursued a divinely guided society through preaching, education, and outreach, the millenarian scenario provided a short cut to a heavenly goal.

Juhaiman al-Utaibi

Juhaiman al-Utaibi's alienation from Saudi society and his hostility toward the government had a decisive effect on the Salafi Group's destiny. A rebellious streak in his personality can be traced to three sources. First, he grew up in an old Ikhwan settlement where he came to know veterans of the militant movement and absorbed their sense that Ibn Saud had betrayed them. Second, he resented how the modern Saudi state had destroyed the power and independence of Bedouin tribes. Third, he blamed his struggles in school on clerics. According to Juhaiman, they needlessly complicated education in order to reinforce their authority as the gatekeepers of religion. His rejection of Saudi clerical authority over the Salafi Group triggered the government's attempt to arrest him and his followers, but he eluded capture for nearly two years. During his time on the run, he led his faction down the path to violent insurrection in anticipation of heavenly intervention in history with the advent of the Mahdi.

The Old Ikhwan

Juhaiman was born around 1938 in Sajir, one of the *hijrahs* (agricultural settlements) established under Ibn Saud for Bedouin abandoning the nomadic way of life.[108] The term "hijrah" alludes to the migration of the Prophet and the believers from Mecca to Medina, from a place of idolatry to a place of belief. When the Bedouin settled in colonies, they were migrating from desert domains of religious error to permanent settlements where Wahhabi clerics would spend a few months a year to instruct them in religious truth, making them "Brethren (*ikhwan*) in Obedience to God," or Ikhwan for short.

The first Ikhwan colony went back to around 1912. At their height in the late 1920s, there were roughly 200 colonies dotting the central Arabian landscape. To attract the Bedouin to a sedentary way of life, Ibn Saud had wells dug for each household and supplied basic provisions and seed to turn the tribesmen into productive cultivators. While some colonies failed for lack of water, the ones that took hold helped Ibn Saud's plans to reestablish his clan's power. The Bedouin who abandoned their nomadic ways were no longer a source of insecurity, raiding towns and caravans, but warriors for Ibn Saud's military campaigns under the banner of jihad against infidels. The warrior ethos of the Bedouin now had religious sanction.

Members of Juhaiman's tribe, the Utaibah, were some of the first Bedouin to settle. The oldest and largest Utaibi colony, named al-Ghat Ghat, was established around 1914. It was the home of the Utaibi chieftain Sultan ibn Bijad, whose martial valor and piety were long remembered. Utaibi tribesmen settled about twenty-five colonies altogether. Juhaiman's town, Sajir, was founded in 1919.[109] No census of the Ikhwan colonies was ever conducted, therefore population estimates for them vary widely. The count for al-Ghat Ghat ranges between 3,500 and 12,000 residents. A description of Sajir in 1928 estimated it had 500 warriors.

The Ikhwan colonies had two features that made them potential threats to Ibn Saud's vision of a stable, unified Arabia under his rule. First, each colony was settled by members of the same tribe. Consequently, tribal solidarity remained intact at the expense of allegiance to Ibn Saud. Second, the colonies became strongholds for exclusivist Wahhabism. This meant that the Ikhwan's support for Ibn Saud was conditional, based on their estimation of his commitment to upholding true belief. When he took a pragmatic course in dealing with the outside world, he collided with the Ikhwan's uncompromising spirit.

Difficulties for Ibn Saud began only two years after the first colonies were set up. Ikhwan warriors attacked Bedouin tribesmen who had not entered the Wahhabi mission's fold. Ibn Saud had to intervene and directly order the Ikhwan to stop such attacks. When they fought in approved military campaigns, they sometimes carried out atrocities that violated the prohibition in Islamic law against killing noncombatants. Political developments on Arabia's northern frontier after the First World War exacerbated friction between the Ikhwan and Ibn Saud. During the war, Great Britain conquered the Ottoman regions that became Iraq and Transjordan. Under the League of Mandates system, ratified in 1920, London was responsible for the defense of the newly formed countries. From the perspective of the Ikhwan, the new international border was merely an infidel invention that could not restrict the duty to wage jihad against infidel tribesmen. In their view, jihad into territories under British mandates was the same as jihad in Arabia against Ibn Saud's enemies.

In 1926, Ikhwan leaders held a meeting to air their grievances with Ibn Saud over his dealings with infidels. They blamed him for sending his sons on diplomatic journeys to England and for lax treatment of Shiite Muslims, allowing them to retain their religious beliefs and practices. The Ikhwan also objected to the introduction of modern inventions such as automobiles, telephones, and the telegraph. One complaint straddled the line between religion and the material interests of Bedouin: They accused Ibn Saud of imposing taxes on nomads that were not allowed in Islamic law.

To head off a crisis, Ibn Saud invited Ikhwan leaders and senior Wahhabi clerics to a meeting. The clerics sided with the Ikhwan when they maintained that Shiites would have to undergo instruction in Wahhabi doctrine. On the issue of taxes, the clerics granted that they were not in accord with religious law but maintained that the ruler was allowed to collect them if he deemed them necessary. On modern inventions, Ibn Saud agreed to ban the telegraph. When it came to what was probably the most significant question for Ibn Saud—who decides when to wage jihad—the clerics upheld the traditional Sunni doctrine that reserves that decision to the ruler. The clerics maintained that the Ikhwan were like other believers: they had the duty to obey the ruler.

Some Ikhwan rejected the restriction on jihad and insisted that raids into Iraq were part of the holy struggle against infidels. The refusal to accept Ibn Saud's authority over jihad involved more than religious principles. The transition from nomadism to a sedentary way of life was not complete as some tribesmen still depended on the nomadic economy, which included raiding. Meanwhile, Ibn Saud was starting to assert control over wells and grazing land, in essence removing the economic resources that sustained the independence of Bedouin tribes. Furthermore, powerful tribal chieftains felt that Ibn Saud should have rewarded their participation in his conquests by making them regional governors. It was therefore a mixture of religious and material motives that fueled a raid into

Iraq, in defiance of Ibn Saud and the Wahhabi clerics. The British retaliated with aerial bombardment for the violation of a recent border agreement between Saudi Arabia and Iraq.

Ibn Saud convened a second conference to head off a confrontation with rebellious Ikhwan, but to no avail. A devastating attack on a caravan of Saudi merchants, killing men faithful to the Wahhabi mission, was the last straw for Ibn Saud and he mobilized a force of townsmen and loyal tribesmen to stamp out the rebels. Last-ditch efforts to reconcile failed on the eve of the fateful battle of Sabilah on March 30, 1929. Ibn Saud's forces quickly routed the rebels—contemporary accounts report that the fighting lasted little more than thirty minutes. It took nearly a year before the last rebels surrendered, but Sabilah is remembered as the decisive defeat of the Ikhwan. In its aftermath, Ibn Saud took steps to disband the militant tribesmen. He dispatched powerful chieftains such as Sultan ibn Bijad to prison where they perished. Rebel tribesmen had their horses and livestock confiscated. Colonies whose warriors joined the revolt were demolished while others withered away. The Ikhwan chiefs who stood by Ibn Saud became court advisers, district governors, and commanders of a new force called the White Army, a forerunner of the Saudi National Guard. Ibn Saud paid subsidies to tribal leaders to distribute to ordinary tribesmen. By doing so, he preserved tribal bonds but made the tribal leaders dependent on his largesse.

Long after Sabilah, some former Ikhwan never shook the feeling that Ibn Saud had manipulated them to serve his personal ambition. In their version of history, they were heroic religious figures, entering battle under banners emblazoned with the testimony of faith, "there is no god but God and Muhammad is the messenger of God." They played a significant part in the conquest of the holy cities, whose possession imbued Ibn Saud with religious prestige. After a decade of exhorting the Ikhwan to wage jihad to bring unbelievers into the fold, Ibn Saud reversed course and ordered an end to jihad. Even worse, he cooperated with a Christian power to thwart tribesmen continuing to wage jihad. After the battle of Sabilah, monthly stipends for Ikhwan veterans purchased acquiescence, but there remained a sense that Ibn Saud had forsaken religious principles in favor of material interests.[110]

According to Huzaimi, Sajir residents and other former Ikhwan believed that Ibn Saud had betrayed them. Members of Sultan ibn Bijad's tribe resented that they never avenged their chieftain's death in Saudi custody. Juhaiman, whose father was Sultan ibn Bijad's friend and participated in his revolt, inherited his tribe's suspicious attitude toward Saudi rulers and developed a rebellious, vindictive attitude. When Huzaimi accompanied Juhaiman on journeys in the desert, he met veteran Ikhwan, including men who participated in the battle of Sabilah. At their gatherings, these old men would tell tales of the jihad and the miraculous military feats they witnessed in ways that called to mind the heroic conquests of the Prophet's Companions and the Pious Ancestors. These tales, often related in a formulaic, memorized way, formed an important part of their culture and mentality.

When Juhaiman was a fugitive, he said that he would not surrender because he feared the government would deal with him the same way it did with Ibn Bijad. He felt strongly about the treatment of Ibn Bijad and often repeated that the Ikhwan who died at Sabilah were martyrs. In his writings, he described how Ibn Saud and Wahhabi clerics had called on the Ikhwan to give him their allegiance on the basis of the Quran and the Sunnah. The Ikhwan waged a jihad of conquest because they considered Ibn Saud the legitimate ruler. Once he achieved his aims, however, he called on the Ikhwan to end the jihad against infidel Shiites in Iraq and later requested assistance from Christian powers (Great Britain and the United States) to develop Saudi Arabia's economy. Since then, the Saudi government has not lived up to its claim to stand for true belief. Instead, it has allowed Muslims to mingle with Christians and Shiites, while suppressing true Muslims who rejected mingling with infidels and wished to combat Shiite idolatry. According to Juhaiman, the true foundation of the Saudi government was the worship of money.

Bedouin

The Ikhwan's fate was connected to the decline in the historic position of Arabia's nomadic tribesmen, the Bedouin. In Arabic, *badawi* refers to someone inhabiting the desert, as opposed to someone inhabiting a village or city. The Bedouin way of life—economy, social relations, cultural norms, and political dynamics—had developed through adaptation to the arid ecology of the Arabian desert.[111] Juhaiman grew up at a time when political and economic forces were bringing about the end of that way of life.

As the son of a former Bedouin, Juhaiman identified with Bedouin ways, felt that he belonged to the desert, even though he grew up in a small town rather than roaming the desert, and had strong pride in his tribe, the Utaibah. He boasted that the Bedouin were superior to settled folk because the Bedouin are tough: they can endure extreme desert conditions in which townsmen would perish. He had blind faith in Bedouin superiority, treating tales of tribal heroism as self-evident truths. Juhaiman also inherited a Bedouin's pride in the superiority of his own tribe. He would boast of the Utaibah's virtues and denigrate the shortcomings of other tribes. Juhaiman's pride in his tribe was not entirely unwarranted. In the mid-1800s, the British traveler Charles Doughty described the Utaibah as "an honourable and hospitable Bedouin nation ... rich in sheep and camels ... never subject to any, save to the old Wahhabi princes."[112] Juhaiman's attachment to the idea of Bedouin superiority fostered resentment toward Saudi Arabia's transformation into a mostly urban country where former Bedouin were relegated to shanty towns and impoverished desert settlements.

Bedouin Economy and Independence before the 1900s

Bedouin pride rested on tribesmen's fighting prowess, which they celebrated in a poetic tradition that expressed an ethos vaunting courage and daring exploits.[113] Their military power enabled them to thwart efforts by settled rulers to impose their authority. Throughout Arabia, the Bedouin were divided into tribes, and each tribe constituted something like an independent state. Relations among tribes and between tribes and settled authorities were negotiated and malleable. The tribe's primary concern was maintaining autonomy. The settled ruler's primary concern was protecting trade routes and guarding towns and village lands against Bedouin raids. Settled rulers commonly paid tribal leaders to refrain from raiding, an arrangement bordering on extortion.

In addition to military power, Bedouin independence was rooted in an economy that maximized Arabia's scarce resources. The economy's main pillar was raising livestock, primarily camels, whose milk, butter, and meat were staples of diet. The Bedouin traded animals and animal products in market towns for food and merchandise. They also supplied camels to caravans to carry people and goods. Familiarity with the desert made the Bedouin essential guides for caravans traversing Arabia to Yemen, Iraq, Syria, and ports on the Red Sea and the Persian Gulf. Raids on other tribes replenished herds diminished by drought or disease, and attacks on villages and caravans could yield rich plunder. Bedouin tribes typically included clans that were not pure nomads. The seminomadic clans spent part of the year cultivating date palms and other crops, part of the year on the move with livestock. Some tribes had clans that were permanent cultivators. One of the powerful tribes expressed pride in its composite membership: "Bedouins, sedentary folks, and semi-nomads. All ways of life join in their homeland."[114]

The Saudis and the Bedouin

Western writings on Saudi Arabia frequently characterize it as an expression of Bedouin power and culture. That is completely wrong. Al Saud were not Bedouin but chieftains of an oasis settlement. Their political order rested on the manpower, resources, and interests of townsmen and cultivators. The Bedouin were a threat to Arabia's sedentary world.[115]

When it came to religion, Juhaiman believed that Bedouin were virtuous believers. Muhammad ibn Abd al-Wahhab, however, regarded the Bedouin as idolaters to be fought and brought into the fold of belief. The Bedouin did not maintain mosques in the desert and they did not much frequent them when visiting towns for trade. Nor did the Bedouin observe Islamic law. Instead, they followed their own set of customs to regulate social life.[116] A more accurate way to characterize the history of Saudi Arabia, then, would be the story of how townsmen conquered the Bedouin.

The battle of Sabilah was a milestone in the military subjugation of the Bedouin. Ibn Saud had already taken steps to end the Bedouin way of life in order to bolster his power and to establish secure conditions in his realm. First, he banned raids between tribes and attacks on settled areas. A core piece of the proud warrior ethos was turned into criminal behavior.[117] Second, he abolished tribal domains, or *dirahs*.[118] The tribal domain was territory that was recognized as belonging to a particular tribe. The division of Arabia into tribal domains regulated control over resources essential to raising livestock: pasture and wells. A tribe's independence depended on its ability to establish and defend its domain.[119] Apart from military pacification and political subjugation, the introduction of motor vehicles spelled the end of camel caravans and reduced demand for camels as transport animals.[120]

By the early 1940s, the perennial mainstays of the Bedouin economy were in decline. Some tribesmen joined the National Guard. Some used their unique knowledge of the Arabian desert to work as truck drivers or to smuggle goods from Kuwait. Some found work with the American oil company and saved their wages to purchase pickup trucks that they then used to either return to raising livestock or invest in livestock and hire foreigners to tend to them. During a prolonged drought in the 1950s, many former Bedouin moved to Riyadh, where they set up shanty towns of tin shacks, wooden huts, and tents and sought handouts from the king and princes. The Saudi government tried various schemes to convert the tribesmen into cultivators, but without the religious mission of the Ikhwan's colonies.[121]

Nostalgia

In modern Saudi Arabia, Bedouin tribes no longer possess political autonomy, no longer follow the migratory life with their herds, and no longer live according to their historic customs. The end of these markers of Bedouin distinctiveness did not spell the end of identification with a Bedouin past. Tribal ties remained strong and there emerged a general Bedouin identity shared by members of different tribes and that distinguishes them from Saudis descended from settled folk.[122]

Not all former Bedouin missed the hardships of the nomadic way of life: unpredictable weather, drought, loss of livestock to disease, and endemic insecurity in the absence of a strong ruler. In the words of one poet,

> In the olden days, before our rightly-guided government established its rule, the people of the Wadi [Valley] and the tribes used to pillage each other. As the saying goes, "Najd[123] is for the one with the strongest mounted force," the strong trample upon the weak. Today, God be praised, our rulers are just and moreover people have learnt to distinguish right from wrong. God, the Sublime and Exalted, led them on the right way so that instead of looting each other they became like brothers.[124]

The material advantages of settled life had its appeals as well: modern health care, education, sewing machines, radios, and motorcycles. Settled Bedouin were poorer than most Saudis, but their lives were easier than those of relatives who remained in the desert raising livestock.[125]

Nevertheless, many men of Juhaiman's generation lamented the passing of the era of Bedouin heroism, when one's prestige rested on fighting prowess and courage rather than connections to princes. Because poetry had long been the Bedouin art par excellence, poetry naturally served as the way to express alienation from a world where the warrior had to kowtow to the effete townsman. One poet in particular, Bandar bin Srur, captured that sense of alienation, the yearning for an idealized bygone epoch of the Bedouin hero, and tribal pride.[126] The rebellious poet and Juhaiman were like many other tribesmen of their generation forced to find new livelihoods. They served in the National Guard, worked as truck drivers, and engaged in smuggling between Kuwait and Saudi Arabia. They also felt pride in their respective tribes and harbored resentment toward the Saudi state. Juhaiman, however, differed in holding a grudge against the rulers for corrupting religion. His blending of Bedouin nostalgia with religious zeal did not represent a deep-rooted part of Bedouin culture but the intense, short-lived, and decisive phase of Saudi history when the Bedouin raid was transformed into jihad, endowing the warrior ethos with religious heroism. Perhaps Juhaiman's insistence on Bedouin superiority and the Ikhwan's loyalty to the original Wahhabi mission was a way to compensate for the decline in the status of Arabia's nomadic tribes by asserting their fidelity to religious purity.

Struggles in School

The memoir points to Juhaiman's struggles in school as another source for his rebellious personality. It seems he did not attend school while growing up in Sajir. At some point, he joined the Saudi National Guard and worked as a truck driver. To qualify for promotion in rank, he was required to complete elementary school, but he quit his studies after fourth grade. His next attempt at formal learning was no more successful. He enrolled in the Medina Hadith Institute's elementary level but dropped out during his first term because he struggled in his classes.

Huzaimi observed that Juhaiman's handwriting was illegible and that he never learned correct spelling and grammar. How then do we account for the polished religious essays published in Juhaiman's name? For one thing, he attained enough literacy to read the major hadith collections and the commentaries on them. More importantly, he possessed a powerful memory that enabled him to cite Quranic verses and hadiths to support his ideas. The essays that were published under his name were composed by two members of the group with a firm command of Arabic grammar. Juhaiman would dictate his ideas and they would write the essays.

Challenging Clerical Authority

Juhaiman's difficulties in school may have shaped his critical attitude toward the Sunni idea that restricts authority in Islamic law to men with specialized education. He asserted there were no grounds in the Quran, the Sunnah, or the ways of the Pious Ancestors for the idea that a believer must possess specialized knowledge to figure out legal rules. Rather, any believer could examine the Quran and hadiths to come up with legal rules. Requiring specialized knowledge was just a pretext for clerics to dominate ordinary believers. To support his position, Juhaiman cited a hadith about how quickly and easily the Prophet instructed a Bedouin about the essential elements of religion, assigning one of his Companions to spend a single day with the Bedouin to give instruction on how to pray, fast, and pay alms. Nowadays, instead of the Prophet's simple approach, clerics use technical jargon that baffles commoners and needlessly complicate religious education to justify their insistence that believers accept their authority.

Clerical Corruption and Hypocrisy

Juhaiman felt that Saudi clerics in the religious establishment were corrupted by the temptations of power and wealth. While advocates of clerical authority like to cite a famous hadith that calls them the "heirs of the prophets" and they refer to a verse in the Quran that exhorts believers to turn to the learned, critics point to hadiths that warn against the corrupting influence of serving rulers. According to one hadith, one sign of the End of Time is when clerics come to depend on rulers, "permitting for them the forbidden and forbidding for them the permitted and furnishing them with legal opinions according to what they desire."[127] This hadith reflected a suspicion that clerics would sacrifice religious principles for the sake of placating rulers. In Juhaiman's view, that is exactly what happened when the clerics betrayed the Ikhwan by taking Ibn Saud's side against them. In a sense, Juhaiman's challenge to the Saudi clerics of his day mirrored the original Wahhabi rejection of established religious authority in the 1700s. Muhammad ibn Abd al-Wahhab's preaching aroused harsh criticism from fellow clerics who condemned his ideas as the fruit of ambition and deficient learning. Ibn Abd al-Wahhab wrote that, in their hearts, the clerics recognized the truth of his message, but their appetite for prestige and wealth prevented them from admitting it.[128]

Preaching to Bedouin and Former Bedouin

Juhaiman's affinity for Bedouin and his lack of confidence in his educational attainment show up in Huzaimi's description of his preaching tours. He avoided towns because he did not have a firm command of classical Arabic, which was expected of religious teachers, and because he was aware that his limited religious education might expose him to difficult questions he could not answer. Juhaiman was comfortable preaching to Bedouin and former Bedouin at their encampments and villages. Moreover, he was familiar with Bedouin customs that were not in accord with Islamic law. For example, he exhorted Bedouin to abandon a marriage custom that skirted the obligation to pay a dowry to the bride. He also urged them to observe the requirement in Islamic law to wait three months to remarry after the death of a spouse.

Quitting the National Guard

Juhaiman left the Saudi military when he came under the influence of an exclusivist Wahhabi cleric, Sheikh Hammud al-Tuwaijiri. In 1963, the sheikh published a treatise[129] condemning imitation of non-Muslims, a common theme in older Wahhabi works that warned against taking residence in infidel lands because it endangers a believer's faith. The idea that Muslims must not imitate infidels is based on a hadith: "Whoever imitates a people or group is one of them." In early Islamic times, the hadith was frequently understood to refer to imitation of infidels, in particular their dress. Tuwaijiri applied the hadith to Western military salutes that had become part of Saudi military etiquette. To use the Western salute not only imitated infidels. It also meant abandoning forms of greeting sanctified in the Quran and the Sunnah. Furthermore, it was part of a general laxness about imitating infidels that corrupted morality and spread repugnant Western customs.

Domineering Personality

Given Juhaiman's limited education and rustic background, it is hard to account for his rise to leadership of a group dedicated to a religious vision based on a voluminous set of texts. Part of the explanation has to do with his domineering personality. Before Huzaimi ever met Juhaiman, Salafi Group members described his iron memory, his sound understanding of texts, and his manners in nearly mythical terms that called to mind the Prophet's Companions. Apparently, Juhaiman possessed the instincts of a charismatic leader able to mesmerize men with advanced degrees and draw them into a poorly planned venture such as the ill-fated attack on the Grand Mosque. In the aftermath of the Mecca uprising, these men wondered what had happened to their ability to reason. At times he manipulated members by pretending to ignore them, as occurred to Huzaimi when he began to distance himself from Juhaiman's faction. Other times, Juhaiman would denounce a member's ideas in front of the group. If the member tried to defend himself, Juhaiman would say he was not talking about him, but everyone knew otherwise. One of the Salafi Group's founders eventually quit the group over such manipulative behavior.

Juhaiman's ascent was not only a matter of personality. He was also an effective grassroots activist, devoting all his time and energy to the cause. He became a familiar figure to members throughout the country by touring desert settlements, attending prayer circles in small villages, and accompanying members to Mecca for the lesser pilgrimage. The other founders had little time to spare because they had regular, six-days-a-week jobs—Friday was their only day off. Consequently, members got excited when word spread that Juhaiman was on his way, but the other founders were mere names.

Around the time Huzaimi joined the group, the relationship between Juhaiman and the other founders was beginning to sour.[130] Consensus on the original principles animating the Salafi Group had sustained a unified leadership for about a decade, but Juhaiman's increasing assertiveness created strains with two of the other founders. They thought it was presumptuous of him to command members to shun anyone who disagreed with the group's doctrine or opposed its unorthodox religious practices. Even worse, he became outspoken in criticizing anyone who attended a public school or held a government job because the schools taught subjects he considered contrary to religion, and reliance on a government salary made one reluctant to stand up for religious belief. This quite naturally annoyed the two founders who taught at public schools. One member holding a government job became friendly with official clerics and started voicing objections to some of the Salafi Group's peculiar religious practices. He was expelled from the group's house in Medina.

The Rupture with the Saudi Clerics and the Schism in the Salafi Group

In Huzaimi's account, Juhaiman became leader of a dissident faction that adopted irregular worship practices.[131] The Salafi Group's departures from authorized religious practices appear minor—members used slightly different wording for the call to the dawn prayer; they allowed the worshipper to wear sandals at prayer (this resulted in scuffles at the Mosque of the Prophet); and they sealed off a portion of the mosque that indicates the direction of prayer toward Mecca.[132] The Salafi Group's clerical supervisor, Abu Bakr al-Jaza'iri, received complaints about its unorthodox ways, and in the summer of 1977 he arranged a meeting at the group's house in Medina in an attempt to persuade them to return to regular ways of worship. Several leading members of the group attended, but Juhaiman stayed away.[133] At the meeting, Jaza'iri informed the group that anyone who refused to obey his guidance would have to move out of the house. To ensure conformity with regular worship, Jaza'iri appointed an official cleric to pronounce the call to prayer and to lead prayers at the group's mosque.

Jaza'iri's steps to rein in the group backfired. Most members moved out of the house rather than submit to what they considered misguided clerical authority. Juhaiman's home became their main gathering place, and as a result, the group's home was no longer under government supervision, so the authorities put preachers in Juhaiman's faction under surveillance. When reports about the meeting with Jaza'iri spread to other towns, most members sided with Juhaiman, now the unquestioned leader of a dissident faction. The Salafi Group's other founders lost influence with his followers and could do nothing to stop the momentum toward a confrontation with the government.

The Fugitive

In December 1977, Huzaimi was having lunch with Juhaiman at his home in Medina when a fellow tribesman who worked for the provincial authority stopped by to warn him that the government planned to arrest him and other members that evening.[134] Juhaiman and Huzaimi took flight, avoiding checkpoints by following unpaved tracks into the desert. They found refuge with members of the Salafi Group who had abandoned city life to live as shepherds in the desert. Juhaiman asked that they try to find out if the arrests had been carried out. A few days later, they learned that the authorities had detained some two dozen members in different parts of the country and that they were searching for Juhaiman. His home town Sajir was under surveillance and security forces were posted at his brother's farm. At that point, Juhaiman suggested they go their separate ways because Huzaimi was not wanted by the authorities.

While Juhaiman was in hiding, he arranged the distribution of his first collection of essays. Huzaimi describes a secret meeting in the middle of the night with Juhaiman at a member's home where several members were amending printed copies. Juhaiman instructed Huzaimi to perform the lesser pilgrimage with members of the Riyadh branch as a cover for handing out copies of the essays in the Grand Mosque to members from other towns.

In one of the essays, Juhaiman described a plot to deceive Muslims and lead them astray. The "people of falsehood" constantly enticed believers with new temptations. When radio was introduced, it would broadcast only recitations of the Quran and news reports, but eventually, women began broadcasting and seductive songs were played over radio. Then, the authorities allowed women to appear on television without a veil. These sorts of changes had taken root in other countries decades before, but in a social climate under the eye of Wahhabi clerics, they made many uneasy. Juhaiman stood out in considering these changes to be portents of Judgment Day. During his time as a fugitive, isolated from all but a few trusted followers, Juhaiman came to believe that Judgment Day was nigh and that he had a role to play in the events foretold in the ancient prophecies. This was the conceptual pivot that turned his followers from a dissident faction into an apocalyptic sect.

Was Juhaiman's Faction a Sect?

Sects in Islam

In the history of Islam, "sect" usually refers to three groups that represent divergent views on who qualifies for rightful leadership and what qualities the rightful leader possesses. Those three groups are the Sunnis, the Shiites, and the Kharijites. There are also subsects of Shiites and Kharijites.

A Theory of Sects

In the field of religious studies, sect is defined in a number of ways. The definition proposed by Rodney Stark and William Sims Bainbridge fits the Salafi Group and Juhaiman's splinter group: "A sect is a religious group that rejects the social environment in which it exists." They write that sects live in greater or lesser degrees of tension with society: "The ideal sect falls at one pole where the surrounding tension is so great that sect members are hunted as fugitives."[135] They go on to suggest that "Because sects are schismatic groups they present themselves to the world as something *old*. They left the parent body not to form a new faith, but to *reestablish the old one*, from which the parent body had 'drifted ….' Sects claim to be the authentic, purged, refurbished version of the faith from which they split."[136] Because sects consider society to have strayed from true religion, they withdraw from society and form a distinct subculture based on rigid rules for its members' behavior.[137]

The Salafi Group as Sect: A Summary

The Salafi Group stood out for members' extraordinary efforts to shape personal behavior according to detailed rules in the Sunnah. They believed that Saudi society had strayed from true Islam and that they were reviving Islam in its ancient, original form. Consequently, they withdrew from society to live in their own neighborhoods, to worship in their own mosques, and to abide by stricter rules than mainstream society. A few members attempted a more complete separation by moving to the desert, but conditions were too harsh and they returned to the city. Ultimately, Juhaiman and his followers became outlaws, pursued as fugitives by the Saudi authorities.

The Wahhabi Mission as Sect: Historical Echo of the Salafi Group?

Muhammad ibn Abd al-Wahhab claimed that Muslim societies had lapsed into pre-Islamic spiritual ignorance and that he sought to reestablish Islam as practiced by the Prophet and the Pious Ancestors.[138] Because central Arabia was not under the rule of the dominant Middle Eastern power of the time, the Ottoman Empire, the Wahhabi mission did not have to withdraw from society. Rather, with the backing of Saudi power, it filled the space in Arabia on the fringes of the Ottoman orbit and established a religious regime where Wahhabi clerics reigned over religious practices and public morality, creating a distinct subculture based on rigid rules.

From the perspective of Ottoman religious scholars, Muhammad ibn Abd al-Wahhab's religious movement looked like a schismatic sect and they characterized it in sectarian terms, labeling it Kharijite and Carmathian (the Shiite sect that attacked Mecca in 930). The term "Wahhabi" was coined by Ottoman religious scholars in order to indicate that they considered Ibn Abd al-Wahhab's teaching to be his personal, eccentric opinion, beyond the pale of the Sunni consensus. For their part, Wahhabis resorted to the language of sect in the way they defined themselves. They would cite a hadith that says that at the end of time, Muslims will be divided into seventy-two sects, only one of which will be on the right path and saved from hellfire—and they were that "saved sect."[139]

Under the second Saudi state, Wahhabi clerics erected a barrier of separation from the Ottoman realm that corresponded to the way sects withdraw from society. Wahhabi clerics disapproved travel to and residing in Ottoman lands, which they called infidel lands, and they barred outside influence. Intentional isolation meant cutting ties to centers of religious learning in Cairo, Damascus, and the holy cities, where central Arabian religious pupils and scholars had studied for centuries.

Tension with the outside Muslim world began to ease in the late 1800s when Sunni religious scholars began to reevaluate the Wahhabi mission and argued for including it in the Sunni consensus as part of the Hanbali legal tradition. In the 1920s, Ibn Saud pressed the clerics to go along with opening the country to foreign Muslims and non-Muslims. While most Wahhabi clerics fell in line with accommodationist moves to curtail isolation from other Muslim societies, a strain of the original exclusivist impulse survived. The revolt of the Ikhwan in the late

1920s and the emergence of the Salafi Group in the 1960s can be read as efforts to restore separation between realms of religious purity and corruption and to revive "the authentic, purged, refurbished version of the faith."

The Salafi Group: From Mainstream to Sect

The Salafi Group was in tension with Saudi society, rejecting the infiltration of Western influences as sources of moral corruption. Nevertheless, members recognized the authority of the religious establishment, seeking and obtaining approval from a leading Saudi cleric, Abd al-Aziz ibn Baz, who agreed to serve as their guide, proposed the name for the group, and paid rent for its house in Medina. Ibn Baz later steered funds from a donor to build a mosque for them that he placed under the supervision of one of his deputies. There was nothing secretive or rebellious about the group.

Rigid Rules

Huzaimi's first acquaintance with the Salafi Group took place about ten years after its establishment. His description of the group's deliberate habits calls to mind the sectarian inclination to observe rigid rules. For instance, he considered the Saudi Salafis to be more austere and detached from worldly matters than the Salafis he knew in Kuwait. In a telling anecdote, Huzaimi relates that the Kuwaiti Salafis sometimes went out for ice cream, but that was the sort of "luxury" which had become a regular part of daily life for most people that the Saudi Salafis did not indulge.

The Saudi Salafis also differed from the Kuwaitis in adopting a spartan way of life. Their house in Mecca was erected on the site of an abandoned animal pen. It lacked a foundation and the floor was bare, rocky ground. Its two small rooms were covered by a flimsy wooden roof. There was no bathroom, so residents used toilets at a nearby mosque. Likewise, in Medina, they lived in small, cinder block houses sparsely furnished with cheap rugs and cushions. The only possessions were collections of religious books. Such austerity stood in contrast not only to the Kuwaiti Salafis but also to the direction of Saudi society during the 1960s and 1970s, when increasing revenues from oil production gave rise to higher consumption and materialism.

When Huzaimi moved to Mecca, he earned money by peddling watches to pilgrims. The brand of watch that he sold, West End, was objectionable to the Salafis because the watch face bore a design in the shape of a cross. One day, Huzaimi was walking through Mecca with the watches when he ran into a fellow Salafi. The man looked at the watches and declared it was forbidden to sell merchandise bearing the cross, presumably because it is a sign of polytheist belief (according to the Muslim view of Christianity's doctrine of the trinity). The man added that believers have a duty to break crosses and wipe out their image. Huzaimi decided to return the watches to the wholesale merchant. Salafis later told him he should have acted on the duty to forbid wrong by erasing the cross on the watch face before returning them. He discovered that the Salafis were preoccupied with watches and wristbands and would talk about them frequently at their meetings. For instance, they might use a West End watch but only after making it permissible by smearing out the cross. If a watch came with a metal wristband, they would replace it with a leather or plastic band because they believed that wearing something made of steel is forbidden. Yet others would leave the steel wristband but carry the watch in a pocket to avoid violating the prohibition on wearing steel.

The Salafis were just as scrupulous about the prohibition on human images on currency, identity cards, newspapers, and magazines. Their authority for rejecting images is in the Sunnah. A hadith from al-Bukhari's collection has the Prophet stating: "Angels do not enter a house in which there is a dog or a picture." According to another hadith, "Whosoever makes an image, him will God give as a punishment the task of blowing the breath of life into it; but he will not be able to do this."[140] In modern times, the taboo on images resulted in a long interval between the introduction of photography to the Middle East in the 1830s and its approval by religious authorities in the 1920s. Defenders of photographs argued that the prohibition on images did not pertain to photographs because they did not actually create images but only reproduced them.[141] In Saudi Arabia, customary opposition to images led clerics to protest the introduction of drawing classes in 1930, but Ibn Saud overruled them.[142] Juhaiman considered photographs one of the "new temptations" that were spreading in Saudi society.

Huzaimi reports that the Salafi Group discussed the question of images at meetings. Some members would keep money and identity cards bearing their photographs in the glove compartment of a car. Some Salafis inked out the image on paper currency while others refused to carry paper currency, because it bore the king's image, and only used coins. Huzaimi writes of a member who kept a bag of coins weighing twenty-five kilograms in the back seat of a car. His companion told him that he had three more large bags of coins at his home. As for identity cards, most Salafis refused to carry one bearing their photograph. New members would destroy their cards. Some members obtained permission to have identity cards without photographs. Because of the prohibition against images, the Salafis would not bring magazines or newspapers into their homes, and some would pick up loose scraps of newspaper from the ground to cut them up.

Rejection of Public Schools

Another sign of the Salafi Group's estrangement from mainstream society was its rejection of public school. One Salafi treatise claimed that public schools disobeyed God because they tolerated images and compelled students to silently accept the authority of misguided teachers. Huzaimi points out that the Salafis borrowed their arguments against public schools from exclusivist clerics who had opposed them because they were not fully devoted to religious instruction and taught "infidel ideas," like the earth is round and revolves on its axis. Juhaiman extended disapproval from government schools to government clerics, arguing that you could not learn anything worthwhile from them. Given the certainty

Saudi clerics felt about their grasp on religious truth, Juhaiman's position was a direct assault on their authority.

The Buraidah Ikhwan

The Salafi Group was not alone in warding off modern influences by keeping aloof from mainstream society. During the 1940s, a small colony of puritans had taken shape in Buraidah, a medium-sized town north of Riyadh. They were known as the Buraidah Ikhwan and they followed the teachings of Saudi clerics opposed to the innovations allowed by the rulers. They refused to send their children to public schools because they disapproved of teaching English, geography, and the heliocentric view of the heavens. Instead, they set up their own private school. They refused to use modern inventions such as the telephone and television. And they refrained from working for the government. The Buraidah Salafi clerics had worked out a modus vivendi with the authorities— the clerics recognized the government's legitimacy and the government left them alone, even accommodating their aversion to images by issuing them identity cards without photographs. The memoir does not provide a clear sense of how the Buraidah Ikhwan and the Salafi Group differed, but both fell in the spectrum of sectarians in their objections to mainstream social practices that the religious establishment accepted.[143]

Withdrawal from Society

Huzaimi's description of Salafi neighborhoods points to the sectarian impulse to isolate from mainstream society. In Mecca, Medina, and Riyadh, they chose to live at a distance from the nearest neighbors. As Huzaimi puts it, their house in Mecca was "out of the sight of prying eyes." In Medina, the Salafi Group developed its own neighborhood some distance from the city center in a district called the Eastern Harrah, part of a vast lava flow that covers 20,000 square kilometers south of the city. The district was home to low-income residents, many of them immigrants from other parts of the country, some from other Muslim lands. Surveys of Medina in the early 1970s indicated that a fairly high proportion—as many as half—of its residents came from other countries and other parts of Saudi Arabia.[144] The Eastern Harrah was attractive to the Salafis because land there was inexpensive and its distance from the city center meant that they could erect shacks and flimsy houses with little or no official oversight. During the 1970s, when the Salafi Group's neighborhood developed, houses lacked piped water and electricity.[145]

By the time Huzaimi joined the group's Medina branch, its leaders were living in a newly constructed two-story house in the Eastern Harrah. He describes it as resembling a fortress designed to accommodate nearly fifty residents: each story had eight rooms that could hold three residents. The Salafi Group built more houses in the same neighborhood on land obtained by squatting. They put up houses without obtaining building permits, undertaking construction at night and sometimes bribing inspectors to look the other way. As their numbers grew, they put a puritanical imprint on the neighborhood: no tobacco shops or cigarette smokers in the streets, no televisions in homes.

In essence, the Salafi Group formed a separate society, with its own mosque where members could freely worship according to their own rules, giving the call to prayer in their preferred formula and sealing the mosque's prayer niche. The niche is a feature of mosque interiors that indicates the direction toward Mecca that Muslims face when performing prayer. While the niche was a feature of very early mosques dating from the 600s, it was not part of the original mosque of the Prophet in Medina.[146] Consequently, the Salafi Group followed a fatwa issued by Sheikh Albani declaring the niche an illegitimate innovation and sealed off the niches in their mosques.[147]

Back to the Desert

Members of the Salafi Group saw themselves in opposition to a corrupt society. In their minds, moral decay came about in the course of the country's abandonment of Arabia's historical nomadic roots and the rise of modern cities. Nostalgia for a pristine pastoral past imbued with moral purity is, of course, not unique to the Salafi Group. In European and North American history, we find the yearning for an idyllic past of organic social relations, upright morality, and harmony with nature.

Members of the group talked among themselves about living in the desert as a way to stave off moral corruption. When Juhaiman fled the authorities, he found refuge with Salafi Group members in the desert living in tents and raising sheep. Their children did not go to school; instead, the parents taught them the Quran and basic literacy. They preferred a simple, austere way of life far from the city, which stood for temptation and corruption. Huzaimi does not obscure the folly and conceit of "back to the desert" adepts. A Kuwaiti Salafi living in the desert exhibited exaggerated pride in the Bedouin way, even though he was originally a townsman. Huzaimi visited members who had decided to quit Medina to settle in the desert a short distance away. He described the encampment as barren and gloomy. Indeed, he wondered why anyone would bother trying to live there. The men and their families were lice-ridden, short on water, and, all in all, incapable of thriving. We do not hear how long the experiment lasted, but the members wound up returning to Medina.

From Tension to Rupture

According to sect theory, sect members live in greater or lesser tension with their surrounding society. The Salafi Group seems to have been at the lesser end of the spectrum for about a decade before it drifted into greater tension as a result of Juhaiman's assertion of leadership. The summer 1977 meeting between the Salafi Group and Saudi clerics forced members to either follow Juhaiman or obey the clerics' insistence that they give up their irregular religious practices. Some members affirmed the Salafi Group's original acceptance of clerical authority but most sided with Juhaiman. After the meeting, he escalated criticism of government jobs, arguing that if someone depended on a government salary, he would be inhibited from forbidding wrong. He also urged members to avoid Saudi clerics, berating Huzaimi for attending lessons with Ibn Baz, whom he called "one of Al Saud's sheikhs," that is, someone whose ties to the rulers compromised his integrity.

An Apocalyptic Sect

Complete rupture between Juhaiman's faction and the government came in December 1977, when authorities decided to arrest him and his followers. In terms of sect theory, they were now "hunted as fugitives." Pressed by government persecution and living in a society under the domination of corrupt rulers and clerics, they saw the world as so filled with evil that it meant the End of Time was nearing. Juhaiman's reading of Saudi Arabia's moral decline meant that preaching was not enough to redeem the world. Only divine intervention through sending the Mahdi could reverse the course of history. Seizing the Grand Mosque was the necessary first step to trigger a divinely ordained series of events. Juhaiman and his faction had no political program, neither gradual change nor revolutionary revolt; instead, they turned to an apocalyptic vision of divine interruption in the flow of time.

Apocalyptic Thought

Apocalypse is derived from a Greek word that means revealing or uncovering. The religious sense is revealing or uncovering true reality, with the implication that events have hidden meanings that are normally obscured.[148] The apocalyptic thread in monotheistic religions anticipates the revealing of true reality at the End of Time.

Ancient Middle Eastern and Mediterranean myths and religions imagined a cosmos divided into natural and supernatural realms where the forces of good and evil waged constant battle. The forces of good upheld order and morality that the forces of evil strove to disrupt. Over time, the balance between good and evil, between order/morality and disorder/corruption, is in flux. The ancients of Babylon, Persia, and Greece divided history into a sequence of ages, with order giving way to disorder as the human condition declines from a golden age of harmony to later times of discord. Ultimately, history, and the natural realm, will come to an end when good destroys evil. In some traditions about the end of the world, a state of harmony will be restored. In other stories, the destruction of evil precedes the Last Judgment.[149]

In the Abrahamic religions, dreams and visions are windows into the hidden meanings of events that augur the End of Time, when a cataclysm will erase the disorder prevailing in the world and God will send a savior to restore order.[150] Apocalyptic verses in the Quran depict cataclysmic events that will occur at the

End of Time: Nobody can predict when it will arrive, but when it does, it will be sudden. Mountains will be pounded to dust, the seas will boil, and the sun will go dark. God will then resurrect the dead, judge individuals according to their deeds, and either reward them with eternal peace in the Garden or punish them with eternal torment in the Fire.[151]

Interpreting Hadiths about the End of Time

Juhaiman was preoccupied with portents signaling the approach of the End of Time. He believed that evil temptations such as television and personal images on paper currency were such portents. In his essay about the End of Time, he drew connections between hadiths and recent history. For example, one passage cites the following hadith:

> When we were sitting with the Messenger of God, he talked about trials, mentioning many of them. When he mentioned the one when people should stay in their houses, some asked him what that was. He replied, "It will be flight and war. Then will come a trial which is pleasant. Its murkiness is due to the fact that it is produced by *a man from the people of my house, who will assert that he belongs to me, whereas he does not*, for my close ones fear God. Then the people will unite under a man who will be like a hip-bone on a rib. Then there will be a *little black trial which will leave none of this community of believers without striking a blow*" (translator's emphasis).

Juhaiman interpreted the phrase "a man from the people of my house" to mean Sharif Husain, the ruler of Hijaz and the holy cities during and after the First World War. Because Sharif Husain was an enemy to Muhammad ibn Abd al-Wahhab's mission, Juhaiman asserted that the phrase "who will assert that he belongs to me, whereas he does not" pertains to the sharif. "Then the people will unite under a man who will be like a hip-bone on a rib" refers to Abd al-Aziz ibn Saud because he pacified Arabia, ending strife and banditry. The "little black trial which will leave none of this community of believers without striking a blow" refers to the present time.[152]

Dreams and the Apocalypse

Dreams and visions played a large part in ancient Middle Eastern traditions about revelation and future time. In Egypt and Mesopotamia, they were considered omens of imminent events. In the Book of Numbers, God declares that he sends revelations through dreams and visions. Other books of the Hebrew Bible contain passages describing dreams and visions that occurred to Abraham, Jacob, and Solomon. Because dreams and visions seldom have a clear, literal meaning, it was common for an intermediary mystical figure, such as an angel, to explain their meaning. In Islam, the Prophet's earliest revelations came from an angel. In later Muslim tradition, the Prophet appeared to believers in dreams and visions to explain their meaning. Apocalyptic ideas surfaced in the Hebrew Book of Daniel, where dreams and visions foretell divine intervention to bring about the End of Time. Daniel's mixing of dreams and the End of Time became part of Christian and Muslim apocalyptic lore where dreams make it possible to interpret past events as predictions of events to come.[153]

Dreams and the Salafi Group

Dreams played an essential role in the Salafi Group's shift from an agenda for righteous living to preparing for apocalyptic violence. Members frequently discussed dreams and how to interpret them. Juhaiman in particular was preoccupied with dreams. Members regularly told him their dreams and sought his interpretation. For a group opposed to any but a literal interpretation of texts, assigning dreams the same authority as texts seems paradoxical, but members considered hadiths affirming the veracity of dreams to be authentic and they judged dreams to be reliable guides for acting in the world.

Dreams of the Mahdi

Huzaimi considers Juhaiman's time as a fugitive, when he was isolated from all but a few trusted associates, the turning point in his path to insurrection, for it was during his flight that he had dreams where fellow member Muhammad al-Qahtani appeared as the Mahdi.[154] Juhaiman already believed the world was in moral decline. The Mahdist dreams signified that the End of Time was at hand and it was time to act, in accordance with the hadith, "When the End of Time nears, the believer's dream will not be false, for the believer's dream is one forty-sixth of prophecy, and whatever is part of prophecy is not false." Other members of the group were also having dreams where Qahtani appeared as the Mahdi. Talking with one another about their dreams intensified their preoccupation with the End of Time.

Hadiths about the Mahdi cited by Juhaiman:[155]

"In this house, meaning the Kaabah, a group of people will take refuge who have no power, number, or arms. An army will be sent against them; until when they are in a desert of the earth, they will be swallowed up."

A'ishah said: "The Messenger of God moved his hands in his sleep. So we said: Oh Messenger of God, you did something in your sleep which you used not to do. He said: how amazing some people of my community will be heading toward the House because of a man of the Quraish who sought refuge in the House; until, when they are in the desert, they will be swallowed up. Then we said: Oh Messenger of God, the route may bring together the people. He said: yes, among them there will be the judicious and the constrained and the wayfarer. They will all perish in the same way, but will be sent forth from different points of origin. God will raise them according to their intents."

"Hafsah informed me that she heard the Prophet say: verily, an army will be heading for this House to raid it, until when they are in a desert of the earth, the one in the middle of them will be swallowed up, and the first of them will call to the last. Then they will be swallowed up, and no one will be left but the fugitive who will give information about them."

Qahtani

Muhammad al-Qahtani was not the source for rumors that he was the Muslim savior. In fact, he initially dismissed the idea as a joke. But as more members described their dreams to him, he began to take it seriously. He told Huzaimi that he came to believe he was the Mahdi only after he had a dream affirming it, in accordance with the hadith, "God will set him right in one night." Huzaimi and others were skeptical of such talk, but Juhaiman decided the dreams were true and that Qahtani was indeed the Mahdi.[156] Soon, Qahtani's brother and other members were preparing for the impending apocalypse by selling their farms to raise funds to purchase weapons. Members then began to collect and store weapons to attack the Grand Mosque. Huzaimi sensed that a collective delusion was taking hold among members obsessed with dreams, portents of the End of Time, and the advent of the Mahdi. As Juhaiman's band armed itself for millenarian battles, Huzaimi cut his ties with the group.

Dreams and the Mahdi in the Uprising

In the uprising's early minutes, the man Juhaiman chose to deliver a sermon presented Muhammad al-Qahtani and declared that he had been seen in more than fifty dreams attesting that he was the Mahdi. According to Huzaimi's informant of events during the siege, people who gathered at the sanctuary and who were not part of Juhaiman's band and had never before seen Qahtani excitedly proclaimed that they immediately recognized him from their dreams. The preacher went on to cite hadiths about dreams and the End of Time:

> Nothing remains of revelation except for good tidings, a true dream that a believer sees or is seen about him.
> The believer's dream at the End of Time will not be false.

The insurgents continued to have dreams throughout the siege. Juhaiman cheered on the defenders, reminding them of dreams where the earth swallowed up enemy forces. A rumor spread among the defenders that a fighter on the front lines was close enough to the besieging forces to hear a radio broadcast describing huge losses suffered by the attacking army when the earth swallowed it up. In the last days of the siege, when they were confined to underground cells, members circulated reports of still more dreams about the End of Time, until the last sixty fighters surrendered to government forces.

Seizure of the Mosque and the Mahdi Script

In Huzaimi's final analysis, the Mecca uprising came about from a mixture of dreams and interpretations of recent events as the fulfillment of hadiths about the End of Time. Once the Salafi Group gained control of the Grand Mosque and swore allegiance to the Mahdi, God would take care of the rest in a divinely scripted scenario: an army would march from northern Arabia to attack the Mahdi, but the earth would open to swallow it up in the desert. The Mahdi would then go to Medina to fight the Antichrist. After defeating the Antichrist, the Mahdi would lead his forces to Palestine to fight the Jews. Then Jesus would return to earth and pray behind the Mahdi. His forces would move on to Syria and pray at the Umayyad Mosque in Damascus, whereupon the Resurrection would take place.

Juhaiman and his band staked their lives on the salvationist vision laid out in hadiths. They had no strategy, no plan to establish a government. As things turned out, the Mahdi was killed on the third day of fighting in the Grand Mosque, but Juhaiman refused to believe it and browbeat members to deny it. Instead, he insisted that the Mahdi could not be killed, that he was trapped somewhere and would eventually reappear. But at the end of the two-week battle, Juhaiman and sixty of his men emerged from the underground cells to meekly surrender. One month later, the survivors were beheaded in public, dispelling ghosts of the old Ikhwan and dreams of the Mahdi.

THE MEMOIR

Memories of Childhood

My oldest, foggy memory is of water glistening in a muddy stream that I was trying to touch with my hands while riding in a small, pink wooden wagon for children called a *qasiriyyah*. I remember the water glistening and the wagon's color and my effort to touch the water with my hands. I have confirmed the memory by asking my mother, may God lengthen her life, and she assured me that it was in Basra when we lived there in the al-Balush quarter. I remember the darkness of the rooms, the aroma of incense associated with Hindu temples.

What is there to say about my childhood? It was not tormented or deprived. I was not an orphan. I did not suffer from a family wracked by divorce or strife. Nor did I suffer the complex of a middle brother. I was the oldest child and had four siblings. We were two boys and three girls. Because I was the oldest and two girls came after me, for a time, I enjoyed the privileges of a favorite only son, in accordance with the Eastern mentality. These privileges have some importance in shaping one's personality, especially in patriarchal societies.

As a child, I was headstrong and unruly, more likely to fool around than do anything creative or inventive. There was nothing about me to indicate either excellence or distinction.

My world was not as narrow as might be supposed of a young boy. Rather, I was aware of a very expansive world: the world of the market. And what a market! The vegetable market was the largest in our town, Zubair.

My father had an office job in Kuwait, like many others from Zubair. He rented a small mud house like most houses in Zubair. It was close to my maternal grandfather Yasin al-Huzaimi's large house. In the dark of the night, before the dawn prayer, I would go out of the house, taking advantage of my sleeping mother, open the door on its hinges, and leave it ajar. I went out without paying heed to the dogs in the alleys. They were the first thing I would encounter because the market had a butcher shop, and wherever there was a butcher shop, there were dogs and cats. My grandfather's shop was at the end of the street along three roads, so I would head over there. His lamp would be aglow while its owner went to the al-Naqib Mosque to give the call to prayer and to lead the prayer. I would play in his shop until he returned from the mosque. He would take me by the hand to our home and argue with my mother for not keeping an eye on me. To keep me from going out and sneaking away at dawn, she blocked the door, but I could open it and my grandfather again would take me home and scold my mother. Then locks were put on the door and my mother kept the keys under her head. But that only prevented me from going out early, before the call to dawn prayer.

A World Full of Secrets

The vegetable market was my heaven and earth, a market stretching from east to west, with small streets branching off, busy with coffeehouses, horses and donkeys pulling wagons, pushcarts filled with vegetables, shopowners, and customers. I would meander among the stores and street vendors. Everyone knew me or knew that I was the Mullah's grandson. At least that is what I imagined. The only place that I dreaded passing was the front of Zubair Mosque and the western end of the market. The reason for that was the group of poor folk who used to sit beneath the wall of al-Zubair ibn al-Awwam's mosque. Each one of them had a plate or a small metal tray that he would raise in front of every passerby. There were so many of them at that spot because some generous soul had donated funds for a dervish lodge on the north side of the mosque to serve the poor and the needy.[1] They were usually not townspeople but strangers who happened to wind up there. As much as I was afraid of that place, I liked to go into and explore the dervishes' lodge. It was a world full of secrets, as I eventually learned.

As I said, I was an unruly child. My mother started to sense the danger that awaited me if I continued on that path, so she decided to enroll me in kindergarten. The only kindergarten in Zubair at that time was part of the Najat School. Even though the school was far from our home, I was enrolled and rode a bus there for a time. One day, one of my playmates, I recall her name was Hajir, told me that she was going to her home, which was near the school. When the monitor got distracted, we left the school, each one going home. My home was far from the school for a young child, not yet four and a half years old. To get home, I had to cross al-Rashidiyyah Street then go down my road in al-Banat Market and then cross al-Batin Street, then continue walking south until I arrived. When I went inside, my mother was surprised to see me because I was home before the bus came. When I told her what happened, she decided not to send me to such a negligent kindergarten, fearing the automobile traffic.

After a short time, she enrolled me in a government kindergarten that had recently opened near our home. This kindergarten was in the same building as the dervishes' lodge but was newly renovated. I don't know where the poor and old residents went. I remember that this kindergarten had a large tree that dropped almond-shaped fruit with sharp burrs as if they were thorns. My teachers said that they were explosive bombs and that they were lethal. When I was older, I learned it was a castor oil plant and that its fruit was very poisonous. Long ago, book copyists would mix its poisonous juice with the ink they used for writing manuscripts in order to keep harmful insects and worms away from the paper.

I loved liver. In fact, I could not resist it. One day I decided to eat liver at a restaurant that specialized in kebab and liver. It was near the vegetable market. Its owner knew my grandfather. I went in and ordered enough liver to feed a crowd. When I finished eating, I told them to charge it to Mullah Yasin. I kept doing that until the day of reckoning came. The man went to my grandfather to collect the tab for the liver that I had eaten. My grandfather got furious and got into a heated argument with the man. In the end, he paid the tab for the liver that I had eaten, took my hand, and yet again took me to my mother and scolded her. I remember that she tried to punish me in front of him, so I sought protection from him, and he stopped her from hitting me.

My Grandfather's Surprise

One day I decided to go to Basra. It was a big deal for me since I had heard grown-ups repeatedly say that so and so went to Basra. I decided to go to Basra like them. I left the house early in the morning after getting dressed. I had 15 piasters on me. I went to the bus station. The conductor took the 15 piasters from me and I boarded. By a strange coincidence, my grandfather got on board after me. When he saw me, he beckoned me with his hand and asked me: "Where are you going?" I told him, "I'm going to Basra." Then he asked me, "Is anybody with you?" I told him, "No." At that point he flew into a rage, took my hand, and made me get off the bus. He called the bus driver and scolded him for allowing me to ride the bus without someone old enough to look after me, as I could have gotten lost in Basra, especially since I had no other money. Then he took me by the hand and brought me to my mother and scolded her for that.

The Story of the Great House

The great house was my refuge whenever they would not let me go to the market. In fact, the name was apt, for it was a great house, with a broad courtyard and a pen for sheep and chickens. It is strange that I do not remember lunches and dinners in our home as much as I remember them at the great house. My grandfather loved the company of his younger children, like my aunts and my Uncle Ibrahim, who was about one younger than I. As for me, I was practically a permanent guest there. My grandfather's wife, Umm Yusuf, often made tea and pastries to delight our hearts.

When I became old enough to go to school, I had a place reserved at the Talhah ibn Ubaidallah primary school. When I started going there, it was a completely different world for me. My classmates were older boys. I think I was the youngest student there. In fact, some students who had been there were my cousin's classmates. Then he advanced and I arrived and became their classmate. Then I advanced and my brother Khalid came after a while and advanced while they remained behind. Children typically began first grade when they were 7 years old, but it was also common for some to start elementary school when they were young adolescents. I knew some classmates who left school in the first year to become unskilled workers at hard jobs.

Professor Hasan Zabun taught me in first grade. He was one of the kindest and most patient teachers with students. His many former students still talk about him with gratitude. He, may God grant him long life, had ways to clarify lessons that young boys loved, like acting and using simple tricks. After twenty years or more of teaching, he was drafted to fight in the Iraq–Iran War. He went missing during the war and we had no news about him. Iraq lost so many men of rare talents during the war. Then Hasan returned from the war as part of a prisoner exchange agreement, carrying bitter memories of war and imprisonment. He returned hating war but did not lose his incandescent spirit.

Music and Movies

After spending a year in the first grade at the Talhah School, around 1965, we went to live with my father in Kuwait.[2] There I resumed my studies. Based on an exam, I was not ready to join the second grade, so I repeated the first year at the Umar ibn al-Khattab School in Khaitan [a suburb of Kuwait City]. It is a very large school that was based on modern style of education, for it included a theater, several sports facilities of different kinds, chicken pens, and a large dining hall. There I became acquainted for the first time with peas. They were served to us as a delicious dish at lunch. There I got to know a different kind of atmosphere because the school was equipped with everything a pupil would need, from clothes to school books and notebooks and pens. Furthermore, the school had a class period dedicated to music. But all this did not entice me to study or learn. The first year was difficult for me. In the second year, I learned to ditch school. It got to the point that I did not take the final examinations at the end of the year.

In Kuwait I also discovered death, burial, and funerals—that it is a sad thing that makes people cry—I may not have been aware of that before. Two incidents taught me about death. The first event was the death of an older relative, Uncle Yusuf ibn Muhammad al-Huzaimi, the husband of my aunt Shaqiqah. My father went to get ready for the funeral early in the morning. With him was my cousin Muhammad. We went at dawn to the place of condolence. I was to open the door for boys and girls and most of them came into the house crying in grief. The second event was when I attended the burial of the ruler of Kuwait, Abd Allah al-Salim al-Sabah.[3] Men were crying and I was surprised by that. I asked my father and he told me that this man was the father of all of Kuwait. At that time, I learned about car accidents, for I escaped an accident with light injuries to my foot.

Return to Zubair

When we returned to Zubair, I enrolled at a new school, Abu Bakr al-Siddiq Elementary School, but I cut class whenever I had the chance.

The Suitcase Incident

One of the events that befell me around that time was when I was sitting by the door of the house, brandishing a long tree branch, when I saw my Uncle Yusuf, may God have mercy on him, from some distance. I threw away the branch and hurried inside the house. My mother was in the kitchen. I started looking for a place to hide from him as I was afraid of being punished because he had warned me against leaving the house. In our sitting room we had a very large suitcase: I crawled into it and locked myself in. Then my uncle entered the house and asked about me. My mother told him that I was in the street. He told her that he had seen me go into the house. They looked for me on the roof, in the rooms, in the basement. They began to get worried. All this happened while I was in the suitcase listening to their talk and their effort to find me. It was summer, so I lifted the suitcase lid a little to get a breath of air and to cool off. Then my mother came with a thermos of water and she put it on top of the suitcase. The thermos was made of heavy metal, so it was hard for me to lift the top of the suitcase. So I called to my mother from inside and she moved the thermos. She got me out of the suitcase but did not punish me that day. Instead, my uncle said that what happened was enough.

At that time, I learned about friendship, fights with classmates, and social games. One day, around sunset, we were told that there was a cinema showing movies in one of the other neighborhoods. So the boys from our neighborhood went to the other one and indeed we found a cinema showing a movie. The screen was a piece of cloth tied to the side of a car. The movie turned out to be educational, about bilharzia. Nevertheless, the world of entertainment had a kind of wondrous charm for me. After that first brush with movies, I was drawn to movies and plays, and I followed everything that played at the Rashid Cinema or at the Watan Cinema in Basra at an early stage of my life, and that is another story.

Memories of Youth[4]

When I was a boy, I began playing a sport, soccer, in an organized way. I learned about a league at the Qadisiyah Sports Club in Kuwait at that time, around the time of the 1967 war. The Jews were our enemies at that time and I was not aware of the differences between Judaism as a divine religion that is connected with us through historic ties and the Hebrew state that defeated us in the year of the Setback and, before that, the year of the Catastrophe, the 1948 Palestine War. It was jumbled in my mind and far from rational and moderate. Likewise, my mental image of a Jew was childish. Add to that a stereotypical mental image reinforced by reading Abd Allah al-Tall's book[5] where he speaks about the Jewish danger and how they make bread mixed with the blood of Muslims and Christians: his book has a long discussion of that, which is a pure lie. But Tall's book affected me and I took it as a source of information for conversation in salons and gatherings. I was surprised by my mother's attitude toward Jews for she always told me that we lived next to them as neighbors in the al-Balush neighborhood and that we only saw good things from them. She was proud of the gold that she bought from a Jewish goldsmith famous for honesty in all his dealings and never cheating on gold. She preferred him to the Muslim and Christian goldsmiths because of his honesty. I was surprised by this talk and in my depths I doubted my mother's patriotism because of her illiteracy and her ignorance. How could I not, when she did not read or write and was not aware of what was going on in Palestine. The only things she listened to on the radio were the songs of Khadiri Abu Aziz, Nazim al-Ghazzali,[6] and Salimah Murad (Salimah Pasha).[7] Years later, I figured out that my mother was truthful and honest in her feelings toward others, including Jews. I remember that I said to her that Hitler equated Jews with monkeys. She said to me in a reflexive reply, "And what did he think of us [Arabs]?" Truly, I had no answer at that time. My source was what I heard. Her source was her instinctive feeling about how to deal with things.

In 1968, the Baathists came to power in a coup. It changed the general atmosphere to anxiety and turning inward. The government entered a phase of harshness, austerity, and boycotting everything American. At that time, I used to read comic books like *Superman* and *Batman* and *Tarzan*, but now they were prohibited and we could only get them smuggled from Kuwait. My biggest misfortune was the ban on American movies and the abundance of European, Eastern Bloc, Indian, and Arab movies instead. The movie houses went broke with these movies and some resorted to deception to attract customers. They would announce a new movie with posters next to the box office but when we went in, we found a dancer on the stage performing an Oriental dance. That was the first time I saw an Oriental dance in person.

The general atmosphere in the country was to sanctify national feeling in a childish, haphazard fashion. What is even stranger about this period is how it was marked by distraction and fear more than growth and development. At that time, in 1970, champion wrestlers toured throughout all of Iraq, and as a result, Adnan al-Qaisi[8] became a legend hosted by Saddam Husain on television screens and his picture was hung in streets and squares. Every Iraqi wanted to become like Adnan al-Qaisi. No wonder! He beat wrestlers from Europe and America. In the collective Iraqi psyche, this was a victory over Western imperialism. At that time, people had to wait in line for a kilogram of potatoes and other goods. And yet, the excited atmosphere surrounding Adnan al-Qaisi's heroics persisted.

Abu Tubar's gang appeared in Baghdad, using axes to kill people, spreading fear and terror among Iraqis in all parts of the country.[9] Even though the gang was active in Baghdad, rumors reached the provinces and fear crept into every Iraqi household in every part of the country.

In this climate of terror, celebratory parades were held to exalt the Arab Socialist Baath party. It got to the point that celebrations were held at schools on a weekly basis. These celebrations had no educational or moral point. They were just for singing and dancing.

I witnessed all this, watching and hoping ...[10]

My First Acquaintance with Islamic Movements

Before I get into how I joined the Salafi Group and my relationship with the Group's leader, Juhaiman ibn Muhammad ibn Saif al-Utaibi al-Dann, I should give some background to that relationship.[11]

My first brush with Islamic groups was around 1974 when I was a youth in the southern Iraqi town of Zubair, not as a member but as a pious youth on their fringes. That time was the true beginning of the Religious Awakening and the wave of religious politics that advanced in the Muslim East, while progressive forces, and the Left in general, were in retreat, and Arab nationalism was losing its appeal to the masses. As for secularism and liberalism, they could not compete in terms of organization or popularity. The unimaginable leap in oil prices after the October 1973 war had bolstered conservatives in general as there was financial support for anyone opposed to the communist bloc or the Arab nationalists, who had adopted the socialist line by and large. An official silence prevailed toward the political activities of religious groups even though they were not at all customary. In the broader arena of the Cold War, reviving political Islam looked like a good choice.[12]

In those days the taped sermons of Egyptian preacher Sheikh Abd al-Hamid Kishk were very popular.[13] From them I learned about the tribulations of the Muslim Brotherhood in Egypt during the Nasir era.[14] Likewise, I came to believe that Islam had many enemies wishing it harm, especially those who paid lip service to Islam but did not act according to it or apply it either in public affairs or in private matters.

I became acquainted with Sayyid Qutb's *Milestones*,[15] but I did not like it because I did not understand it at the time, and with Sayyid Sabiq's *Law of Sunnah*,[16] especially the part about worship. Then I got to know Muhammad Nasir al-Din al-Albani's *Characteristics of the Prophet's Prayer*.[17] At that time, I heard that he was a "Salafi" who adhered to sound Prophetic Traditions.[18] I did not understand what people meant by "Salafi" except in a superficial fashion, but since I did not want people to think I was ignorant, I did not ask anyone to explain it to me.

In 1976, I went to Kuwait where I got to know the Salafi Group[19] and its leading lights, such as Abd Allah al-Sibt, Abd al-Rahman Abd al-Khaliq, and Abd al-Rahman Abd al-Samad.[20] I started attending their discussions held in salons known as *diwaniyyah*s. By listening to them, I came to understand the Salafi way and rejected the authority of the four Sunni legal schools[21] and the views of the legal schools' classical scholars with the implicit blessing of this Group. Likewise, I came to understand this Group's definition of belief in one God. Out of the various religious movements, I adopted the views of this particular group and not those of the Muslim Brotherhood or the Tablighi Association,[22] which were the two largest groups in Kuwait apart from the Salafi tendency. I heard about the Islamic Liberation Party[23] but I never met any members. When I still lived in Zubair, I had heard about the Muslim Brotherhood and the Islamic Liberation Party.

While I was in Kuwait, the Salafi Group was a new rising force that formed a single bloc and had not yet suffered schisms. For the most part, its members wanted nothing to do with politics. In fact, apart from Sheikh Abd al-Rahman

Abd al-Khaliq, it is no exaggeration to say almost none of its members had any political awareness at all. Later on, the Salafi Group split into an apolitical faction, the Jamis, and a political faction, the Sururis.[24]

In Kuwait I met a man who would play a role in setting up the Salafi Group in Riyadh, Muhammad al-Haidari. We agreed to meet in Riyadh. In fact, after six months in Kuwait, I moved to Riyadh where I resided in a bachelor flat[25] with some fellow Zubairis in a very small mud and stone building, near Umm Salim Circle. Some of us worked, others studied at the Teacher Training Institute. We were seven in all, living in three rooms measuring six square meters, including one on the roof. As soon as I arrived in Riyadh, I got a job working in a shop that sold materials for electric supplies, earning 900 riyals per month.[26]

Islamic Movements in Riyadh

In 1977, Saudi Arabia's first store for selling Islamic tapes opened in Riyadh in the Dughaithir Building overlooking Batha Street,[27] in a tiny space measuring just four by two meters. It was the only place for Islamic tapes amidst stores selling music recordings, so it was an important step for the Islamists. Some sheikhs visited the place to congratulate the owner for taking that step. They told him that they were ready to support it and offered him their services.

At that time, it was not unusual to hear the din of songs bursting from music stores before the opening of al-Yamamah Tapes, the store for Islamic tapes. After al-Yamamah Tapes opened, you rarely heard music anymore because the owner of the Islamic tapes store opposed it. It was enough for him to play Quran recitation from the Islamic tapes store to entirely silence the music stores. If someone in a music store responded by raising the volume of a song, then he was accused of disrespecting the Quran. Thus, the opening of a small Islamic tapes store made the music stores change their actions and move to new locations.

At that time, there was only one bookstore in Riyadh that specialized in Islamic books, and books by the Muslim Brotherhood in particular, namely al-Haramain Bookstore, located in the same Dughaithir Building [as the Islamic tapes store] overlooking Batha Street. True, there were other stores [that sold Islamic movement books], but al-Haramain Bookstore had a larger selection of books by the Muslim Brotherhood and other Islamic movements. At that time, apolitical Salafi books were very different from the movements' books, which were full of argument and rebuttal. For instance, I did not see Albani's books at the Islamist store with the exception of *The Abbreviation of Muslim's Sound Prophetic Traditions* by al-Mundhiri[28] on which Albani had written a commentary, *The Prophet's Prayer*,[29] and *Wedding Etiquette in the Pure Prophetic Tradition*.[30] As for his book that triggered opposition from the ulama,[31] *The Muslim Woman's Veil and Dress during Prayer*,[32] it was hard to find even though some of the rebuttals to it were around, such as the rebuttal by Sheikh Abd al-Qadir Habib al-Sindi and Sheikh al-Ansari.[33] Usually *The Muslim Woman's Veil* was distributed for free. In it the sheikh argued that it is permitted to show a woman's face and palms because they are not a woman's private parts, in contrast to the predominant opinion of the Hanbali ulama.[34] In general, the ulama of Najd considered this fatwa[35] by the sheikh to be a black mark on his academic career, in addition to the sheikh's call for not following any of the four legal schools—Hanafi, Maliki, Shaf'i, Hanbali—and taking rulings directly from the Quran and Prophetic Tradition.

These matters had effects on later events, especially because the Salafi Group took an extreme position on how to derive legal rulings from the Quran and the Prophetic Tradition, to the extent that the Group ignored ancillary disciplines like legal theory and grammar to interpret these two sources. In fact, some members condemned these disciplines because the Companions[36] did not know them. Likewise, they condemned anyone who depended on opinion, analogy, or other nontextual legal principles, let alone a concept like general welfare or the law of circumstances occurring after the Prophet's lifetime.[37]

At that time, the Committees for Commanding Right and Forbidding Wrong[38] did not have the kind of power that we see nowadays.[39] They were old men who relied on wisdom and fair exhortation,[40] in their dealings with others. Society did not view them as an intrusive presence but an integral part. They were known as deputies or *nawwab*s. Their main role was to remind others about prayer time. The deputy was like a big brother for everyone, a father whose word was heeded, not someone at odds with society. Rather, he would provide guidance and counsel with courtesy, in contrast to deputies nowadays who view their society with so much doubt that they are suspicious of everything. Now just about all they do is follow people to catch them sinning. As a result, they have created an abyss between themselves and the rest of society, and now people think of the duty of commanding right and forbidding wrong as something like the Spanish Inquisition.[41]

I spent a lot of time reading the six canonical books[42] of Prophetic Traditions and treatises on the Science of Prophetic Traditions.[43] In particular, I got to know some works by Nasir al-Din al-Albani as well as *The Book of God's Unity* by Muhammad ibn Abd a-Wahhab.[44]

I got to know some young men who it turned out were members of the Muslim Brotherhood. In Riyadh, the Brotherhood was divided into two factions. The main faction was recognized by the international organization of the Muslim Brotherhood and was distinguished by its robust organization and visionary program. In terms of outlook, the members of the faction gravitated to the writings of Sayyid Qutb, so they did not believe in giving allegiance to the ruler. They are often referred to as the Qutbist wing of the Muslim Brotherhood, or as Qutbists. The other, less organized, smaller faction of the Muslim Brotherhood known as "The Abode of Knowledge Group"[45] mostly followed the writings of Hasan al-Banna and believed in giving allegiance to the ruler. They were known as Bannaists, after Hasan al-Banna.[46] Likewise there was noticeable activity by the Tablighi Association, which focused on the popular lower-class neighborhoods. They had a mosque in a poor neighborhood called Iskirina, so they were sometimes known as the Iskirina Group. Their approach to proselytizing emphasized education and preaching, and they were known for their passive, fatalistic, Sufi orientation.

That time [the mid-1970s] was notable for an intense struggle for the loyalty of religious youth, especially in the schools. Practically every school had two or three religious tendencies, loyal to Qutb, Banna, or the Tablighi Association. Behind the scenes, these tendencies were in an intense competition to recruit followers. Their rivalry sometimes escalated into sharp verbal arguments. Although I never heard of physical violence used against an activist trying to recruit in Riyadh, I did hear from numerous sources of such things happening in Kuwait. Apparently, a Muslim Brother youth invited a Salafi activist to his home and when he arrived, he welcomed him. The Muslim Brother then went inside the house and when he came out a short time later, he was wearing a karate outfit. He then applied all he had learned in the Social Reform Society's martial arts classes, knowing that the Salafi youth was weak.[47] It was a huge scandal. Older members of the two organizations intervened to limit its effects and broke up the affray but did not talk about ways to prevent future incidents.

Riyadh had some mosques whose members were not affiliated with any particular group. Their members simply gathered for religious observances and rituals. They were more like discussion groups or neighborhood cultural centers. Practically every mosque had a room with a library where young men would gather around the imam of the mosque. These were the best places for the Muslim Brotherhood and the Tablighi Association to recruit new members. It was not necessary for these libraries to belong to either group. Some mosque groups did not lean toward any of the Islamic groups but were loyal only to their imam. I became familiar with one of these independent groups and started to go with them on religious retreats.

In 1976, I traveled [to Mecca] with them during Ramadan to perform the lesser pilgrimage for the first time.[48] By sheer chance, I attended a lesson circle where the sheikh used only the Quran and Prophetic Tradition for proofs. A group of students surrounded him, asking him questions, and he answered them in a deliberate, confident manner. The name al-Albani was mentioned repeatedly in the group. Afterward, I asked the name of the teacher and was told he was Sheikh Ali al-Mazrui, a teacher at Dar al-Hadith in Medina.[49] This meeting completely transformed my thought and action.

After completing the lesser pilgrimage, we returned to Riyadh by road on the morning of the Ramadan Feast. I was convinced that I had to study at Dar al-Hadith in Medina with Sheikh Ali al-Mazrui. So I quit my job in the middle of Dhu al-Qa'dah,[50] gathered my belongings, and flew to Medina early one morning. I arrived at Dar al-Hadith and spoke with Sheikh Ali al-Mazrui. He tried to get me admitted to the Dar al-Hadith Institute but it was not easy because the registration period was over. So he wrote on my behalf to the head of the Ikhwan[51] in Mecca, A'id ibn Duraimeeh, and he advised me to go there and ask for him or for Abd Allah al-Harbi. I immediately took a taxi to Mecca.

The Salafis in Mecca

I arrived in Mecca at the time of noon prayer. At the Haram[52] Institute, I asked for either A'id ibn Duraimeeh or Abd Allah al-Harbi. I went to Harbi and we got acquainted. He told me we might find A'id at the Ikhwan[53] House in Hawd al-Baqar, the first house for the Ikhwan in Mecca, so we went over there. The house was merely a piece of land enclosed by cement blocks. It had two modest rooms with a roof made of thin, cheap wood. In general, it was put together at random. It had practically no foundation for the rooms and no support for the walls. The floor was not paved; it was just bare rocks on the hill. Nor did it have a bathroom. If someone wanted to answer a call of nature, he went to the bathrooms in the nearby mosque. Likewise, if someone wanted to wash up [one used the mosque]. The house was lacking in every meaning of the word. I think it used to be a pen for animals because there were traces of them here and there.

I waited a short while for A'id to show up and gave him the letter that Ali al-Mazrui had written for me. He told me that the Institute would resume classes after the pilgrimage and that he would speak on my behalf with the Institute director, Sheikh Salih al-Maqushi. So I left the matter of registering at the Institute to A'id and got involved in the life of the Ikhwan.

I attached myself to Abd Allah al-Harbi, leader of the movement's Mecca branch. He was the one who gathered the Ikhwan, took them on missions to the outskirts of Mecca, and led them to study with sheikhs.[54] At that time I got to know Sultan al-Lihyani and his brother Mansur, who belonged to the Tablighi Association, and their cousin Abd al-Latif al-Lihyani, Suwailim al-Salmi, Marzuq al-Hazli, Husain al-Ghamdi, Salim al-Hazmi, and Nur al-Din, son of our sheikh Badi al-Din ibn Ihsanallah al-Rashidi. These were most of the Ikhwan in Mecca when I got there. The oldest one was not more than 25 years old, except for A'id ibn Duraimeeh, who was over 40. He told me that he had begun teaching himself as an adult, for he had been a Bedouin camel shepherd into his thirties. After teaching himself reading and writing in the desert, he moved to Mecca where he enrolled at the Haram Institute because it did not require an elementary diploma. Instead, it conducted interviews to determine one's academic level. The Haram Institute had evolved out of study circles in the mosque and held its lessons on the floor in the Grand Mosque's porticoes.

It was the time of the pilgrimage season. I was completely overjoyed with this new place: pilgrims from all races and all parts of the world, movement without rest, 24 hours a day, praying before and circling the Kaabah, and walking the concourse between al-Safa and al-Marwah.[55] I spent all my time in the Grand Mosque. A'id ibn Duraimeeh was able to reserve a space in the Grand Mosque's basements for the Ikhwan.[56] It was my favorite place to stay except for evenings when we were not allowed to sleep there due to the potential for floods that might rush down from Mecca's ravines and sweep debris into the Grand Mosque. There was drainage beneath the Grand Mosque but sometimes the basement would be flooded. Visitors to the Grand Mosque, especially people staying in basement rooms, were warned to take precautions in the event of a flood.

Abd Allah al-Harbi told me that the Ikhwan of Medina were going to perform the pilgrimage and we would have to get ready to set up tents in Mina.[57] After a few days, on around 6 Dhu al-Hijjah,[58] their tents came from Medina and we helped pitch them at the location in Mina that was set aside for them. When it was ready, it was a spacious encampment. Then we started greeting them in Mecca. I got to know Ali ibn Musharraf al-Umari, the first Medina member I ever met. I was also very eager to meet some individuals with outstanding reputations, such as Juhaiman. I got to know all of them at the Mina encampment: Nasir ibn Husain, Sulaiman ibn Shtaiwi, Sa'd al-Tamimi, Ahmad Hasan al-Mu'allam, Faisal Muhammad Faisal, Muqbil al-Wadi'i,[59] Radan al-Utaibi, and Mutlaq ibn Sahl from Sajir.[60] I also met Sultan, Fahd, Umar, Abd Allah, and Abbas, all sons of Jarallah from Ha'il.[61] There was also a group of Sudanese from Ansar al-Sunnah[62] that came from Ta'if.[63] Other groups came from all parts of the kingdom. A place was set aside for Sheikh al-Albani, whom I met for the first time. I was in a state of amazement, even intoxication, about meeting him and his large entourage of Salafis from Syria, and about hearing him speak in person. Truly, I was in a state of intense excitement. Could I really be sitting alongside the sheikh whose books I read so closely, whose ideas and opinions I had embraced after hearing them to the point of blind imitation?

The Ikhwan of Mecca had the pivotal task of taking care of all requirements for the tents because everyone in the tents was under the authority of A'id ibn Duraimeeh al-Nafi'i, leader of the Meccan Ikhwan. The Ikhwan shared the tasks. Some worked in the kitchen, while others handled the chore of bringing water. Some brought food. My job, along with Abd Allah al-Harbi, was to bring food. We brought large quantities of bread from a bakery in town for breakfast before the dawn prayer.

Thus, the pilgrimage days passed, between performing the rituals, attending sessions of the Ikhwan and Albani, getting to know Ikhwan I had not previously met, and establishing a relationship with Juhaiman, who appeared very busy. It was at that time that I was beginning to get acquainted with issues that divided the Ikhwan from the followers of the legal schools. When the pilgrimage ended, the Ikhwan returned to their countries and towns, and we went back to the Grand Mosque.

The meeting that took place during the pilgrimage was a kind of turning point for me, for I was now truly a member of the Salafi Group. Their conduct, their nature, their gentle character, their activities, and how they spent their time were deliberate and purposeful. They were different from the Salafi Group in Kuwait for being more serious, more austere, and more withdrawn from mundane concerns. For example, during my time with the Salafi Group, we never indulged in luxuries such as going out for *kunafah*,[64] like we did in Kuwait, where we would go for kunafah at [dining places like] al-Kurd or al-Samadi, or go for ice cream or something else. Instead, each step was counted and regulated, not by written ordinance but as a way of life. The reason for that may go back to their pure Bedouin character. Therefore, you would find them leading a very humble way of life. Their houses in the Eastern Harrah neighborhood of Medina were very small, so that any time I went to one of their meetings, the house had nothing but a rug, some cushions, and a library full of books of Prophetic Traditions and Quran exegesis.

Juhaiman's library contained most of Albani's books, the six canonical books of Prophetic Traditions and their commentaries, Ibn Sa'di's exegesis, Ibn Kathir's and al-Baghawi's exegeses,[65] Sheikh Hammud al-Tuwaijiri's book on the Last Hour,[66] Muhammad Shawkani's commentary on Prophetic Traditions,[67] and Muhammad al-San'ani's commentary on Prophetic Traditions.[68] As for books from the legal schools, they were practically nonexistent. His library included the *Collection of Writings on Monotheism*,[69] books by Ibn Taymiyyah, Ibn Qayyim al-Jawziyyah,[70] and al-Tahawi.[71] That was everything in Juhaiman's library. It was like the libraries of most Ikhwan, except for that belonging to Muqbil ibn Hadi al-Wadi'i or the library of Ali al-Mazrui. Muqbil is unusual for having a mostly modern library with books on modern law. As for al-Mazrui, his library was modern law.

A year after I moved to Mecca, the Ikhwan moved from Hawd al-Baqar to another house located in a neighborhood called al-Sufaira' on the outskirts of Mecca but within the bounds of the *haram*.[72] The walls of the house were made of rough cement blocks. It had three rooms, bathrooms, and a large courtyard, about a third of which was covered by a thin, wood roof. The house was out of the sight of prying eyes as there were no other houses in the vicinity. Except for one house behind it, it was all by itself. Its door opened on to a broad, flat area. The house served as a place of relaxation for Ikhwan from outside Mecca to stay while performing the lesser pilgrimage.

At the Haram Institute, I received a stipend of 150 riyals. Inasmuch as I was deeply influenced by the ways of the Pious Ancestors,[73] seeking knowledge and enduring hardship for their own sake, I was satisfied with that amount, which I spent on a little food, but mostly on books. The bookshop owners allowed us to purchase books on installment to make their acquisition easier, so it was a common practice for students. From time to time, we used to receive some charity designated for religious students in Mecca. I would receive around 2,000 riyals a year. Either the Institute's sheikhs [teachers] or the director, Sheikh Salih al-Maqushi, would hand out the funds. With my share of alms, I paid back the debts that accumulated in dealings with bookstore owners and lived on what remained.

Some of our classmates, especially the foreigners, worked as cleaners at the Grand Mosque while others worked as peddlers. I decided to work as a peddler selling watches during the pilgrimage season. An Ikhwan from Hadramaut [in South Yemen] went with me to a wholesale merchant who supplied me with merchandise, some "West End" brand watches. I took the merchandise and walked around with them among the pilgrims until I ran into one of the Ikhwan. He inspected the watches and said to me, "It is forbidden to peddle such merchandise!" When I asked him why, he told me that these watches contained the sign of the cross, and we are commanded to break and wipe out the cross. As a matter of fact, I held the same beliefs, but I had not noticed the cross on the watches, so I went to the fellow who recommended me to the watch merchant and explained the situation to him. He took the watches from me and returned them to the merchant in the condition I had taken them. That evening, a discussion about these watches took place, noting that I was not allowed to return them to the merchant, and that I was obliged to "forbid wrong with my hands"[74] by erasing the cross before returning them. I later discovered that most Ikhwan erase the cross with a finger smudge. Other Ikhwan believe it forbidden to wear a steel wristband and replace the metal wristband with one made of leather or plastic. The ones who do not change the wristband do not wear a watch but keep one in their pocket, or they attach it to a chain that they keep in a small pocket. I saw a group of Ikhwan who were preoccupied with the issue do that. Wearing metal bands and watches was frequently discussed at Ikhwan meetings.

We were in very difficult financial straits that could drive a student to get rid of his dearest possessions, namely, his books. Something like that happened to me. I craved owning original editions of books. I had obtained a copy of a famous commentary on Prophetic Traditions in the Bulaq Edition.[75] One of my classmates heard about it. I had borrowed some money from him and he offered to redeem the debt of 450 riyals in exchange for the book, but I refused because it was worth more than that. A week later, he came back to me asking for the money [that I owed him], insisting that he needed it. I offered him the commentary on Prophetic Traditions to see if one of the avid book collectors we knew in Mecca might want to buy it. He took the book and came back two days later and said to me, "The book sold for 500 riyals." He gave me 50 riyals and kept the money I owed him. A short time later, I visited him at his residence. As I browsed his book collection, I found the Bulaq Edition of the book that was so dear to me. I left his house right away as I felt cheated. Many things like that occur among students, so my loss was minor compared to students driven by poverty to sell their entire book collections.

I knew a Hadrami[76] who went kind of crazy when his book collection was burned in South Yemen, reportedly at the hands of the communists.[77] This man owned a very large collection containing everything he could lay his hands on in the way of original editions from all parts of the world. The amazing thing is that he memorized the titles of the books, their authors, and the dates and places of publication, the best editions, who abridged them, who wrote commentaries on them, and who wrote on their subject matter. Most of the time, he would sit talking to himself. Sometimes he would pass by a study circle and say to me, "This sheikh teaches students from a deficient edition." Then he would come to the same place the next day and repeat what he had said the day before. I benefited from him as much as I could, even though listening to him was tiresome.

Religious Studies and Tensions over Doctrine in Mecca

Sheikh Badi al-Din ibn Ihsanallah Shah al-Rashidi returned from Pakistan and brought a chair for teaching in the Grand Mosque. The story of the chair is that one of the sheikh's close followers in Sind made it for him to use when he gave lessons in the Grand Mosque.

When the Haram Institute's academic year resumed after the pilgrimage, I began to study in the circle for beginners. We had lessons on the Quran,

Prophetic Tradition, law, grammar, monotheistic doctrine, inheritance, exegesis, and arithmetic. Our day began after dawn prayer. Abd Allah al-Harbi would take us in his pickup truck from the Ikhwan House. On our way to the Grand Mosque, we passed by Sheikh Badi's home. Before Sheikh Abu Turab al-Zahiri[78] gave him his Corolla [automobile], we used to pick him up and pray together in the Grand Mosque. Then we would gather around Sheikh Badi for a lesson— Abd Allah al-Harbi, Sultan al-Lihyani, Marzuq al-Salmi, and myself. We read a number of books about the Prophetic Traditions with the sheikh.[79] We finished them in two months. Then we read an exegesis of the Quran.[80] Actually, I did not benefit as much from Sheikh Badi in the science of Prophetic Traditions as much as I did from discussions with other students.[81] After his lesson, we usually went together to one of the restaurants near the Grand Mosque, except for Sheikh Badi. He would go to a blind sheikh named Sheikh Fathi, a member of Ahl-i Hadith in India[82] and a preacher in the Grand Mosque, where he had a private cell. Sheikh Badi would go visit him and have breakfast with him until it was time for him to teach at the Haram Institute. We would then resume our lesson at 8:00 until the noon prayer. After the noon prayer, we studied for one period lasting about 50 minutes and then went to the Ikhwan House. Sometimes I stayed in the Grand Mosque, especially during my first months in Mecca. I wanted to be in the Grand Mosque an hour before afternoon prayer. I would usually spend the hour with Sheikh Abd al-Aziz ibn Rashid al-Najdi, but that is another story.

After the sunset prayer, I attended Sheikh Badi's lesson on a controversial work on religious law by Ibn Hazm.[33] He was eventually forbidden from teaching Ibn Hazm's book and he replaced it with Ibn Kathir's exegesis. The reason for banning Ibn Hazm's book is that it attacked the four legal schools, especially the Hanafi legal school. Next to Sheikh Badi's circle there was a group of Bukharan[84] students studying the Hanafi legal school. Sheikh Badi would speak loudly so that they would hear his offensive, ill-mannered remarks, like calling them effeminate jurists.[85] He frequently repeated those words to draw attention to the Bukharan students, as if to say, "Look at these effeminates abandoning the Prophet of God's Tradition for the opinions of mere men," and so on, until they complained about him to Sheikh Muhammad ibn Subayyil, the director of the Grand Mosque's religious affairs. They submitted a petition stating that Sheikh Badi was insolent toward the ulama and that he taught the Zahiri legal school, something no one ever did in the two holy places.[86] Sheikh Badi was summoned and asked to temper his language against the ulama of the four legal schools and to stop teaching Zahiri jurisprudence from Ibn Hazm's book. Sheikh Ibn Subayyil recommended that he teach Ibn Kathir's exegesis instead. That occurred after we had already covered a good portion of Ibn Hazm's book, then we began reading Ibn Kathir's exegesis.

One of the most important factors that shaped my religious outlook was studying with Sheikh Badi al-Din ibn Ihsanallah Shah al-Rashidi al-Sindi, even though it was hard to understand his Arabic accent when he spoke the classical language. At first, I found it difficult to understand what he was saying, especially because he spoke fast. I complained to Abd Allah al-Harbi about it. He told me that he had had the same problem and that he got used to his way of speaking after a few days. He also spoke with him [Sheikh Badi] about his fast way of speaking, and he slowed it down a little. In fact, after a while I got used to his accent and his speech became clear. Even though Sheikh Badi had traveled from a young age to Europe and some Asian countries, and even though he mastered a number of languages like Hindi, Farsi, English and Arabic in addition to his mother tongue Urdu, he remained a prisoner of his intellectual heritage. True, he followed the Zahiri legal school, but he denounced Ibn Hazm's treatise on love,[87] and he denounced Ibn Hazm for issuing a legal ruling that allowed singing. Yet, he disputed with zeal anyone who doubted Ibn Hazm's creed and he maintained this position until his death. Some companions told me that Sheikh Badi used to reject the idea that his son Nur al-Din died in the Grand Mosque Incident, and [believed] that he was alive and well. It is strange that he supported his belief with a verse from the Quran (Surat al-Nisa', The Women 4:157), "They did not kill him or crucify him."[88]

If I were asked from whom I most benefited during my studies in Mecca, I would say that I truly benefited from only two people: Sheikh Badi and Sheikh Abd al-Aziz ibn Rashid. As for Sheikh Badi, I benefited from his lessons after dawn prayer. As for Sheikh Ibn Rashid, I benefited from my studies with him about the science of Prophetic Traditions.

I tried to study a number of texts, like a work on logic,[89] which I began with an Indian sheikh. Some of the Ikhwan heard about that, and Abd Allah al-Harbi in particular strongly advised me to stop. He dissuaded me from that subject on the grounds that the *ulama al-salaf*[90] strongly condemned whoever pursued it because it is an innovation,[91] that whoever studies it deeply is not among the ulama, and that the ulama must reject it because it is not one of the sciences of the Pious Ancestors.

As I mentioned, I would spend the period following afternoon prayer in the Grand Mosque and try to meet with Sheikh Abd al-Aziz ibn Rashid al-Najdi, with whom I established a close connection after he learned that I was from Zubair. He told me that [years ago] he set out from Mecca with Abd Allah al-Qusaimi[92] for Zubair to study with one of its sheikhs. They stayed at the Ibrahim Mosque there. After some months, they left Zubair and headed to India after some ulama in Zubair had provided them with introductions to Indian ulama. They then left India and headed to Baghdad where their companion was Abd Allah ibn Yabis.[93] Then they left Baghdad and headed to Egypt to study at al-Azhar.[94] He started telling me about their life in Egypt and the reasons for the changes that came over the ideas of Abd Allah al-Qusaimi. I enjoyed his calm way of speaking and his strong memory. Afterward, I began to study the science of Prophetic Traditions with him, reciting to him after afternoon prayer what I had read after dawn, may God have mercy on his soul. He had a gentle, light touch with young students, who were happy in his company. I used to go to him every day after the afternoon prayer. Even after I settled in Medina, I looked forward to seeing him whenever I visited Mecca.

On one visit, I found him with a cheerful looking sheikh. Sheikh Abd al-Aziz introduced me to him, saying, "This is one of the Ikhwan [of the Salafi Group]." Then Sheikh Abd al-Aziz said, "This is Sheikh Muhammad Amin al-Misri."[95]

I said, "The same Sheikh Muhammad Amin al-Misri who is the sheikh of our sheikh Muqbil ibn Hadi al-Wadi'i?" And he said, "Yes." Then I said to Sheikh Muhammad, "I have heard much about you, I wish I could study with you." Then Sheikh Muhammad said to me, "The council is conspiring against you."[96] At that time, I was familiar with what some sheikhs and students were writing against the Ikhwan, and I said to him, "God will protect us from their evil."[97] This took place a few months before the first arrest.[98]

One time I saw Sheikh Abd al-Aziz hurry to catch up to Sheikh Abd Allah ibn Humaid[99] to stop him and ask why he was banned from teaching while Alawi al-Maliki[100] was permitted. The sheikh had been forbidden from teaching in the Grand Mosque because he followed the Zahiri legal school and because of his attack on allegiance to the four legal schools. He felt bitter about it because he had been opposed in Egypt for his Salafi views on monotheistic doctrine.[101] Some Azhar ulama called him the "Wahhabi Fifth."[102] (They used that term because they considered Wahhabis to have invented a fifth legal school after the four Sunni legal schools: Hanafi, Maliki, Shafi'i, and Hanbali.) When he moved to Saudi Arabia, he was opposed by Hanbali ulama because he was a follower of Ibn Hazm and the Zahiri legal school. For that reason, Sheikh Abd Allah ibn Humaid, the director of the two holy places and head of the supreme judicial council, had banned him from teaching.

Preaching in Villages

On Fridays—the Institute's weekend—we would preach in villages outside Mecca. At that time, our preaching centered on illegitimate innovations that were widespread among villagers. Abd Allah al-Harbi usually was in charge of this mission. We would perform the Friday congregational prayer with them [villagers] or Abd Allah al-Harbi would pray with them. No matter where we went, the Tablighi Association had already gotten there first. That group was noticeably active with commoners in these villages. Therefore, we often encountered villagers who had gone with them on preaching tours, whether for a week inside the kingdom or for forty days outside it. They were well-liked by the villagers for avoiding confrontation and for their gentle manners and humility. It is noteworthy that many of the Ikhwan had belonged to the Tablighi Association before joining the [Saudi] Salafi Group or the Salafi Group in Kuwait. There is a popular saying that if the Islamic State were to come about, the Tablighis would be the commoners, the Salafis would be the religious leaders, and the Muslim Brothers would be the political leaders.[103] I do not remember who coined this saying but I liked it when I was new in these circles and I would repeat it to others, especially since I was in favor of bringing the Islamic groups together.

Meeting Juhaiman

One day, Juhaiman visited us in Mecca. After performing the lesser pilgrimage rites, he sat with us at the Ikhwan House in al-Sufaira'. The meeting centered on discussion of religious knowledge. He then asked me to accompany him on a preaching tour and I agreed. This was my first long tour outside Mecca. I recall that we went to some nearby villages in Hijaz like Rahat and Madrakah, then we went to Ta'if. In his preaching lessons, he mostly talked about forbidden things that Bedouin commoners did like *shighar* marriage,[104] divorce, the waiting period after the death of a spouse before remarriage,[105] the ruling about seeking help from magicians, and rulings about menstruation and impurity. As for discussions at the homes of Ikhwan and their supporters in towns, he would discuss issues related to adherence to the legal schools, particularly the need to reject that practice and to follow scriptural evidence instead. In addition, there would be a lot of discussion of dream interpretation.

After that trip, I often joined Juhaiman on preaching tours until the time of the first arrest. I got to know him well during these trips and became attached to him because I liked his generosity, humility, gentle manners, and devotion to preaching. I did not like his zeal for his Utaibi tribe and the way he often pointed out the shortcomings of other tribes. This matter disturbed me greatly. In spite of Juhaiman's earnestness in preaching, he was weak before his deep-seated tribalism. He would research Prophetic Traditions to verify them, but when it came to stories about his tribe, he would repeat them as if they were glories that everyone knew about, even if it wronged others. Something that I often heard Juhaiman say and that would have a role in shaping his actions: "The Bedouin are distinguished by special abilities that settled folk do not possess, such as courage, perspicacity, stamina, and ability to endure hardship." This was not something I heard once or a few times, but frequently. At the time, I was enchanted by such ideas but after I went to jail and spent time alone, I found them to be superficial, insubstantial ideas that could never give rise to a modern country. I used to wonder what would happen if this group gained power: What kind of government would it be? I imagined that it would eat its children from the settled folk and other tribes and put one tribe in power, namely Juhaiman's tribe, and it would rule through purges and bloodshed. For example, Juhaiman told me that one time he met an official in the Bureau for Religious Rulings, Preaching and Guidance who was impolite with him.[106] He always repeated the story of that meeting. I later learned from an Egyptian named Usamah Awad Ibrahim who joined the attack on the Grand Mosque that when the Ikhwan seized control of the Grand Mosque, Juhaiman saw the same man [from the Government Bureau for Religious Rulings] and ordered that he be thrown in the Grand Mosque's jail along with others who happened to be with him, even though Juhaiman knew this man had committed no crime. The previous encounter with Juhaiman was his crime. This is just one simple example of the behavior of a man who was leading a movement. Can you imagine what a mob would do?

Historical Roots of the Salafi Group

I have been frequently asked about the nature of the Salafi Group and Juhaiman's faction within it. I have read what is said about it. Everyone classifies it according to their own point of view. The leftists classify it as a revolutionary movement; Arab nationalists classify it as a rebellion; others classify it as a protest. All of these classifications are completely wrong because of the difference between these currents and the true nature of the discourse of the "Salafi Group that Commands Right and Forbids Wrong," the group's official name. It was a revolutionary, rebellious, and protest movement all in one, but in its own way and on its own terms. In order to avoid the usual hasty judgment of the Group, we must point out the milieu in which Juhaiman's ideas took shape.

It is known that Juhaiman grew up in one of the settlements called *hijrah*s that were established to settle and educate the nomads, later known as the Ikhwan in Obedience to God.[107] This settlement was called Sajir.[108] All the nomads living in that settlement belonged to the Ikhwan who fought on the side of King Abd al-Aziz but under the leadership of Sultan ibn Bijad,[109] whom the Ikhwan dubbed Sultan al-Din.[110] They later rebelled against King Abd al-Aziz because he pursued modernization. They fought him at the battle of Sabilah and were defeated.[111] Sultan ibn Bijad surrendered to King Abd al-Aziz and died a while later in prison. Among the Ikhwan in general and the people of Sajir in particular this development gave rise to the feeling that they had been duped. A generation grew up that inherited resentment and a rebellious attitude toward the government. As Juhaiman himself told me and others, he used to smuggle goods from Kuwait before he became pious.[112]

This is the rebellious environment that formed Juhaiman ibn Muhammad ibn Saif al-Dann's psyche. Because of it, when he was young, he did not care about loyalty to the state, especially because his father was a good friend to Sultan ibn Bijad and was among those who advised him not to surrender to King Abd al-Aziz.[113] This calls to mind Juhaiman's refusal to turn himself in when he was wanted in the first arrest after 1398 AH/1977 CE because he considered the state to be treacherous since it had betrayed Sultan ibn Bijad in the first place. Therefore, it was legitimate to deceive the state, especially since Juhaiman and his tribe had refrained from getting revenge on the rulers for killing Sultan ibn Bijad. He felt strongly about that and often spoke about it openly.[114]

Creation of the Salafi Group

The Salafi Group was founded after the Breaking Pictures Incident [in Medina], around 1965, when six men gathered on the sand after evening prayer and decided to set up a group based on the commands for preaching and warning in mosques and public places. They were all former members of the Tablighi Association, except for one who was apparently from the Muslim Brotherhood. They believed the Tablighi Association did not pay attention to monotheistic doctrine in its preaching and was lax when it came to duties such as owing loyalty to believers and bearing enmity toward infidels, and forbidding wrong. Therefore, they believed that the Tablighi Association did not call to being guided by the Quran and the Prophetic Tradition. The six were Juhaiman ibn Muhammad ibn Saif al-Utaibi, who worked as a driver in the National Guard and picked up jobs here and there;

Sulaiman ibn Shtaiwi, a student at the Islamic University of Medina;[115] Nasir ibn Husain al-Umari al-Harbi and Sa'd al-Tamimi, both students at the Institute for Teachers; and two whose names I do not know.[116] I never knew them because one of them, a Yemeni, died in unusual circumstances. He had gone on a preaching tour by foot in a distant region, reportedly in al-Nakhil, and he was found dead in a well. The other one left the Group soon after its establishment because he was a Muslim Brother who apparently wanted to recruit some of the Salafis, but he was at odds with the Salafis' rejection of the idea of an activist party. Juhaiman spoke of him as someone working with the Salafi Ikhwan for a specific agenda at odds with the Salafi line already laid down and agreed upon. This is what I heard directly from Juhaiman.

At any rate, this group went to Sheikh Abd al-Aziz ibn Baz[117] to inform him about their decision to form a Salafi group that rejects partisanship for the legal schools and that calls to monotheistic doctrine and adhering to the Quran and sound Prophetic Tradition. They had no worldly goals and they wanted him to be their leader and guide. He agreed to do so. They told him that the group's name would be the Salafi Group. He told them that since they sought reward from God, then their name should be the Salafi Group that Commands Right and Forbids Wrong, and that was done. The Group was not secret, rather it was out in the open in a very clear way. There was even stationery printed with the Group's name. I remember the 1977 pilgrimage when Hizam al-Bahloul, a Yemeni Ikhwan who later became a Muslim Brother, took a microphone and announced the start of the Salafi Group's performance of the pilgrimage. Thus, he openly declared the Group's name.

In Medina

The Ikhwan Neighborhood in Medina

One time I went to the Eastern Harrah neighborhood in Medina. It was not the first time I visited them [the Ikhwan in Medina]. I had been to the old Ikhwan house numerous times before. The house had a wide courtyard and quite a few rooms for lodgers. I heard from Ikhwan at the time that Abd al-Aziz ibn Baz paid the rent for the house.

On this particular visit, I decided to settle down in Medina because the Antichrist could not enter there[118] and because Ali al-Mazrui and Juhaiman were there. The leaders of the Ikhwan lived in a new house that resembled a fortress and was designed in the Arabian style to accommodate a large number of residents. There were two stories and each story had eight rooms surrounding a courtyard. Each room could hold three students. Attached to the house was a mosque built with funds from a donor who stipulated that it be under the supervision of Sheikh Abd al-Aziz ibn Baz. He turned it over to the Ikhwan, under the supervision of Abu Bakr Jabir al-Jaza'iri.[119]

The Ikhwan's houses were all in the Medina neighborhood of the Eastern Harrah. The houses were built at random here and there, possessed through squatter's rights. Construction went on at night, far from the prying eyes of the municipal authority. Some Ikhwan paid bribes to the housing inspector, who would turn a blind eye to the unregulated construction. The neighborhood expanded, houses multiplied, and the Ikhwan came to dominate the neighborhood, so you would not see any tobacco shops or smokers. Likewise, you would not see a television in anybody's home.[120]

The way buildings were constructed in the neighborhood made it easy for fugitives to escape. Each house had two doors. The front door was used mainly by men. Women used the back doors which opened to the back doors of other houses to freely visit each other [without being seen by men]. Those back doors would eventually be used by fugitives to escape arrest. In fact, Juhaiman escaped through such a door in 1398 AH/1977 CE, when he was wanted in the first arrest, but that is another story that will come later.

Once, at the beginning of 1399 AH/1978 CE,[121] I sneaked into Juhaiman's house while it was vacant and under surveillance to retrieve some documents, entering through the back door. A short time before that, we had removed some of Juhaiman's books through the back door as well. Abd Allah al-Harbi was with me that time. All that took place while the two doors facing the street were being watched, but nobody noticed the other door. The security forces are to be excused [for that lapse] because Juhaiman's house had three doors, two on the street and a third opening on a narrow alley, too narrow for more than one person to pass by on foot—that is the one that women used when going to and from the houses of their neighbors, and it is the one I later used after the inhabitants evacuated the house following the first arrest.

The Problem of Excommunication

My daily schedule in Medina was very busy. When I was not with Juhaiman on his preaching tours, I spent most of my time studying with Ali al-Mazrui works on Prophetic Traditions.[122] With Muqbil ibn Hadi al-Wadi'i, I studied technical works on Prophetic Traditions and the Science of Prophetic Traditions. Then I studied Ibn Taymiyyah's *Book of Faith*[123] with fellow Ikhwan member Faisal Muhammad Faisal. I concentrated on studying this book after the *takfir*[124] doctrine took hold with a few Ikhwan due to their interaction with members of the Egyptian Excommunication and Emigration Group (Mustafa Shukri's group whose members called themselves "The Society of Muslims").[125] They had raised questions about sovereignty and the legitimacy of rulers.[126] Their leader was a fellow known to us as Abd Allah al-Misri. He and another Egyptian named Usamah al-Qusi had come during the lesser pilgrimage and then stayed in Saudi Arabia. A number of Islamic University students from Egypt and Yemen were drawn to them as well.

Faisal Muhammad Faisal had become acquainted with similar ideas and adopted them in 1977. As a result, he moved away from Medina to live with his family in a tent in a remote location outside Medina. With him was Isam Sheikh. Ahmad al-Zamil joined them later but did not stay long before returning to live with the Ikhwan in the Eastern Harrah. Isam and Faisal later returned to Medina. Faisal's embrace of these ideas [about excommunication] gave Juhaiman sleepless nights because they resonated with ideas of the Kharijites, a label that greatly alarmed Juhaiman.[127]

One day when Sheikh Muhammad Nasir al-Din al-Albani was visiting Medina, Juhaiman explained to him the problem he was having with Faisal. Albani asked to meet with him, and Juhaiman arranged for it to take place at Faisal Muhammad Faisal's house. The meeting was attended by Yusuf Akbar, Juhaiman, Faisal Muhammad Faisal, Isam Sheikh, and Sheikh al-Albani. They discussed legitimate sovereignty and excommunication, their connection with the ideas of the Kharijites, and the different categories of unbelief. Sheikh al-Albani cited the views of authoritative Salafi religious scholars like Ahmad ibn Hanbal, Ibn Taymiyyah, Ibn al-Qayyim, and others. Yusuf Akbar recorded the meeting on tape cassette. As they left Faisal's house, Juhaiman took the tape from Yusuf Akbar as if to borrow it, but he did not return it and nobody ever saw it again. I later learned from Yusuf Akbar that Juhaiman immediately destroyed it. Juhaiman's view was that government sheikhs were on the lookout for any slip on the part of the Ikhwan. This tape would have been strong evidence that the Ikhwan harbored Kharijite ideas. In any event, Faisal left the meeting with a new, more moderate outlook on excommunication and faith. Consequently, the suggestion to study Ibn Taymiyyah's *Book of Faith* was intended to strengthen the Group against takfiri doctrine. Faisal Muhammad Faisal was the best person with whom to study Ibn Taymiyyah because of his familiarity with him and his specialization in reading and teaching his works.[128]

The Ikhwan in Medina

Among those living at the Ikhwan House during that time was Ahmad Hasan al-Mu'allam, a poet from Yemen.[129] He was the most important person at the House, in charge of managing its affairs, and a member of the Ikhwan's administrative council. He was a teacher at the Islamic University and very close to Juhaiman. In fact, he was the one who put together *The Essays of Juhaiman* and undertook to edit them with Muhammad Abd Allah al-Qahtani, "the Expected Mahdi," who was also a poet. Yusuf Akbar was also with me at the Ikhwan House. He was a youth from Jeddah who studied for a time at the University of Petroleum and Minerals and then quit the university. Id al-Shabihi and Ahmad ibn Muhammad Abd al-Wahhab al-Banna also lived at the Ikhwan House.[130] They [Akbar, Shabihi, and Banna] all enrolled at the Islamic University, but only Ahmad al-Banna graduated from there.

I first heard of Shukri Mustafa's Excommunication and Emigration Group from Ahmad Banna. He told me that shortly before we met, he had come under the influence of their ideas and adopted their main tenets, to the point that he would not pray behind his father, who lived in Jeddah. He had met them during a summer vacation that he spent with relatives in Egypt. When he returned to Jeddah, he was having doubts about his father's belief. In fact, he stopped praying behind his father until he was convinced of his father's belief in Islam. He then spoke to his father about the matter and his father convinced him that he was wrong. Then he returned to the position of the majority of the ulama, the *Ummah*,[131] and the way of moderation.

As for Id al-Shabihi, he became completely immersed in the Salafi mission. He married Muhammad Abd Allah al-Qahtani's[132] sister and was one of the men who joined the attack on the Grand Mosque. Yusuf Akbar left the university and joined the Ikhwan, then was arrested for distributing *The Essays of Juhaiman* shortly before the attack on the Grand Mosque. The strange thing about Yusuf was that he believed that Muhammad ibn Abd Allah al-Qahtani, the Expected Mahdi, did not die but was in occultation.[133] He would express this view later when he was in prison. It was strange. Abd al-Rahman Hamudah had the same view. Khalid al-Shuraimi was someone else I knew well in the Ikhwan House and in jail. I never met anyone less selfish and so completely devoted to serving the Ikhwan.

Interactions with Egyptian Religious Activists

In the later period but before the first schism that caused Juhaiman and his side to lose the Ikhwan House, the Salafi Group would host a group of Egyptians including pilgrims, frequent visitors to Medina, and students at the Islamic University—all opposed to the Egyptian government. It later became clear that some were from the Jihad Group[134] while others were from the Excommunication and Emigration Group or had a connection to it. The most controversial issues with them back then were the Salafi positions on Sayyid Qutb, excommunicating the ruler and working for the state. Long and deep debates took place between them and the Salafi residents of the house. The dispute reached the point that if one of them was not chosen to lead prayer they would hold their own separate prayer after the Salafi Group prayed. I later learned that they did not acknowledge the validity of praying behind someone who does not join them and adopt their ideas. Nevertheless, their members frequented the Salafi Ikhwan House and the Ikhwan did not sense any danger from them, considering their differences to be matters of opinion, not serious enough to cause schism. The Ikhwan felt that they and the Egyptians were all "mujtahid,"[135] doing their utmost to understand religion correctly. We did not feel any malice toward them. I sometimes joined karate lessons on the roof of the Ikhwan House given by a young Egyptian named Maher, who had formerly won the Egyptian Youth Karate championship. Some of them occasionally worked for Id al-Shabihi on excavation jobs.[136]

In Buraidah

During this time, I went to Buraidah to study with Sheikh Abd Allah al-Darwish. Under his supervision, I studied works about Prophetic Traditions and religious law.[137] He was a virtuous sheikh, humble and patient with students. I remember the time when he asked me about my hometown. I told him I was born in Zubair, but my ancestors came from al-Dir'iyyah.[138] Then, he said to me, "Do you believe the earth is round and stationary?" Without even thinking about it, I told him what I had learned in geography class, that the earth is round and that it rotates on its axis and revolves around the sun. He said to me, "You need to correct your belief. I will arrange a lesson for you about Sheikh Hammud al-Tuwaijiri's refutation of modern astronomy."[139]

Abd al-Aziz al-Ulait, God have mercy on him, was taking lessons alongside me.

I would sleep at the Ikhwan School. This group of Ikhwan were students of religion who had set up their own school because they were opposed to government schools and their curriculum, but they had no connection with the Salafi Ikhwan. They borrowed from the Salafi Ikhwan the rejection of legal school partisanship and some other secondary issues. They were essentially ascetics devoting their time to study and worship. After about two months in Buraidah, I left and returned to Medina because I did not feel comfortable in that environment.

Doctrinal Tensions between the Salafis and the Official Clerics

In 1978, the crisis between the government sheikhs and the Salafi Group escalated. It went back to 1976 when Ali al-Mazrui gave a legal opinion at the Meccan Grand Mosque that it is permissible to eat during Ramadan after the dawn call to prayer because the call to prayer does not indicate the arrival of the moment at dawn when food is prohibited in Ramadan but only the moment for the dawn prayer. Discussion and debate [over Mazrui's opinion] resulted in branding the Ikhwan's position as mere opinion and rejection of the authority of the four legal schools. Back then, this sort of controversy was new and unfamiliar to most people. The sheikhs who debated Mazrui were not prepared to answer the questions that he put before them concerning fresh interpretation of the law and adhering to precedent.[140] It was a surprising, unexpected development. These discussions revealed that most sheikhs and religious students were in the grip of blind imitation and unthinking adherence to Hanbali law books[141] and that they had strayed far from the books and science of the Prophetic Tradition. It was rare to find anyone with expertise in researching and authenticating Prophetic Traditions. These sessions were the cause for banning Ali al-Mazrui from teaching at the Grand Mosque and, later on, the reason for putting the Ikhwan under close supervision by a group of sheikhs.

In a similar fashion [to Mazrui's independent thinking], members of the Ikhwan did not seek fatwas from a sheikh without asking for its evidence. If the sheikh cited a Prophetic Tradition, they asked him, "Is that Prophetic Tradition sound or weak?"[142] Such questions annoyed muftis[143] whose knowledge was limited to a single work on Hanbali law,[144] and that was the majority of them. The Ikhwan broke the barrier of awe between mufti and people requesting a fatwa. They made religious knowledge accessible to the masses after it had been the monopoly of sheikhs and religious students. They spread an argumentative spirit among commoners. Eventually, that would have a harmful impact on the pious masses, which became evident in much of the Awakening movement's positions and beliefs.[145] Whereas the ulama once monopolized religious authority over the masses, the masses now made the ulama pay attention to their concerns, and as a result, a more even exchange of influence took place between them. If religious fanatics had been locked out early on, there would not have been a way for them to consider themselves members of the ulama thereafter. But the absence of an enlightened reform project, among legal specialists in general and Hanbalis in particular—that rested on the general purposes of religious law and addressed contemporary national and social concerns—is what generated a collision that had no resolution but a return to the way Islam was practiced in the Middle Ages, with a jurisprudence that was born in times of unrest, schism, and Crusades, embodied by the jurisprudence of Ibn Taymiyyah and his followers, which during the Russian–Afghan War became increasingly consecrated as an obligatory blueprint.

Something else that alienated the hearts of the [official] sheikhs was the Salafi Group adopting fatwas like the one about the phrase "prayer is better than sleep" and whether it belongs in the first line in the dawn call to prayer and not the second.[146] They started giving the call to prayer in this fashion at the Ikhwan mosque in the Eastern Harrah in Medina and in mosques where they predominated. Likewise, they raised the issue of whether the mosque niche is an illegitimate innovation since it was not created until after the age of the Prophet. They closed off the niche in their own mosque and most of their imams did not pray there because they believed it was an illegitimate innovation. Similarly, some young religious students wore their sandals when praying in the Prophet's mosque and that provoked the anger of other worshippers.[147] More than once such practices were the cause of brief scuffles while I was living in the Medina Ikhwan House.

One incident involved a Tunisian student at the Islamic University named Munir al-Tunisi who frequented the Ikhwan house but was not a member. He was a kind of impetuous fellow. When he prayed wearing sandals in the Prophet's mosque, he was apprehended and there was a commotion. The Ikhwan, however, adopted his practice because they had seen that he acted only according to sound Prophetic Tradition and this practice became associated with the Ikhwan very easily. He was suspended from the Islamic University but the Ikhwan interceded for him and got him released.[148]

All these sorts of things, which happened before 1978, made the sheikhs accuse the Ikhwan of fanaticism and of having eccentric ideas about religion, ideas that Juhaiman had embraced.

Tensions between Juhaiman and Founders of the Salafi Group

Ill will arose between Juhaiman and two founders of the Group, namely Sulaiman ibn Shtaiwi and Sa'd al-Tamimi. The cause of the ill will was that Juhaiman started acting like the leader of the Group and giving orders like shunning anyone who did not follow the Group's way of preaching, or who discouraged its unorthodox fatwas. The bigger problem was that Sulaiman and Sad were teachers, that is to say, employees of the state, and Juhaiman was opposed to government jobs and education. He let them hear directly and indirectly his opinion about that, sometimes in a provocative way, and they grew to dislike him, as did Falih ibn Nafi' after he graduated from the Islamic University, because he worked for the government. Falih did not say anything about the Ikhwan's position on government employees when he was at the university because the Ikhwan provided him some financial support. Then, when he got a government job, he started to object to the Ikhwan's provocative, eccentric practices while at the same time he became friendly with the ulama and sheikhs. Following a heated argument with Isam Sheikh and Faisal Muhammad Faisal, he was expelled from the latter's home.

Rupture between Salafis and the Official Clerics

That year [1977] was hot, in every sense of the word. A meeting was held at which Sheikh Abu Bakr Jabir al-Jaza'iri and a group of sheikhs spoke with Ikhwan members Nasir ibn Husain, Ahmad Hasan al-Mu'allam, Sa'd al-Tamimi, Falih ibn Nafi', Ahmad al-Zamil, and residents of the Ikhwan House like me. In brief, the purpose of the meeting was to get rid of the outlandish ideas I already described. Whoever did not like it could leave the Ikhwan House, for Sheikh Abu Bakr Jabir al-Jaza'iri was the deputy of the guide acting as the supervisor for the house.[149] Afterward, Nasib al-Jaza'iri would come to give the call to prayer at the Ikhwan mosque for the first and second calls, and lead their prayers. As for us, we left the Ikhwan House one by one until nobody was left from the group I have mentioned. This incident marked the first major split in the ranks of the Ikhwan. At that time, most of the Ikhwan sided with Juhaiman. He became the absolute leader for all members of the Group and his home became the Ikhwan's meeting place. Moreover, he had concentrated on undertaking preaching tours to all parts of the kingdom.[150] Most of the time, I went along with him.

It seems that the purpose of al-Jaza'iri's meeting with the Ikhwan was for the ulama to distance themselves from the Group rather than to make a sincere attempt to correct its extreme line. Why else would a group of sheikhs meet with a few insignificant young men and then decide to take the house from the Ikhwan, as if the Ikhwan themselves were no more than the house? At that time, every town had a house—Riyadh, Jeddah, Mecca, Ta'if, Raniyah, Ha'il, Ahsa—all these centers had not heard that a meeting was going to take place. But when they heard about what happened there, they gave their allegiance to Juhaiman. So the meeting did nothing to improve conditions in the Group. In fact, quite the opposite—it made things worse by making Juhaiman, in effect, the absolute leader. In any case, al-Jaza'iri's primary purpose was to get out of the predicament of having to lead a group that refused to obey, where he was only the titular guide and where the group's organization, activities, and ideas were in Juhaiman's hands.

Like I said, Juhaiman's trips became more frequent and so did his criticism of the government and of working for the government. It became shameful for Ikhwan to work for the government. Opposition to official jobs extended to studying in schools and to the idea that one could learn anything from books and sheikhs. He intensified his denunciation of anyone who tried to get any learning. For this reason, teenage runaways joined the Group, mainly to get away from schoolwork, and also on the pretext that their families' homes had abominations like television and photographs. Wherever they went, the Group made them feel welcome.

Fugitives in the Desert

One day I prayed the noon prayer with Juhaiman in the mosque near his home as usual.[151] Then we had lunch and we sat in the outer courtyard near the men's entrance that opened on the street. We were drinking tea and talking about a book when suddenly a red GMC bearing the Medina Province emblem drove up and a man called out, "Hey Abu Hadhal." Juhaiman went out to speak with him for five minutes, and then the GMC drove off. When Juhaiman returned, his face had completely changed color. He said to me, "This man is one of my people,"[152] and said that a wire had come to the Medina provincial authority with the names of Group members who were to be arrested that night. Juhaiman's name was at the top of the list. The plan was for someone he had never met before to pray with him and to greet him at the afternoon prayer to make sure that the authorities had the right person. Indeed, when we prayed the afternoon prayer, he greeted a man we had previously seen in the Eastern Harrah neighborhood. We stood with him while he asked Juhaiman about a minor legal issue. Then we returned together to the house as usual. The news [about the plan to arrest members] had reached a number of the Ikhwan. Juhaiman went outside to speak with Dahham al-Anazi and then returned to me and said, "Do you want to leave with me until this clears up?" I agreed and rode with him in Dahham's pickup truck.

We set off after afternoon prayer and as a precaution we stayed off paved roads in order to avoid checkpoints. We followed a route that Dahham knew well and went deep into the desert.

All I recall about the route that we took was that we followed a way that runs northeast of Medina. We spent three nights in the desert. We all hunted some lizards,[153] then cooked and ate them, except for Juhaiman. He was anxious to hear the news of the planned arrests, whether they had in fact taken place, and who had been arrested. Dahham suggested that we go to stay with Ubaid and Abid, members of the Ikhwan from the Mihlani clan who were living in tents in the desert and herding their flock of sheep. So we headed to their camp up north. Dahham asked some Bedouin living in tents about them and he was then able to find them. We went up to them and told Ubaid and Abid about the situation. They had not heard anything about it up to that point. Juhaiman asked that they not repeat his name. In fact, we started calling him Abu Muhammad. He asked Ubaid to go to the Qasim region[154] to bring some news. Ubaid went to Qasim while we stayed with Abid waiting for his return. They were generous and discrete, asking us few questions. They taught their children the Quran, writing and reading in the desert. Their spontaneous, natural way of teaching was in accord with the surrounding environment. They inclined to an ascetic, spartan way of life. They had their sheep and a pickup truck to bring water to them and their sheep. They lived far away from cities because they believed that they were full of corruption and evil temptations.

We waited some days until Ubaid returned from Qasim with news. He told us who all were arrested in different parts of the kingdom. They numbered about twenty-five members, including Ali al-Mazrui, Muqbil ibn Hadi al-Wadi'i, and Sulaiman ibn Shtaiwi in Medina; Sheikh Badi al-Din ibn Ihsanallah Shah al-Rashidi and A'id ibn Duraimeeh in Mecca; Muhammad al-Haidari and Muhammad Abd Allah al-Qahtani, the Mahdi, in Riyadh; Umar al-Ulait in Buraida; and Radan [al-Utaibi] in Sajir. The authorities were still searching for Juhaiman. His brother Nayef's farm was under surveillance around the clock. Ahmad Hasan al-Mu'allam was wanted but still at large. This news made us gloomy, especially Juhaiman. He was worried about his mother. After a few days, Juhaiman said to me, "You are not wanted. I think it best we separate."

So I went with Ubaid to Ali al-Hudaini in al-Imar, which is about 100 kilometers from Sajir. One reason Ubaid went with me was to reassure Juhaiman's mother, who lived on the way to Ali al-Hudaini, with whom we stayed. Ahmad al-Zamil and Mutlaq ibn Sahl were also there. Ali told us that all of Sajir was under surveillance and there was an around-the-clock stakeout on the house of Juhaiman's older brother Nayef. The authorities set up a tent on his farm to keep watch from there. The three of us then went in a GMC pickup truck with one of Mutlaq's acquaintances and set off toward Sajir after the afternoon prayer. I was with Ahmad al-Zamil in the back of the GMC while Mutlaq was in front with the driver. As we neared Sajir, we collided with a Toyota pickup truck. We got out to look at the damage. The others asked a passerby to inform the highway patrol about the accident. The three of us rode with this person and we got off at Sajir while Mutlaq stayed with the driver. Ahmad al-Zamil and I walked some distance until we arrived at Shu'aib, then we headed to the home of an Ikhwan named Madukh al-Utaibi. He and his brother Mish'al were Ikhwan. We stayed with them overnight then headed to Riyadh early the next morning.

Back to Riyadh

Consequences of the Arrests

As I said, we headed in the early morning for Riyadh, arriving there about fifteen days after the arrests of Ikhwan members. The general climate of opinion about the arrests was divided between sympathy and resentment. These were the first mass arrests in the kingdom. Never before had an Islamic group or organization had its members arrested. Young Salafis were in a celebratory mood because they had a connection with the detainees, a status that before then was the sole possession of the Muslim Brotherhood.[155] One Ikhwan said, "Now, nobody is better than another. Just as they, namely the Muslim Brotherhood, have people under arrest, we too have detainees in the cause of calling to God." This is an important point. For the psychological and intellectual reputation that had spread and continued to spread via numerous channels in favor of the early Muslim Brothers and other detainees and prisoners made a later generation regard them as holy warriors and strugglers in the way of the word of truth, as exemplars who must be followed. To be more precise, it made them an elite group with its own followers and helpers.

I think the government's decision to rein in the movement by imprisoning members did a lot of harm in the long run. It would have been better to follow a policy of positive containment by rehabilitating the organization's leaders using different methods, according to the inclinations of this or that particular leader. This applies as well to rehabilitating returnees from Afghanistan.[156] King Abd al-Aziz, may God sweeten his grave, provided an ideal example for successful rehabilitation when he created new battalions and enlisted the Old Ikhwan to fight on his side in order to unify the kingdom. He did not leave them to their fates and whims.[157]

As I was saying, Riyadh's Islamic groups were beset with questions that demanded answers, especially concerning the fate of the detainees. I learned from an Ikhwan that some back channels through government sheikhs were active. Two weeks later, we were invited to a meeting that Ahmad al-Mu'allam organized in the countryside along the Riyadh-al-Majma'ah Road. A large group of Ikhwan attended. Ahmad Hasan al-Mu'allam spoke about what had happened to the detained Ikhwan and said this was a trial from God to test his servants. Ahmad al-Mu'allam was the senior leader at the meeting, a member of the Group's Consultative Council. Along with Juhaiman, he was the only Council member still at large, so the Ikhwan paid close attention to him.

In the course of the meeting, a pickup truck stopped alongside the group and Muhammad al-Haidari stepped out of it. He was leader of the Ikhwan in Riyadh and had been one of the detainees. He told us that the Ikhwan had been released and asked us to break up the meeting for he had taken an oath to join no organized groups or political parties. We gathered that he would no longer be a member of the Ikhwan. In fact, his position was courageous at that moment and in those circumstances. I have not encountered him since then After the meeting, we tried to find out who was still under arrest and who was released and we learned about some who were released. Muqbil ibn Hadi al-Wadi'i had been released and allowed to defend his master's thesis before he was exiled from the kingdom, about two months after he got out of jail. I attended his thesis defense at the Islamic University on al-Daraqutni's collection of Prophetic Traditions.[158]

At that time, the Ikhwan were enjoying a revival; large numbers of young people were joining. Some Muslim Brothers joined as well and helped spread the Ikhwan's reputation, especially in Islamist circles, for the arrests had turned the Ikhwan into heroes endowed with a magnetic appeal that attracted everyone, with some finding the Group's ideas convincing and others driven by curiosity to follow the Group and its ideas. Then, after the first essay was distributed, the appeal of the Ikhwan grew exponentially, but that is a topic we will discuss later.

During this period, my ties with Sheikh Abd al-Aziz ibn Baz were growing stronger via Khalid al-Shuraimi. We asked that he give us lessons on al-Tirmidhi's collection of Prophetic Traditions.[159] I began to study with him after the dawn prayer, along with Khalid al-Shuraimi, Abd al-Aziz al-Sadhan, and some other religious students studying other books with the sheikh. At the same time, I was attending meetings of the Ikhwan held at the Ikhwan House [in Riyadh] or at a member's home.

Publishing Juhaiman's Writings

One day I ran into Abd al-Latif al-Dirbas, an Ikhwan I knew quite well. He had Kuwaiti citizenship and had burned his identity papers some time ago and settled in Medina. Then he moved to a tent in the desert, and even though he was originally a townsman, he praised Bedouin life in an affected and crude way. That is the nature of converts, be it religious or social, such that you see them desperately trying to prove they are worthy of their new position. Abd al-Aziz al-Sadhan mentioned to me that one time he was at the Ikhwan's tent in Kuwait with Abd al-Latif al-Dirbas, and he, Abd al-Aziz, put out breakfast. One of the men in the tent acted like the food was disgusting. Al-Dirbas then stood up as a rebuke against that person and threw dirt on the food. He said, "Eat it." Abd al-Aziz al-Sadhan replied that that was contrary to Sunnah. Dirbas said, "What is your evidence?" So Sadhan recited the Prophet's words to a man who was eating dates and when he dropped one, the Prophet told him, "Remove its dirt and eat it." Al-Dirbas said, "You want to confuse me about my religion."

Anyway, Sadhan told me that Juhaiman had composed an essay called *Removing Confusion about the Religion of Abraham*[160] and that it would be printed in Kuwait. He said that Abd al-Latif took it first to the Dar al-Qabas publishing house, but it asked for a large payment to print it, so then he took it to the leftist Dar al-Tali'ah publishing house. When al-Dirbas told them about the difficulties of writing it and that the author was wanted by Saudi security forces, the publisher became enthusiastic and printed it for a small price, less than one riyal per copy, while Dar al-Qabas had asked for three riyals per copy. So the essay was printed. Dar al-Tali'ah was asked to leave out the name of the publisher and the place of publication, and it did so. The same publisher that printed this essay printed some others as well.[161]

There were, however, some serious printing errors. For instance, in some print runs, the back cover had the name of the publisher Dar al-Tali'ah and the place of publication in Kuwait. The Ikhwan used razors to cut out the publisher's name from every copy. They did not want the publisher and the place of publication to appear because they wanted to avoid detection of the route they were using between Kuwait and Saudi Arabia via Hafr al-Batin to smuggle the essays into the kingdom. Ikhwan who did not have passports or identity papers used the same route for clandestine travel to and from Kuwait. Almost all Ikhwan destroyed their identity papers due to their fanatical attitude against images and their position on existing regimes. In their view, establishing national borders and shackling them with passports are signs of tyranny that are not ordained by God. It is better for Muslims to disobey and oppose such tyranny.

Sometime later, Iqab al-Utaibi came to tell me that Mutlaq ibn Sahl wanted to see me. So I headed to Sajir with an Ikhwan and we went to Mutlaq's farm.

We found with him an Ikhwan suspected of being sent by the security forces to infiltrate our group. He was staying with Mutlaq and his family. I think his name was Ahmad. Mutlaq took me aside and confided to me that Juhaiman wanted to see me and that he would arrange a meeting at a later time because Juhaiman was not around then. I understood that Juhaiman was the reason Mutlaq had sent for me, but I had not asked because of the need for secrecy. Two nights later, Mutlaq woke me from sleep at about 2:00 a.m. and told me to come with him. I went with him in a GMC to Iqab's house and in the back room I found Iqab, Id al-Shabihi, and Hamid al-Ahmadi talking together. After greeting them, I sat with them talking about various things. After a few hours, Juhaiman showed up. After greetings, we entered a large room and sat on the rug. The room was full of red bags piled up to the ceiling. At first, I thought they were bags of onions. Later I found out that they were copies of *Removing Confusion*, the first of Juhaiman's essays to be printed. Juhaiman was looking over a copy stamped with two additional lines of text. He told me that the essay had been read to Sheikh Abd al-Aziz ibn Baz[162] and that Ibn Baz had added a paragraph after it was printed. At his insistence, they added the paragraph by making a stamp of it because it was too difficult to reprint the entire book. As I sat and spoke with the group, I stamped the paragraph on the margin of the copy in front of me. Juhaiman told me to perform the lesser pilgrimage and to urge the Ikhwan in Riyadh to do it as well during Ramadan in order to distribute copies of the essay in the Grand Mosque on the night of the 27th.[163] He said that I would find Ikhwan members there. He then excused himself and departed.

After that, Mutlaq came to take me to his farm. From there I returned to Riyadh. I told some Ikhwan I trusted about Juhaiman's instructions. During Ramadan, I performed the lesser pilgrimage and I met some Ikhwan who were renting an entire building with their families. In a room on the ground floor, I found a large number of red onion bags. When the night of the 27th arrived, I took the agreed upon number of essays to the Grand Mosque. Immediately, some were sent to Ta'if, Jeddah, and Medina. I handed out some to Ikhwan on their way to the Grand Mosque and stored some in the basement cells. At the end of the prayer, we started to hand them out right in front of the worshippers. At the very same time, copies of the essay were distributed in all parts of the kingdom. The book clearly bore Juhaiman's name. It was surprising that while I was carrying a bunch of copies, some youths who were not Ikhwan volunteered to distribute them. I am certain that some people who helped distribute the essays did not know what they were passing out or who Juhaiman was. After the dawn prayer, I sat in the Grand Mosque and I saw people leafing through copies of the essay.

Then I returned to Riyadh. Sheikh Badi Ihsanallah al-Rashidi wrote a rebuttal against the essay, saying that Abraham's religion does not have ambiguity or confusion.[164] I think he published it in *al-Nadwah* newspaper[165] and that is what caused the Ikhwan to break with him, which is one reason why he returned to his native Pakistan soon after.

Tensions between Nasir and Juhaiman

At this point, I was spending more time at the lessons of Sheikh Abd al-Aziz ibn Baz and starting to feel that the Ikhwan were on a path to chaos. I tried to stay organized. One day Ahmad al-Zamil stopped by to see me in Riyadh and asked me to accompany him to Ta'if, where he was staying with his family in a rented house. I went with him without asking for an explanation because I knew that it was Juhaiman who had sent for me. I went with him but did not meet Juhaiman until three days later. After our greeting, Juhaiman scolded me sharply and said

> What do you want with Sheikh Ibn Baz? This sheikh lost his eyesight and his intellectual discernment, so why are you eager to attach yourself to him? He is one of Al Saud's sheikhs. Sheikh al-Albani warned us about him at a private meeting where he said, "Sheikh Ibn Baz is easily deceived by those around him, so do not rely on him on matters that touch on the Group's security. He got us into trouble already."

I just listened to him without daring to defend Ibn Baz or respond to Juhaiman. The meeting ended two days later and I returned to Riyadh to study with Sheikh Ibn Baz along with some other youths including Khalid al-Shuraimi.

One day I ran into Ahmad al-Zamil and he said Juhaiman wanted to know why I was still studying with Ibn Baz. I did not answer. Attending the lessons of Sheikh Ibn Baz probably helped me and other Ikhwan later on inasmuch as we did not accept the idea of the Mahdi and its implications, such as taking weapons into the Grand Mosque and firing them.

In spite of the pressure I came under for studying with Ibn Baz, my relationship with the Ikhwan was not severed. Instead, it grew stronger, although I did not become involved in handing out the essays that were later published: *The Four Essays* and *The Seven Essays*.

Juhaiman did not send for me until one of the Ikhwan told me they were going to Medina and asked if I would like to join them. That time I did not think that we were going to meet with Juhaiman. So I left for Medina. Along the way, one of the Ikhwan wanted to rest a bit at the foot of Mount Tamiah.[166] So we stopped, got out some things to sit on, and made tea. A Japanese pickup truck stopped unexpectedly and Ahmad al-Mu'allam got out of it. He was wanted at the time. I had thought he was in Kuwait. After greetings, he told us that he and other Ikhwan were staying on the other side of the mountain. When we went up to their place, we found Juhaiman and Muhammad Abd Allah al-Qahtani. We greeted them. At that time, I sensed that Juhaiman was not his usual self with me in terms of small talk and politeness. I knew why he was like that. It was his way of addressing me indirectly, a way that he had when he wanted to denounce particular ideas or positions. If you objected, he would say, I was not talking to you. He would needle you that way, but you could not respond. You knew that he was directing his words toward you, and whoever he seemed to be addressing knew it as well, and so did everyone else who was present. This habit is what drove Sulaiman ibn Shtaiwi to leave the Group.

The group was gathered around Juhaiman in order to write his essays that were to be printed. Muhammad Abd Allah al-Qahtani and Ahmad Hasan al-Mu'allam did the writing. It is well known that these two wrote Juhaiman's essays. They were both poets and fairly proficient in Arabic prose, contrary to Juhaiman who refused to learn grammar and spelling as a boy. Indeed, he would speak of his refusal to those around him. It is commonly believed that Juhaiman graduated from the Islamic University or that he was a student at Dar al-Hadith in Medina. But the truth is Juhaiman dropped out after fourth grade in elementary school. The reason he went even that far was his desire to get promoted in his work as a pickup truck driver in the National Guard. That is the truth and anything else is a bunch of lies. Everyone who thinks that [Juhaiman studied at the Islamic University or the Hadith Institute], says "How could he write these essays with a fourth-grade education?" As a matter of fact, these essays were based on his dictation of his ideas to others. Juhaiman did not even write a rough draft because he hated writing and he had bad handwriting. He would dictate his ideas and then Ahmad al-Mu'allam or Muhammad Abd Allah al-Qahtani would write them up. What helped Juhaiman with his dictations was that he possessed a powerful memory that allowed him to recall references[167] whenever he needed them.

Dreams, the End of Time, and the Mahdi

In 1399 AH/1979 CE, there was a lot of talk about the frequent recurrence of dreams and the idea that the End of Time was near. Of course, this kind of talk was noticeably present even before this for a while. As I indicated before, the Group's discussions even before the first arrest were permeated by questions about the End of Time and the interpretation of dreams that some members experienced. Inasmuch as the Group was certain that we were at the End of Time and that recent events affirmed it to be so, this kind of talk became more frequent and went so far as to discuss hypothetical scenarios about the End of Time and the advent of the Mahdi. One of the portents of his advent is the multiplication of dreams about him. This preoccupation with the End of Time and the Mahdi became a collective delusion among members of the Group.

At this point I must cast light on the idea of "portents" or the tribulations and portents of the Last Hour according to Juhaiman in his essay, *The Tribulations, Reports of the Mahdi, the Descent of Jesus, and Portents of the Last Hour*. The subject of the essay is the plan or scenario of events that will occur. Juhaiman explained that the importance of the plan would become clear in the essay. At the beginning of the essay, he wrote,

> I have tried to collect Prophetic Traditions that are sound, Prophetic Traditions about tribulations and portents of the Last Hour due to the tremendous need for such a collection today. I undertook to organize the Prophetic Traditions according to the time and place of their occurrence, striving for consistency between the texts and documenting their reliability in a complete way to accomplish that benefit.[168]

Juhaiman then justifies the reason for his compilation:

> Many other scholars have gathered [Prophetic Traditions] and written on this subject, but I noticed two things in their books. First, they do not limit themselves to sound Prophetic Traditions but combine the sound with the weak. It is well known in our religion that one has to establish what is reliable if one is to believe it and act according to it. Second, there is inconsistency [between Prophetic Traditions] and a lack of connection between the meanings [of Prophetic Traditions] and their application to concrete situations. Consequently, the books contain contradictions, and on some topics, it is impossible to understand what they are talking about. But they [the authors of such books] are to be forgiven for not knowing that because they do not comprehend as I do.[169]

At that time [early 1979], I was still with the Group in body, but in my mind, I was not convinced by what they were starting to repeat to each other [about the End of Time]. Things got worse for me when the subject of the Expected Mahdi arose and Muhammad ibn Abd Allah al-Qahtani was identified as the Mahdi, and when members of the Group began to encourage each other to obtain weapons to prepare for a situation they assumed was inevitable. The possible and the certain got so mixed up that it became difficult to tell them apart. In this way, the Group marched toward catastrophe. The Group became consumed with the ideas of salvation, the Mahdi, dreams, and visions.

Around that time, I ran into Muhammad Abd Allah al-Qahtani and asked him, "Are you truly convinced that you are the Expected Mahdi?" He told me, "At first, I was not convinced by what the Ikhwan were saying about my being the Expected Mahdi. After a while, I withdrew from them and asked God about it, praying that He make the correct path clear to me. My heart opened to it one night."

I asked him, "Who was the first to indicate that you are the Mahdi?" He told me, "This idea was held by some Ikhwan at the Ruwail Mosque before I joined the Ikhwan. They sometimes repeated it and I would smile to myself thinking it was a joke until the dreams began to multiply and then I took them more seriously."

As we see, it seems the question of the Mahdi began for them as a joke and ended as a serious matter that led to catastrophe. I asked Sa'd ibn Abd Allah al-Qahtani about the identification of Muhammad Abd Allah al-Qahtani as the Mahdi and how he could be the Mahdi when their family was from the Qahtan tribe and among the portents of the Mahdi is that he is Quraishi from the line of the Prophet, that is, he is a descendant of one of the Prophet's grandsons.[170] He told me that they were not originally Qahtan but became Qahtan through marriage. Their great-grandfather was a sharif from Egypt who came with the Turks during Muhammad Ali's military campaign, and he settled in Jizan, then in Asir.[171] They were known as the Turki family.

At this point, I was trying to make a living and had a job at a household goods store. My ties to the Ikhwan began to diminish and I no longer paid attention to their meetings or their news. I kept going to Sheikh Abd al-Aziz ibn Baz's lessons, while I kept in touch with Khalid al-Shuraimi. One day, after the hajj season,[172]

I ran into an Ikhwan at the congregational mosque. He told me about the Ikhwan decision to invade the Grand Mosque on the first day of 1400[173] when they would pledge allegiance to the Mahdi Muhammad Abd Allah al-Qahtani between the Yemeni Corner of the Kaabah and Abraham's Station.[174] He asked me, "Are you going with them?" I told him I did not believe in the Mahdi story. He told me that all of the Ikhwan had performed the hajj this year and stayed over in Mecca to await this event. Then we parted.

I knew that some members of the Ikhwan, including my two sheikhs—Ali al-Mazrui and Hamid al-Ahmadi—and Faisal Muhammad Faisal and Abd Allah al-Harbi, were not convinced by the Mahdi story and the plan for an armed invasion of the Grand Mosque. Faisal and Abd Allah had some unusual things happen to them. As for Faisal, he told me in person that he participated in the invasion of the Grand Mosque with the others even though he was not convinced of the Mahdi story or of bearing arms.[175] Faisal said:

> I was coming from Medina and passed by Ali al-Hudaini's farm to fill up on water and to rest the family. I ran into Ali and after greeting, we sat together, sipping coffee. I told him about my opinion about the Mahdi and bearing arms in the Grand Mosque. He then went inside and returned after a short while. Then he said to me, "Do you want to see Juhaiman?" I said that I did. Then after a short while, Juhaiman came out to us, and after greeting, we sat together drinking tea. Then Juhaiman said to me, "Faisal, you are a man whom all respect and listen to. Why have you withdrawn from the Ikhwan?" I told him, "Juhaiman, you know that I told you that God did not put my heart at ease on this particular question and there are many legitimate differences over it. For me, the issue is unclear. I cannot make out what is right or wrong." Then Juhaiman said to me, striking his chest, "Come along, it is on me." Then I took my family to Najran and returned and invaded the Grand Mosque and pledged allegiance to Muhammad Abd Allah. Except for the first few days, I did not fire a weapon, then when we lost Muhammad Abd Allah, I returned to the underground cells and spoke to Juhaiman about losing the Mahdi. We received a report from some Ikhwan that Muhammad Abd Allah had been killed. Juhaiman got angry and said, "It is impossible that Muhammad Abd Allah was killed because he is the Expected Mahdi. The truth is that he is trapped somewhere in the Grand Mosque."[176] He accused the Ikhwan who saw Muhammad Abd Allah killed of lacking conviction in Muhammad Abd Allah's standing as the Mahdi, and of spreading rumors in the ranks of the Ikhwan. So after that nobody dared say that the Mahdi was killed or captured for fear of being accused [by Juhaiman].

I asked Faisal about what he did in the basement chambers of the Grand Mosque. He told me, "I was isolated in a corner of the cell with the wounded. It was weird that so many of us were hearing rumors and seeing visions about the earth swallowing the army coming from Tabuk,[177] which I asked you about." Faisal had asked me when I first entered the prison cell with him about the soundness of the Prophetic Tradition about the swallowing of the army coming from Tabuk.

I told him it is not sound and furthermore that nothing in the Prophetic Traditions about the appearance of the Expected Mahdi took place [during the Mecca uprising]. He was surprised by that. He said,

> In the cells [of the Grand Mosque], every day, there were dreams and rumors. Juhaiman was the one who spread the rumor about the earth swallowing the army. He said that one of the Ikhwan heard such a report on a radio that belonged to besieging forces in forward position. Such reports had no basis in fact and were a mix of lies, errors, and delusion.

As for Abd Allah al-Harbi, his story is stranger than Faisal's. Abd Allah withdrew from the Ikhwan because he too was not convinced of Muhammad Abd Allah's standing as the Mahdi or of bearing arms in the Grand Mosque. He withdrew from the Ikhwan a few months before they invaded the Grand Mosque. When the Grand Mosque was stormed, Abd Allah was overtaken by a sort of fervor and he decided to attempt to relieve the siege on the Ikhwan by launching an operation to storm the Prophet's mosque in a similar manner to the storming of the Mecca Grand Mosque. He went to Sajir seeking assistance from Juhaiman's tribe but along the way he ran into a security checkpoint where he was told to stop. He refused repeated orders and warnings and fled. He then resisted by opening fire on the security forces. After repeated warnings, the security forces exchanged fire with him and he was killed. I heard the story from Ahmad al-Askari, a Yemeni Ikhwan who worked on a farm in Sajir but did not invade the Grand Mosque. He was with Abd Allah Harbi in that incident and urged him to surrender but he refused.

The Invasion of the Grand Mosque

Before delving into how they invaded the Grand Mosque, I must point out that everything that I relate here is based on what I heard from Faisal Muhammad Faisal and some others who were in prison with me who were part of the group that invaded the Grand Mosque.

I learned about the Group's firm intention to invade the Grand Mosque during Muharram[173] by chance when I ran into one of them in Riyadh as I was leaving the congregational mosque in the second half of Dhu al-Hijjah [November]. After greeting, he asked me, "Are you going to Mecca and pledging allegiance to the Mahdi?" I told him that I did not believe in Muhammad Abd Allah al-Qahtani's mahdiship. He told me the Ikhwan had agreed to gather in Mecca to invade the Grand Mosque at dawn on 1 Muharram 1400 AH/November 20, 1979 CE, and they were going to give allegiance to the Mahdi between the Yemeni Corner and Abraham's Station. After that, the event took place on the aforementioned date. Heated arguments broke out among members who held back from invading the Grand Mosque because they were not convinced on the question of the Expected Mahdi.

The newspapers were the only source I could get to follow the Grand Mosque uprising. While the battle inside the Grand Mosque continued, I was afraid to get in touch with other Ikhwan for fear it would lead to my arrest. I remained in this situation until I was arrested on 15 Muharram AH/December 5, 1979 CE. After my interrogation and deposition, I was transferred to a newly built prison on the road between Mecca and Medina, where they put me in a cell with Faisal Muhammad Faisal al-Yami. I was surprised to find him there because I knew about his [skeptical] attitude about Muhammad Abd Allah al-Qahtani being the Mahdi. I already indicated how he joined the invasion of the Grand Mosque, so now let me finish his story.

Faisal said:

I took my family to Najran and returned to Mecca while the Ikhwan's plans to invade the Grand Mosque were in full swing. To smuggle supplies into the Grand Mosque without attracting suspicion, they used two water tank trucks. Vehicles frequently drove into the basement of the Grand Mosque to carry out water from a well that Meccans use for drinking water. The Ikhwan filled one of the water tank trucks with dates, and another with weapons and ammunition. In addition, they filled the two trucks' primary and secondary fuel tanks.

A few days before the attack, Ikhwan from Mecca brought some light arms and hid them in a number of cells in the basement of the Grand Mosque. The plan was to bring weapons in three different ways according to a specific time sequence. The first group was to enter the Grand Mosque with their individual weapons or obtain weapons hidden in basement cells of the Grand Mosque. Their mission was to secure [the Grand Mosque] and to get the trucks inside during the first hour. Next, Ikhwan were to enter the Grand Mosque carrying fake funeral biers on their shoulders. Most of them were women's biers because they are covered with domes, concealing what is underneath and able to carry more weapons. And this is in fact how the events unfolded. The biers were brought in before the first *takbirah*,[179] and then moved to the Place of Qusayy[180] in the Grand Mosque after the first takbirah. At that point, preparations for the attack were complete.

Imam Sheikh Muhammad al-Subayyil[181] began the first takbirah. The Ikhwan had dispersed to the Grand Mosque's entrances, posting one or two men at each one. Usamah Awwad Ibrahim al-Qusi was an Egyptian in the last year of his studies at the College of Medicine in Cairo who served as a medical aid for the Ikhwan inside the Grand Mosque. He joined the invasion of the Grand Mosque and pledged allegiance to the Mahdi. He told me that they began to close the Grand Mosque gates as soon as the imam began reciting the prayer.

One of them told me that he heard gunfire. Later, we learned that the shooter was an Ikhwan who opened fire because of an argument with one of the unarmed guards at a gate. This gun backfired and killed the man who had opened fire. Reports of this incident spread among the Ikhwan, and that man became known as the first martyr in the Grand Mosque uprising.[182] One of the Ikhwan told me that he heard the sound of *takbir* from some enthusiastic Ikhwan during the prayer. I do not know if this takbir was a password to take action or if it came spontaneously.

After the imam gave the greeting and began reciting the prayer for the dead, a group of Ikhwan went up to the microphone and took command of the situation amid shouts of "God is great" and "praise to God." The imam Sheikh Muhammad al-Subayyil tried to appeal to their consciences, but they would not listen to him. Instead, he and some soldiers were led to the administration section of the Grand Mosque, where they were put under guard in one of the rooms.

Some weapons were handed out. Then Khalid al-Yami began to give his written speech which set forth their goals and justifications for storming the Grand Mosque (See Appendix Two, *The Grand Mosque Sermon*.) Juhaiman would interrupt the sermon to give instructions to his followers for them to disperse to assigned positions inside the Grand Mosque or to give instructions for a particular situation [during the battle]. After that, arms and ammunition were handed out in the Grand Mosque courtyard. Muhammad ibn Abd Allah al-Qahtani, the Expected Mahdi, stood between the Yemeni Corner and Abraham's Station, exactly as the Prophetic Tradition foretold. Juhaiman was the first to pledge allegiance, followed by the other Ikhwan around him.

Nur al-Din ibn Badi al-Din ibn Ihsanallah Shah al-Rashidi translated the sermon into Urdu for a group of Pakistanis. A witness told me that Nur al-Din was reciting the sermon to the Pakistanis, holding up his pistol and brandishing it in the air. After he finished, a group of Pakistanis stood up crying, "Mahdi! Mahdi! Mahdi!"

The group in the Grand Mosque courtyard pledged allegiance, then Muhammad Abd Allah al-Qahtani, the Mahdi, was told that there was a group of Ikhwan that had not pledged allegiance because they had taken up defensive positions and could not afford to abandon their positions. Muhammad Abd Allah decided to go to them and take their pledge. Some were in minarets, some were in the al-Mas'ah concourse,[183] and some were on the roof of the Grand Mosque at the entrances. Muhammad Abd Allah went and took their pledge of allegiance and urged them to be patient in battle.

At this point, there was sniping from the minarets on the forces outside [the Grand Mosque] and those forces returned fire. The exchange of gunfire became intense. An armored car from the al-Mas'ah concourse tried to enter from the side of al-Marwah. It was blown up by Molotov cocktails made out of clay Zamzam[184] vessels—normally used for drinking water—filled with gasoline and lit with a fuse made from cloth.[185]

They laid down barricades of folded up carpets in the al-Mas'ah concourse and some other places. They stored water, dates, and ammunition in some cells to make them a place for supplies, refuge, and rest during the first three days, which Muhammad Abd Allah al Mahdi spent with the fighters posted in defensive positions. After that, there was no word of him. Someone told Juhaiman that Muhammad Abd Allah had been injured in al-Mas'ah. Someone else told him that he had been killed in al-Mas'ah. Juhaiman got angry and told them, "The Mahdi cannot be killed before the mission for which he was chosen as Mahdi is accomplished. He has not been killed, he is only trapped." Word spread among the Ikhwan that the Mahdi was trapped somewhere in the Grand Mosque.

Faisal Muhammad Faisal said,

After the end of the third day, nobody saw Muhammad Abd Allah the Expected Mahdi. Rumors swirled and clashed about his death, his wounding, and his being trapped. Juhaiman barred anyone from repeating reports of his death, and he argued with me over that. I asked him to surrender and stop the fighting for one basic reason, namely the fate of the Mahdi was now unknown, we were in the Grand Mosque, and it is not allowed to use firearms there, so [I asked him] if he would consider a ceasefire. He got angry at me and told me that this kind of talk would spread a mood of defeat among the Ikhwan, that the Mahdi was not killed and would not be killed until the rest of the foretold portents were realized, that we are now waiting for the second portent which is the swallowing of the army coming from Tabuk to fight us, that the Mahdi is trapped somewhere in the Grand Mosque, and we will release him.

Faisal told me, "At that point, I dropped my weapon and retreated to a cell to wait for the swallowing of the army coming from Tabuk."
Faisal went on to tell me,

Two days after my conversation with Juhaiman and what occurred on the third day [when Muhammad al-Qahtani disappeared], Juhaiman came to tell us that dreams were multiplying about the army coming from Tabuk and it had been swallowed by the earth. Two days after that, one of the Ikhwan came to us in excitement to bring good news. He said that last night an honest, pious Ikhwan fighting on the front lines had been able to clearly hear a report from a radio among the troops [outside the Grand Mosque] that the army coming from Tabuk to fight the Ikhwan in the Grand Mosque had been swallowed up when an earthquake erupted under them, and they suffered huge losses. The Ikhwan shouted, "God is great."

The reason Faisal and I dwelt on this topic is that he asked me when he saw me in prison whether the radio report about the swallowing of the army coming from Tabuk was true. I told him it was not. I told him that conditions in the country were stable [during the uprising] and that in Mecca itself, life returned to normal just one month after the uprising.
I understood from several of them that every day they heard about dreams and rumors circulating among them, reinforcing the idea of the Mahdi or the swallowing of the army, or urging patience and perseverance. I believe the Group was under the spell of a collective delusion or hallucination.
At the end of the week, they were trapped in the Grand Mosque's cells. Juhaiman would go out with some of his men and shoot at the basement doors. Meanwhile,

the fighters on the minarets and roofs retreated to the second floor, then they retreated to the first floor and the basement, and then from the entire basement to some of its rooms. On the last day, they were trapped in one or two rooms. An opening was made in the ceiling and tear gas grenades were dropped on them. At all places of the confrontation, loudspeakers were calling on them to surrender and lay down arms.

Juhaiman's Ideas

I have often been asked about Juhaiman ibn Muhammad ibn Saif al-Dann al-Hafi al-Utaibi, how this man invaded the Grand Mosque with arms in the holy month of Muharram in the sacred abode of God, and how he desecrated its sanctity with forbidden blood. All these forbidden acts led people to wonder about him and to seek explanations for his action, making him the subject of rumor and conjecture. That was because Juhaiman had been a relatively obscure personality, known to very few activists in the Islamic movement.[186] That was before 1978, but in that year and after, Juhaiman's name became well known to activists devoted to Islamic mission work[187] as an Islamist fugitive from justice for writing a few pamphlets. That was a new kind of mission work in contrast to the well-known style typically represented in mosque sermons. Afterward, his reputation spread far and wide due to the attack on the Grand Mosque, but all that people really knew about him was his name without any details, and consequently, their lack of information about him resulted in lies, errors, and guesses.

Juhaiman's Limited Formal Education

Juhaiman grew up in the Sajir hijrah, one of the hijrahs that King Abd al-Aziz set up for the original Ikhwan.[188] He enlisted in the National Guard as a truck driver. He then tried to get his elementary school diploma to qualify for promotion at work, as he told me himself. He told me that he left school in the fourth grade. He then entered Dar al-Hadith's elementary section for a very brief time, without finishing the first semester. He then left the Institute because he lacked the ability to go on with his studies. He departed the Institute full of resentment toward its program and style of teaching. From that experience, he became an opponent of formal education, which he expressed in later years. When it came to writing, he was practically illiterate. I looked over some of Juhaiman's early writings. Unless one tried very hard to read them, they were basically unreadable because of his bad handwriting and the many spelling and grammatical errors. His book collection includes volumes with his notes and comments on the margins. Many of these wound up in the essays that he later wrote. What really helped Juhaiman a great deal [when he wrote his essays] were his powerful memory, his ability to cite proofs for his ideas, and his rigid insistence on literal interpretation of texts.

Simple, Accessible Conception of Religion

At this point we must note that Juhaiman was averse to any subject that he could not master. He was against subjects that complement the religious sciences like grammar and legal theory, resorting to a pretext that carries weight in the Salafi mentality, namely, that the Pious Ancestors did not learn these subjects.[189] Juhaiman and other Ikhwan would claim that piety substitutes for learning these subjects, noting that God, may He be exalted, said, "Fear God and God will let you know" (Surat al-Baqarah, The Cow 2:282). In fact, Juhaiman would use that verse in his essay, *The Explanation and Detail on the Obligation to Know the Legal Proof*.[190] He wrote,

> "A bedouin[191] came from the desert to ask about Islam and he sat by the Prophet, peace and blessings be upon him, at a meeting one day. He left knowing what would get him into heaven, if he were truthful." Taken by al-Bukhari and Muslim from Talhah ibn Ubaidallah, God be pleased with him.[192] He said, "A man from Najd came to the Messenger of God, peace and blessings be upon him. The man was furious, and we could hear the echo of his voice but could not make out what he was saying until he approached the Messenger of God, peace and blessings be upon him, when he asked 'What is Islam?' The Messenger of God, peace and blessings be upon him, said. 'Five prayers in a day and a night.' The bedouin said, 'Is there anything more?' The Prophet said, 'No. Only that you obey, and fast during Ramadan.' The bedouin asked, 'Is there anything more?' The Prophet said, 'No. Only that you obey.' And the narrator said that the Prophet mentioned alms to him. So he asked, 'Is there anything more?' He said, 'No. Only that you obey.' And the narrator said that the bedouin went on his way saying, 'By God, I will add nothing to this or leave anything out.' The Prophet said, 'Be saved if you are truthful, or enter heaven if you are truthful.'"
>
> Do you see how this bedouin learned to pray? He learned to pray with one of the Companions, God be pleased with them, praying in front of him because the Prophet instructed him to do so, as in the saying "Pray as you see me pray." Transmitted by al-Bukhari. It took the Companion little time to pass on to him the Prophet's many sayings about alms and fasting. He spent one full day to learn all that and returned to his people knowing the religion of God, be He exalted, reporting it as he heard it.

Juhaiman wrote,

> I say if this bedouin came to today's law experts, they would confuse him and hide from him what God revealed, and they would tell him, do this and do that, and they would enumerate the pillars and the duties and the conditions, and the things that nullify, and the duties until he was completely baffled. He would never find guidance or proof. If he said, "I would like to seek knowledge and to know all about the Prophet and his Companions." They would say, "Hah! There is an abyss between you and them. But memorize these books, then read

these commentaries, memorize the Quran, read the exegesis, learn language and grammar and so on. If you spent two years of your life like this, then you would have the right to draw inferences from the texts about various issue. Otherwise, you have nothing but to blindly follow whatever your sheikh tells you. And never tell yourself that you can discuss an issue with him, let alone oppose anything he says."[193]

Juhaiman discussed all the conditions of ijtihad[194] and refuted them with a very simple procedure that the Salafis depended on.

As for the conditions [of ijtihad], that you find them buzzing about and stipulating to allow someone to study the texts and derive rulings from them … all it requires is that the proofs be taken from the Book[195] and the Sunnah. The two sound collections[196] establish a saying of the Prophet of God, peace and blessings be upon him, "Why do people make so many conditions that are not in God's book, since whatever condition is not in God's book is false, false, false … if they were a hundred, they would be false."
Some of them enumerate ten conditions, others thirteen, and others a different number.[197]

The way the Salafi Group and Juhaiman rejected any condition [for ijtihad] that is not in the Book of God was not merely in order to discover the true path for believers. It was also their protective armor against any development or improvement. It was their distinctive mark to strive to follow the Sunnah in terms of a simple, common person's, or even Bedouin's understanding of Islam.

Juhaiman wrote,

What separates the religious student from the lay person, what separates the qualified from the unqualified cannot be precisely defined in order to determine who is a religious student or someone with qualifications. It is enough for him to rule and judge between God's worshippers based on the duties God demands of all of them. There is no proof from God and his Prophet [for defining qualifications]. This difference [in qualification] did not exist among the Companions of the Prophet, peace and blessings be upon him. Why? The commoner had to be a seeker of knowledge. The Prophet said, "Seeking knowledge is a duty for every Muslim. Everything prays for the seeker of knowledge, even the whales in the sea." (Related by Ibn Abd al-Barr[198] in *Explanation of Knowledge and its Virtue*[199] and it is sound). Therefore, why did God create him? Only to worship Him according what He lays down for him.[200]

This is the Salafi way of thinking. They have ready-made molds for proofs, like their saying, "This condition is not in God's Book or his messenger's Sunnah," and their saying, "The Salaf did not do this, and we only do what they did." Some of them call allowable change harmful innovation and say every innovation is harmful. As for the general interest, ensuring general welfare, and updating ideas, none of that is anywhere in their discourse, no matter where you look. Rather you find in their discourse prohibitions for the sake of prudence and forbidding what God allows because it might lead to committing a sinful action.[201]

Salafi Preoccupation with Prophetic Traditions

If you looked at the book collections of the Ikhwan in the Eastern Harrah or on their farms in Sajir and Ha'il, you would find that they are all the same. First of all, they contain Albani's books and his research on the men who transmitted Prophetic Traditions, then the six books or the ten books of Prophetic Traditions,[202] then some books of commentary on Prophetic Traditions,[203] books about scholars of Prophetic Traditions,[204] and other books on the transmitters of Prophetic Traditions. These are the books usually found in their collections. In fact, collecting books became a kind of pastime for them. You would find them boasting about their collection even though they knew and cared nothing about seeking knowledge. Some of them collected books with red leather covers and so you would see a mostly red book collection.

When a new member joined the Ikhwan, they would begin by teaching him how to do research in the books about men who transmitted Prophetic Traditions and how to look up the chain of transmitters of Prophetic Traditions.[205] If there were time, they would read a bit about the science of Prophetic Traditions. I never knew the Group to devote a single day to correct recitation of the Quran even though the Group's many commoners made obvious mistakes in Quran recitation when they preached and later on when they mounted pulpits in mosques.

Juhaiman's Opposition to Government Schools

It is worth emphasizing that Juhaiman did not preach in villages and towns, that is to say, in places not inhabited by Bedouin. Rather, he usually preached in Bedouin encampments. He did that in order to avoid criticism for his poor command of Arabic grammar and religious knowledge.

Another point about Juhaiman to note is his position on schools and government education. Muhammad Abd Allah al-Qahtani al-Mahdi said,

> We must point out the corruption of education in the schools, institutes, and colleges that deceive many people. They are false in so many ways that one could devote an entire essay to them, but for now it is enough to mention that they are based first of all on disobedience to God because they display forbidden images. The student has evil classmates. The student does not learn anything about the Quran and the Sunnah, only unthinking imitation of the teacher.[206] You cannot count all the repugnant things. The students silently endure and go along with what is forbidden. To give examples and evidence for this would take a long time. You can find them in these essays and refer to them. Then, if you look at the graduates of these schools, the matter will be clear to you, God willing.[207]

Of course, this was Juhaiman's view and it was widely shared by the Ikhwan. It was also the outlook of opponents to the establishment of schools in Saudi Arabia years ago, when some leaders and religious students gave the same proofs and arguments against schools for boys. Some sheikhs believed that public schools that were not wholly devoted to religious subjects would teach students infidel ideas like the earth's spherical shape and its revolving on its axis and things like that. Many of the proofs that the Ikhwan used for such issues were taken from ulama who had already addressed them. This kind of talk encouraged everyone who wanted to drop out of school to join the Ikhwan. Therefore, you found the Ikhwan full of youths. In fact, some ran away from their families and joined the Ikhwan, like Abd al-Aziz al-Sadhan, the well-known sheikh.

Flight from Materialism and Moral Corruption

Juhaiman cited a poem by Muhammad Abd Allah al-Qahtani at the end of his essay, *Removing Confusion*, in which Qahtani described the situation of Abd al-Aziz al-Sadhan and why he ran away from his family.[208] Juhaiman said,

> We wish to end this essay with a poem composed by an Ikhwan. It is the story of the situation of a young believer whom God, may He be exalted, guided to seek beneficial knowledge and to support the Sunnah and to come out with it in this society which does not welcome the Sunnah and its truth, or act according to it, this society in which temptations multiply, temptations that deflect people from the path of God. The poet wrote:

A secret servant on a dark night,
With his piety, fleeing abominations
Fleeing the temptations surrounding him
The temptation for better or for worse.
A young servant at the dawn of his youth
Who knew the Guidance[209] and his way to purity,
Who read the Quran with understanding and reflection,
And was thus guided to the unblemished Sunnah
And saw happiness in the life of the righteous
With blessing morning and night.
He yearned for such happiness himself.
His yearning began to rock him [as a baby] in secret
Until he committed to the Guidance, with firmness,
For God, without any whim.
The temptations of misguidance called him forcefully,
Beckoned him with adornment and seduction.
The material world made itself lovely in its outward guise
With its smiles and mascara glances.
It started beguiling people with its allure
Until the vast majority went astray.

He grew up in a society where the Guidance was mixed
With the forces of ruin and the light with darkness,
People taking from it according to whim.
If you happened upon him, he would be far away.
If you came with the clear truth to uphold
And you came out with the pure Sunnah,
They would not recognize it because of their ignorance
Or because it was not handed down from their fathers.
Their day of resurrection arrived and their gathering terrified them.
They look at you as an innovator[210] and one who leads astray with temptation.
"Would you substitute something else for the religion of our sheikhs
"And the way of the mighty and illustrious?
"When did you learn the Guidance and religion of the Prophet?
"Only yesterday you were an ignorant youth."
If you came to them with proofs of the Guidance
And you refuted their error clearly,
They would say, "Your Guidance is repugnant and extreme.
"If you persevere in it, you are a hypocrite."
When the young man came to them with the Guidance
They ran away like foolish asses.
They mocked his behavior and his way of worship.
They tempted him away from the Guidance with harmful things.
If they saw him soften, they sought to
Get him to listen to them and they enticed him with temptation
To turn away from the path of the Guidance, with the temptations of youth
Harming him with worse temptations.
His mood became vexed
As his faith was vexed in evil desires.
And he turned his back on upright schoolwork
Mixing bad things that were common in lessons
Giving advice in open and in secret
To his friends and companions
Especially his family and relations.
They ignored him when he called on them with courtesy
But they did not listen to the word of Guidance
When it came from the youngest son.
Rather they fought him with every shameful thing.
They accused him of being crazy and dumb.
In the face of their spite, he would only say:
"God is my Lord, in my appearance and my heart."
They increased pressure on him so he resorted
To complain to his Lord of the great tribulation
Saying, "O lord, I am your believing servant
"I fear the temptation of the masses
"I fear going astray, and

"I beseech you to accept me and my feeble prayer:
"Save the one drowning in darkness, who is fearful of
"The awesome waves and the terrifying darkness;
"The waves of the storm whose darkness leads astray.
"If the Guidance is obscured, hidden
"What is upright and how can I conceal
"The clear truth out of fear and hope?
"It must be brought out with the weapon
"Of knowledge, to tear apart the arguments of the ignorant.
"Temptations stirred in the east and I went west,
"Seeking the Prophetic Tradition in blessed Mecca.
"By that I mean the people and the party of the Prophetic Tradition,
"Living by its purified guidance."
This is the story of the people of guidance
In the midst of temptation and seduction.
O Lord, preserve them and make them firm,
Vindicating the Guidance and the pure Sunnah.
Give them sustenance and enliven them with foresight
Give them sustenance with patience to endure hardship.
Give us an abundant share of that too.
O Lord, give us victory over the enemies,
The enemies of Ahmad's Sunnah, who replace
The Guidance of the chosen to mislead after purity.
O Lord, make us among the saved
When you punish them with disastrous convulsions.
O Lord, you promised us either Hasan or Husain.
O Lord, resurrect us with the fortunate ones.

Juhaiman then went to live in Medina, but why Medina? Juhaiman said, "I chose to live in Medina for its many virtues and because the Antichrist would not enter it." He mentioned that he accompanied a group of Tablighi members and later found out that there were members of the Muslim Brotherhood in the group trying to recruit young men from the Tablighi. That is what I gathered from Juhaiman. Through that group, Juhaiman decided along with some others whom I previously mentioned to set up the Salafi Group.

Opposition to Serving in the Military

Back then, Juhaiman was a sergeant in the National Guard working as a truck driver. Before he became pious, he worked for transport companies as a truck driver and as a smuggler between Kuwait and Riyadh, driving a Ford. He held these jobs at the same time. When he was still a soldier, he first became alienated from the military and from government positions in general. He eventually left the military when he came under the influence of the writings of Sheikh Hammud al-Tuwaijiri, in particular his book *The Clarification and Explanation of What*

Befalls the Majority Who Imitate the Polytheists.[211] In this book the author harshly condemns whoever acts like non-Muslims, and in some passages, he practically excommunicates them. Tuwaijiri writes:

> The twenty-third kind of the ways that one acts like the enemies of God, may He be exalted, is to wave your hand when greeting, or to salute by raising the palm to the face above the right eyebrow as the police and others do. Likewise, the way police strike their ankles together. This military greeting is forbidden, because it is borrowed from Westerners and other enemies of God, may He be exalted. It resembles mockery and sarcasm more than a greeting. What is to be done with those whom Western civilization has changed and corrupted with its morals and its habits to the point they esteem the habits of Westerners and other foreigners that are repugnant to those with sound minds and upright character? These unacceptable greetings must be changed because they are forbidden, according to the Prophetic Tradition of Abd Allah ibn Umar,[212] God be pleased with them. He said, "The Prophet of God said, 'Whoever imitates a people is one of them.'" Imam Ahmad and Abu Daud transmitted it.[213] Ibn Hibban and others affirmed that it is sound.[214] In al-Tirmidhi's Collection of Prophetic Traditions, Abd Allah ibn Amr,[215] may God be pleased with them, reported that the Prophet of God said, "Whoever imitates others is not one of us. Do not imitate the Jews or the Christians. The greeting of the Jews is to gesture with the fingers. The greeting of the Christians is to gesture with the hands."[216]
>
> According to works by Abu Ya'la, al-Tabarani, and al-Baihaqi, the Companion Jabir, may God be pleased with him, reported that the Prophet of God said, "Greeting a man with one finger is a Jewish custom." Al-Haithami said that Abu Ya'la's transmitters are sound. And al-Mundhiri said its transmitters are sound.[217]
>
> In al-Baihaqi's version, "Do not give the greeting of the Jews and the Christians. They greet with gestures of the hands and the eyebrows." Al-Baihaqi said the chain of transmitters is weak.
>
> I said to him, "Look at what came before and what will come." This is what al-Nasa'i reported with a good chain from Jabir, may God be pleased with him, "Do not give the greeting of the Jews. Their greeting is with the head and a gesture."[218]
>
> Al-Hakim reports the Prophetic Tradition of Ibn Juraij from Muhammad ibn Qais ibn Makhramah from al-Miswar ibn Makhramah, may God be pleased with them, where the Prophet said, "Our guidance conflicts with their guidance," meaning the polytheists. Al-Hakim said it is sound according to the agreement of the two sheikhs[219] even though they did not trace its transmitters; and al-Dhahabi agreed with it in his collection of Prophetic Traditions.[220]
>
> In his collection of Prophetic Traditions,[221] al-Shafi'i classified the Prophetic Tradition of Ibn Juraij from Muhammad ibn Qais ibn Makhramah, as unreliable.[222] His version of the text is, "Our guidance conflicts with the guidance of the idol worshippers and the polytheists."
>
> If you know this, then God distinguished the Muslims with the best, the purest, and most perfect greeting, and that is the greeting that God taught to

Adam, the father of humanity, when he breathed into him the spirit and gave him the tidings of his progeny. The collections of al-Bukhari and Muslim and the collection of Ahmad ibn Hanbal contain the Prophetic Tradition from Abu Hurairah,[223] God be pleased with him, when the Prophet said, "God created Adam in his image, sixty cubits in height, and when he created him, He said, 'Go and greet that group of angels who are sitting, and listen to how they greet you, for that will be your greeting and the greeting of your descendants.' He said, 'Peace be upon you.' They said, 'Peace be upon you and the mercy of God,' and they added 'the mercy of God.'"

God, be He exalted, laid this down for his people to greet each other with this blessed, pure greeting. God, be He exalted, said, "O believers, do not enter one another's houses until you take leave and you greet its folk. That is better for you so that you be reminded." (Surat al-Nur, The Light 24:27).

And He said, "If you enter the houses, then give a greeting from God." (Surat al-Nur, The Light 24:61).

Sa'id ibn Jubair and al-Hasan al-Basri and Qatadah and al-Zuhri said, "Greet one another."[224]

In al-Tirmidhi's collection of Prophetic Traditions,[225] Abu Tamimah al-Hujaimi[226] reported that a man from his tribe reported, "I asked the Prophet," and he recited the Prophetic Tradition. The Prophet said, "When a man meets his Muslim brother, let him say *al-Salam alaikum warahmatallah wa barakatuhu*, [Peace be upon you and the mercy and blessings of God be upon you]."

On this subject, we also have Abu Tamimah al-Hujaimi from Abu Jurayy Jabir ibn Sulaim al-Hujaimi, may God be pleased with him, "I went to the Prophet and I said *Alaik al-salam*, and he said, Do not say, *Alaik al-salam*, but say, *al-Salam alaikum*."

With this blessed greeting the Lord greets the believers when they enter paradise, as He said, "Peace, a saying from your merciful Lord" (Surat Ya Sin, 36:57). And He said, "Greetings to you on the day they will be greeted with peace" (Surat al-Ahzab, The Confederates 33:44).

Ibn Majah[227] reported in his collection of Prophetic Traditions and Ibn Abi Hatim[228] and al-Baghawi in their two exegeses of the Quran from Jabir ibn Abd Allah, may God be pleased with them. The Prophet said, "The people of paradise are in bliss, a light will shine on them, they will raise their heads and the Lord above them will say, *al-Salam alaikum*, people of paradise. That is God's word, *Salam*, a word from the Lord of mercy."

With this blessed greeting the angels greet the believers who enter paradise, as He said, "The angels come to them from every gate. Peace on you for what they endured and the blessings in the afterlife" (Surat al-Ra'd, Thunder 13:23–24).

We have already cited the way the angels greeted Adam with this blessed greeting.

Just as "Salam" is the greeting of the Muslims to one another in this world, so it is the Hereafter, as He said, "Their call therein will be 'Glory to you, O God,' and their greeting therein will be 'Peace.' And the end of their call will be 'Praise to God, Lord of the Worlds.'" (Surat Yunus, 10:10). And He said, "And those who believed and did good works will be admitted to gardens beneath which rivers flow, forever abiding therein by permission of their Lord, and their greeting therein will be: Peace." (Surat Abraham, 14:23)

If the virtue of "Salam" is recognized, that it is the greeting of Muslims in both worlds, then it is also known that nothing is more foolish than to want a different greeting and to replace "Salam" with the gestures and clicking heels of the Westerner.

May God grant success to the rulers of the Muslims to prevent actions that are contrary to Muhammad's shari'ah.

This passage was taken as an excuse to quit the military. Most of the Ikhwan used Sheikh Abd al-Aziz ibn Baz's *Book of Religious Advice*[229] to reinforce Sheikh Hammud al-Tuwaijiri's position.

The Manifesto: Removing Confusion

Removing Confusion is considered the manifesto that contains the ideas that caused the rift among the Ikhwan and that resulted in the departure of some Ikhwan from the Group.[230] In the essay, Juhaiman chose to openly declare his clash with the government and the rulers as part of a religious mission that commands right and forbids wrong and that openly proclaims belief on the model of Prophet Abraham. Juhaiman explained his conception of Abraham's religion:

> Abraham's religion stands on two principles. First, devoting worship to God alone. Second, staying completely clear of idolatry and idolaters, and exhibiting enmity toward them.
>
> The Prophet was commanded to follow it. God said, "Then we revealed to you, to follow the religion of Abraham, inclining toward truth. And he was not one of those who associate other creatures with God."[231]
>
> God said, "Say: Indeed, my Lord has guided me to a straight path, a correct religion, the way of Abraham. He was not one of those who associate other creatures with God."[232]
>
> There is no doubt that we are commanded to follow this religion and whoever does not wish to do so makes a fool of himself. The two prophets Abraham and Muhammad took that path and attained friendship [with God] through it, as we hear in the collection of Prophetic Traditions by Muslim, may God have mercy on him, when the Prophet said,
>
> "May God take me as a friend just as He took Abraham as a friend."
>
> The religion of Abraham is the religion of our Prophet, it is our religion, it is the example for our Prophet and our example, as God said, "There has already been an excellent example in Abraham and those with him, when they said to their people: Indeed we have nothing to do with you and whatever you worship apart from God. We have denied you and there has appeared between us animosity and hatred forever until you believe in God alone." (Surat al-Mumtahanah, The Woman to be Examined 60:4)

It is apparent from these proofs that the religion of Abraham is free of any idolatry and its people, separating from them, and shunning them. Showing belief in Islam is not achieved except by acting on this part, namely separation from others in the land, as we see in the long Prophetic Tradition of Jabir that al-Bukhari reported in *The Book of Holding Fast to the Quran and the Prophetic Tradition*, "Muhammad divided the people."[233] And it is in the Prophetic Tradition of Abu Sa'id al-Khudri[234] about true dreams.

In this essay Juhaiman criticized three groups of religious activists who fell short of the standard Abraham set:

For anyone in confusion about this issue, be it intentionally or by ignorance, let us set forth the beliefs and actions of the three groups to make them clear.

One group says that the way to uphold religion is by combating tomb worshippers,[235] showing enmity to them, and warning against them, and by combating Sufis and innovators.

A second group agrees with the first and adds opposition to blind allegiance to the legal schools and the call to protect the Prophetic Tradition and to purify it of accretions, and that is their primary concern.

The third group is preoccupied with refuting communism and proving the existence of the Creator, and with a serious effort to gain control over important positions in governments with the aim of seizing power.

The first group refers to Ansar al-Sunnah.[236] The second group refers to the Salafi group that follows Albani in Syria and Kuwait. The third group refers to the Muslim Brotherhood.

Juhaiman wrote,

The first and second groups and those who resemble them, in our view, undertake the truth, undeniably, but they do this only with people who have no power and they are silent about rulers when they trample God's religion. That path led others before them astray.

The last group does not follow the Prophet's guidance. They pursue a path to dominate the field of ideas. One of their principles is to hide behind all kinds of veils. They try to fool anyone who works under their influence. The Prophet said in the collection of Prophetic Traditions by Muslim, "There is no treachery in Islam." Ali said in a Prophetic Tradition in al-Bukhari about the Battle of Khaibar,[237] "Call them to Islam."

When they see someone calling to monotheism, condemning polytheism and innovation in their different forms, and explaining the true Sunnah and purifying it, you find them accusing him of falling short in understanding Islam, and they criticize him, claiming there is a more serious matter, namely communism.

Debates took place among members of the Group, often dwelling on withdrawing from evil temptations and from society. The cause of this debate was the decision taken by Muhammad al-Zamil, Faisal Muhammad Faisal, and Isam Sheikh to leave Medina and move to the desert and to live in tents in order to withdraw from society. Here they fell into a contradiction between the Prophetic Traditions that urge withdrawal from society and those that urge living in Medina because Medina banished its wicked people.

In sum, this group went out and struck camp near Medina in a location not suited to camping or living. It was a gloomy place, barren of trees and plants. When I went to stay with them, I got lice. The place was truly wild, a black mountain and black stony earth, with no services. I do not know why someone would torment himself and his family. Things got worse as time went on. When I joined them, I found them bewildered, complaining about lice, shortage of water, and the inability to get used to their surroundings. The only activity I saw was firing rifles for target practice. I stayed with them for a few nights. It was truly tortuous. Then I left them and went to Medina, then from Medina to Riyadh. I sought treatment for lice. An expert in lice advised me to use Tide detergent and to put it on my head like a paste. That was the only way I could get rid of the lice. After that, Ahmad al-Zamil went to Medina and did not return. Faisal and Isam followed him, so the experiment ended in complete failure.

Millenarian Rule in Juhaiman's Thought

One of the things we notice in Juhaiman's[238] thought is its simplistic discussion of government and its lack of a comprehensive vision for understanding the real world. In his *Essay on Rulership*,[239] he wrote:

> If you ponder the news and examine the real world, you find simple cause and effect. When the rulers do not govern according to God's Book and do not seek what God revealed, Muslims fall into misery. Division and discord multiply. One group tries to show that the other is wrong, and they divide into sects and parties. God forbade them all that. It is all the result of suspending rule according to God's Book and seeking what He revealed.

It is true that Juhaiman had some scraps of knowledge on this matter, which is one of the most important issues to preoccupy reformers and preachers, but such sweeping treatment does nothing to advance intelligent discussion. Then he wrote further,

> "Know that ever since the early centuries, few pious, ascetic believers have been concerned with this issue," by which he means sovereignty.

To grasp what Juhaiman is saying, we must understand that he saw Muslim rulers as passing through four phases, not as a matter of historical or modern events, rather as the realization of millenarian prophecy.[240]

In *The Distinction between Caliphal Rule on the Prophetic Model and Tyrannical Monarchy*,[241] Juhaiman cited the Prophetic Tradition of al-Nu'man ibn Bashir,[242] may God be pleased with him.

The Prophet said, "Prophecy will be among you as long as God wishes. Then God will remove it when He wishes. Then there will be the caliphate on the model of the Prophet as long as God wishes. Then He will remove it when He wishes. Then there will be usurped monarchy as long as God wishes. Then He will remove it when He wishes. Then there will be tyrannical monarchy as long as God wishes. Then He will remove it when He wishes. Then there will be the caliphate on the model of the Prophet." Then he was silent.

Ahmad[243] reported it and it is a reliable Prophetic Tradition.

This is the sequence that was the basis for Juhaiman's thought and his program of action. He did not treat the great caliphate [of early Muslim history] as a historical subject, rather, he treated it as a millenarian prophecy that was inevitable and certain to occur according to the following sequence:

First comes prophecy or apostleship, then it is removed or comes to an end.
Second comes a caliphate on the model of the Prophet, meaning the state of the four rightly-guided caliphs, then it comes to an end.
Third comes usurped monarchy, then it comes to an end.
Fourth comes tyrannical monarchy, which Juhaiman believed to be prevalent in his time, as he was seeking to prove.
Fifth comes a caliphate on the prophetic model.

If we examine Juhaiman's essay, we find that it mostly deals with tyrannical monarchy and the caliphate on the prophetic model as paving the way to the future scenario that he treated as an absolutely certain, scriptural necessity, namely, giving allegiance to the Expected Mahdi.

Tyrannical Monarchy

The term for tyrannical monarchy occurs in the Prophetic Tradition of al-Nu'man ibn Bashir cited above. I do not know if Juhaiman mentioned it elsewhere. According to the sequence outlined above, it is the fourth type of rule that the Ummah will pass through, coming after usurped monarchy and before the caliphate on the prophetic model. Some scholars interpret it as the rule of the victor.

Juhaiman wrote,

If you look at its application to the current situation, you would see that today we live under tyrannical monarchy in which Muslims do not get to choose the ruler, rather he imposes himself on them, and they are forced to give him allegiance. It does not follow from their dissatisfaction with this ruler that he resigns. On the contrary, rule is imposed by force. Today's rulers of Muslims do not receive the allegiance of the people the way that the Companions of the Prophet did, when they could speak the truth and uphold religion in any circumstance. Instead, today's rulers govern according to institutions and laws that have nothing to do with religious law apart from what happens to suit their selfish desires. In other words, it is not a caliphate on the prophetic model.

Then he dealt with the pledge of allegiance under a tyrannical king:

Today, tyrannical kings rule the Muslims without the pledge of allegiance, and that is contrary to God's law in several ways. First, the rulers are not from Quraish.[244] Second, they do not uphold religion, rather they ruin it and fight religious people. Third, they do not take the pledge of allegiance from their subjects with the handshake, support from the heart, obedience, and choice, but by force and oppression. With this you can see it is not obligatory to pay them allegiance and obedience.

The most important point Juhaiman mentions is the issue of Quraishi descent. It was the basis for preparing to attack the Grand Mosque.

Caliphate Based on the Prophetic Model

Here he means the Expected Mahdi.

The Other in Juhaiman's Thought

In general, the Other is divided into different degrees according to how near or far one stands from the Salafi Group's program. His attitude toward the Muslim Brotherhood, the Tablighi Association, Ansar al-Sunnah, and certain religious students is mentioned in *Removing Confusion*. He was most violent toward anyone opposed to him on matters of doctrine, be they Shiites or Christians, without regard for the fact that the first represent people living in the same country with the same civil rights and duties as he has. He wrote,

Our government is marked by much confusion because of the government itself and its religious scholars. It may call itself "the government of monotheism," but in fact, it brings together Muslims, Christians, and polytheists, and recognizes the religion of each one, like the Shiites.[245] The government fights whoever opposes that,[246] and it fights whoever fights the idolaters who call to Ali and Husain in prayer.[247] It fought those who fought the worshippers of tombs and domes,[248] and laid down the foundations for worshiping the riyal.

The closest and clearest example is the founder of their country, King Abd al-Aziz and the sheikhs who supported him. He called upon the Ikhwan,[249] may God have mercy on them, those who migrated to various villages in a hijrah[250] to God. He called on them to pay him allegiance according to the Book and the Sunnah. They were waging jihad and conquering towns in the belief that he was the legitimate leader of the Muslims. Then when he consolidated power and he achieved his aims, he allied with the Christians and prohibited jihad in

God's path outside Arabia when they went to fight polytheists in Iraq, who were praying to Ali, Fatimah and Hasan, along with God.[251]

This passage recalls the reasons why the Ikhwan rebelled against King Abd al-Aziz: he prevented them from fighting Shiites and he asked Christians for help in modernizing the country's industries, which is something that religious law allows. That is evidence for the extent to which Juhaiman was influenced by the Old Ikhwan and their attitudes.

Appendix I

THE DREAMING NATION: THE ROLE OF THE DREAM IN SANCTIFYING SALAFI ISLAMIC DISCOURSE, BY NASIR AL-HUZAIMI

Ahmad ibn Hanbal said, "If someone told Sufyan about a dream, he would say he considered himself well acquainted with dreams."[1]

My reason for writing this book[2] is that I used to belong to the Salafi Group, I am familiar with how it elevated and glorified dreams and how dreams charted a path that the Group followed to the end when it invaded the Grand Mosque and pledged allegiance to Muhammad Abd Allah al-Qahtani between the Yemeni Corner of the Kaabah and Abraham's Station and introduced him to the Islamic world as the Expected Mahdi.

Before the Grand Mosque incident, the Salafi Group was like any Islamic group established for the sake of calling to God according to traditional methods of "warning in the mosques and public places." Likewise, since it was established in the mid-1960s, it rejected following the legal schools and gave special attention to the Sunnah. It adopted al-Albani's positions on the reliability of Prophetic Traditions and the compilations of Prophetic Traditions, probably because some of al-Albani's students, such as Sulaiman ibn Shtaiwi, were among the founders of the Group.

In general, that was the Group's program. Before I discuss how dreams shaped their concept of salvation, I first shed light on the place of dreams and visions in Sunni Salafism.

Dreams in Salafism

The problem with dreams is that the wording in Prophetic Traditions about them is inconsistent. Let us look at al-Bukhari's collection of Prophetic Traditions, which contains the most important references to dreams and which most Sunni ulama consider the most reliable compilation. One example:

> "From Urwah ibn al-Zubair,[3] from A'ishah Mother of the Believers,[4] that she said, 'The beginning of the revelation to the Messenger of God took the form of true dreams. Whenever he had a dream, it came like the break of dawn.'"

This Prophetic Tradition is in the Book of the Start of Revelation.[5] Thus, the true dream is a revelation from God—one of the ways that the Messenger received revelation. Most ulama believe that it was limited to the prophets, like the dreams that Prophet Abraham and Prophet Joseph had in their sleep.

This Prophetic Tradition is the basis for other Prophetic Traditions that have long posed significant problems, such as this Prophetic Tradition:

Abu Qatadah[6] from the Prophet, who said, "The true dream is from God and the nightmare is from Satan."[7]

And this Prophetic Tradition:

Abu Sa'id al-Khudri heard the Prophet say, "If one of you has a dream that you like, then it is from God. Praise God for giving it to you and tell others about it. If you have a different kind of dream that you hate, then it is from Satan. Seek refuge from its evil and do not mention it to anyone to avoid harm from it."[8]

Al-Bukhari has a chapter called "True dreams are one of 46 parts of prophecy." The chapter includes a Prophetic Tradition: "Abu Qatadah from the Prophet, he said, 'A good dream is from God and a nightmare is from Satan. If you have a nightmare, seek refuge with God from it, and if you spit on your left, it will not harm you.'"

However, the most important text in this chapter is from this Prophetic Tradition: "Ubadah ibn al-Samit[9] reported that the Prophet said, 'The dream of a believer is one forty-sixth of prophecy.'"[10]

And the Prophetic Tradition: "Abu Hurairah reported that the Prophet said, 'The dream of a believer is one forty-sixth of prophecy.'"[11]

And the Prophetic Tradition: "Abu Sa'id al-Khudri heard the Prophet say, 'A true dream is one forty-sixth of prophecy.'"[12]

And in the Chapter of Good Tidings from al-Bukhari's collection of Prophetic Traditions, "Abu Hurairah said I heard the Prophet say, 'Nothing remains of prophecy but *mubashsharat*.' They said, 'What are *mubashsharat*?' He said, 'True dreams.'"[13]

These Prophetic Traditions taken from al-Bukhari's collection formed the basis for an implicit, unspoken inspiration that became a justification when someone needed to bolster a legal or doctrinal position.[14] We should not be surprised when one of them [Salafis] declares a position with fatal consequences on the basis of a dream. On the basis of infatuation with these Prophetic Traditions, one might resort to violence and killing. History gives us many examples of that.

It is astounding that dreams and this kind of simple-minded belief in them were basic tenets in the doctrine of the godfather of Salafi thought, Ahmad ibn Hanbal. In *The Ranks of the Hanbali Scholars*,[15] there is a passage about the doctrine of the "Tradition Folk."[16]

Abu al-Abbas Ahmad ibn Ja'far ibn Ya'qub ibn Abd Allah al-Farisi al-Istakhri said that Abu Abd Allah Ahmad ibn Muhammad ibn Hanbal said, "These are the positions of the people of knowledge, the companions of Tradition, and the people of Sunnah who hold steadfast to its well-known roots, and act according to it, from the Companions of the Prophet to our day. The ulama of Hijaz, Syria, and elsewhere were known for it. Whoever differs with these positions in the slightest way or challenges them or denounces them is an innovator who is not part of the consensus and strays from the path of the Sunnah and the path of truth. Their position was that belief consists of word, action, and intention; belief entails adhering to the Sunnah; belief may increase or decrease; and one may qualify a statement of belief with the phrase, "If God wills it," as long as it does not stem from real doubt, in which case it is a customary practice of the ulama. Dreams from God are true. When the seer sees something in his sleep that is not jumbled up, he should tell it to a religious scholar and believe in it. The religious scholar should interpret it in a sound way and not twist its meaning, for the dream is true. The prophets' dreams were revelations. Only the most ignorant person in the world could deny dreams and claim they are not real. I heard that some who believe this do not wash after a nocturnal emission. It was reported from the Prophet that the dream of the believer is a word spoken by the Lord to his servant, and he said the dream is from God."[17]

The Salafis consider their position about dreams to be indisputable. Whoever disagrees or challenges it is deviating and straying from the truth. They often tried to keep it quiet, especially when dreams failed to come true, as in the Grand Mosque incident.

The general Salafi discourse says we are near the End of Time, when the world is in moral decline.[18] In al-Bukhari's collection of Prophetic Traditions: "Muhammad ibn Sirin[19] told us that he heard Abu Hurairah say that the Prophet said, 'When the End of Time nears, the believer's dream will not be false, for a believer's dream is one forty-sixth of prophecy, and whatever is part of prophecy is not false.'"[20]

Many Salafis and salvationist groups apply this Tradition to the real world and conclude that we are at the End of Time when the Mahdi will appear.[21]

Ever since I got to know the Salafi Group, it glorified dreams and made a big deal out of them so that it was common for them to describe and interpret dreams. Talk about dreams frequently occupied meetings dedicated to religious learning. I do not remember ever being in Juhaiman's company while on the road or staying somewhere without someone asking him to interpret a dream.[22]

Likewise, the Group carried out an operation that mixed together dreams and Prophetic Traditions about tribulations and the portents of the Last Hour. The Group used the dreams and Prophetic Traditions to interpret current conditions and based its actions on them. Dreams multiplied for members of the Group and reinforced their fascination with Prophetic Traditions about tribulations and the Last Hour. In fact, every member of the Group had a copy of Sheikh Hammud al-Tuwaijiri's *Gift to the Community on the Tribulations, Apocalyptic Battles, and Portents of the Last Hour*.[23] Juhaiman said of that book:

I advised our Brethren to read books written by some ulama, including *Gift to the Community* by Sheikh Hammud al-Tuwaijiri, but to exercise caution because it contains weak Prophetic Traditions. He discusses some of them and he excels in refuting people with deviant attitudes who afflict Muslims. Try to benefit from the book. The sheikh has a firm foundation on this topic.[24]

As people in our Group talked more and more about the End of Time, and dreams about it became more frequent, Juhaiman applied the Prophetic Traditions about tribulations to the present. I heard him talk about it at meetings of the Group sometime before 1395 AH/1975 CE, that is, before he was wanted by the authorities.[25] I emphasize the point so no one will think it was the result of being boxed in by the authorities from 1398 AH/1977 CE until the attack on the Grand Mosque in 1400 AH/1979 CE.

As I said, Juhaiman applied Prophetic Traditions about tribulations to the present. He wrote in *The Essay on Tribulations*:

Abu Daud's Book of Tribulations 4242 gives a Prophetic Tradition with a sound chain from Abd Allah ibn Amr who said, "When we were sitting with the Messenger of God, he talked about tribulations, mentioning many of them. When he mentioned the one when people should stay in their houses, some asked him what that was. He replied, 'It will be flight and war. Then will come a tribulation which is pleasant. Its murkiness is due to the fact that it is produced by a man from the people of my house, who will assert that he belongs to me, whereas he does not, for those close to me fear God. Then the people will unite under a man like a hip-bone on a rib. Then there will be a little black tribulation which will not spare a single person in this community of believers without striking a blow.'"

Juhaiman commented on this Prophetic Tradition as follows:

As for the Prophet saying that the pleasant tribulation's murkiness will come from the feet of a man from his house, it is none other than Sharif Husain, who ruled Hijaz before King Abd al-Aziz. He was from the Prophet's house and in his time people circumambulated tombs the same way they walked around the Kaabah. It is said that he accused Sheikh Muhammad ibn Abd al-Wahhab of dividing people. Therefore, it seems to me we can apply to him [Sharif Husain] the Prophet's saying, "He claims he is from me but he is not." The Prophet explained that when he said, "Those close to me fear God." The man under whom people will unite, it seems to me, is King Abd al-Aziz, because before him Arabia was full of wars and highway robbery, and neither Muslim nor infidel was safe. Then both Muslim and infidel alike enjoyed security, and now you find Muslim, Christian, and Shiite mingling together, all secure from each other. The Prophet saying that people will unite under a man like a hip-bone on a rib is applied to that. We are now in the little black tribulation which spares no member of the community of believers without striking a blow. Whenever it is said to be over, it spreads further. Our present time witnesses that, because you see people of falsehood coming to attack us every day with new temptations. First, they introduce them, then they spread them further. At first, radio only broadcast the Quran and news and you did not hear a woman's voice at all. Then time passed until women began to broadcast programs alongside men and singing seductive songs. Then they put them on television screens without the veil. Then photos and other temptations came along. That is how it is in all of their schemes, if you have some sense and think about it.

In that same essay, where he gets to the Prophetic Tradition of Awf ibn Malik[26]—"I came to the Prophet, and he said, 'Count six things before the Last Hour … then a tribulation that will not spare the home of any Arab,'"—Juhaiman interpreted it to refer to images on currency. He wrote,

As for the evil temptation that will enter the home of every Arab, there is some obscurity in this Prophetic Tradition. If you think about the present time, you see that evil temptation has entered the home of every Arab and that evil temptation includes the images found on currency and elsewhere. It has entered the home of every Arab.

Such assumptions are the basis for claims about the appearance of the Expected Mahdi among salvationist Islamic groups, especially the Salafi ones. If some of them are quiet about it for a time, it is still present in their souls and minds. It is merely postponed until the hour of need, just as the issues of jihad and martyrdom in God's path were postponed for a time and then came into view at the first opportunity in the form of terrorist actions that have no goal or logical justification except to demand the Taliban form of government, something that is not acceptable in religion, politics, or society.

These sorts of ideas were always discussed at the Group's meetings and I often heard them from different members. For instance, some members were ashamed to carry coins because they have images on them. Most of them put coins in a car drawer along with identity papers bearing personal photographs. Some of them were able to have some ulama make special exceptions for them to receive identity cards without photographs, while some others carried only coins. One day I was riding in a car with one of them when he put a canvas bag weighing twenty-five kilograms in the back seat. He had filled it with metal riyals to use for shopping. He told me that he had three more bags like it at home. Some of them ink out images on money. All that in order to escape the evil temptation that will enter every home. Likewise, they never bring magazines and newspapers to their homes. Some even cut up scraps of newspaper lying on the ground.

Some of them fled city life and pitched tents in the desert near Medina so they would be able to get to Medina quickly in accord with their belief that when the Antichrist comes, he will not enter Medina because the angels protect it. Juhaiman often ended his paragraphs with the saying, "Nothing remains but the Antichrist." In these ways, they were preparing for the arrival of the portents of the Last Hour. This was going on, as we said before, in 1398 AH/1977 CE. Dreams were the basis for all of that. Every day we heard about a dream about the expected savior. That kind of collective delusion inevitably reaches its utmost limit with the same kind of thinking.

Then, the issue of the Expected Mahdi was raised, and it was suggested that he was Muhammad Abd Allah al-Qahtani, a young man whose ancestors came with Muhammad Ali Pasha of Egypt's military campaign.[27] One of his ancestors settled in Jizan. I asked Muhammad Abd Allah's brother Sa'd Abd Allah al-Qahtani how Muhammad could be the Mahdi when he was from the Qahtan tribe [not the Prophet's clan of Quraish]. He told me that they were not originally from Qahtan by blood but by affiliation. He said that their ancestor was a sharif in Egypt who came with the campaign of Muhammad Ali and settled in Jizan.[28] That was how they proved their relation to the sharifs: His name and his father's name—Abd Allah—are the same as the Prophet's name.[29] They thought their dreams strengthened his momentous claim. That became the talk of the Group's meetings. Dreams that alluded to it explicitly and implicitly increasingly occurred. Then Juhaiman took it up and tried to convince the Group. Within the Group there was much talk that Muhammad Abd Allah himself was not convinced that he was the one mentioned in the scriptural text, so he stopped attending the Group's meetings. Then after some time, he did become convinced that he was the Expected Mahdi described in the scripture.

I asked Muhammad Abd Allah about that and he told me that he saw a true dream that affirmed him as the Expected Mahdi and that he was put at ease one night after he prayed repeatedly to God to help him decide, and it was the confirmation of the Prophet's saying, "God will set him right in one night."

Some members of the Group and I were not convinced of that, especially because I heard that my sheikh Ali al-Mazrui was not convinced.

My relationship with the Group continued as before, but Juhaiman did not ask to meet with me again as he used to, as when I helped organize distribution of the Group's writings or guided the Group in Riyadh.

The Group then entered the phase of collecting weapons. They discussed how to collect and store them. I heard that some of them sold their farms to buy weapons, such as Sa'id ibn Abd Allah, the older brother of Muhammad ibn Abd Allah. At this point I was overcome with dread and fear. So I quit the Group and stopped going to its meetings. For me, the issue had gone much too far. It ended with the Group invading the Grand Mosque and holding out for fifteen days.

They were driven by dreams, even when they were trapped in the basement cells of the Grand Mosque. Faisal Muhammad Faisal was with the Group until the last day of the Grand Mosque incident. When we shared a prison cell, he told me that [during the uprising] some Ikhwan believed that the army coming to fight them sank in the earth, and he wanted to know if I had heard about that. I told him that nothing like that had happened. He said to me, "We heard about a lot of things while we were in the basement cells," but he did not know their source.

Dreams comprised the driving force for the Group and I believe they will remain the driving force for other salvationist groups. If it happened with the Salafi Group, without doubt it will happen with other salvationist groups that can use dreams when need arises.

Appendix II

THE GRAND MOSQUE SERMON

Delivered by Khalid al-Yami
Instructions to the Group by Juhaiman al-Utaibi

"God's book is the truest word, the Prophet's (peace and blessings be upon him) guidance is the best guidance, inventions [in religion] are the worst things, every invention is an innovation, every innovation is misguidance, and every misguidance is in the Fire."

O Muslims! Hear now the sound Traditions of the Prophet (peace and blessings be upon him) concerning the Mahdi and his advent, so that the Muslim may have clear proof, and so that no one is misled by a proclamation. These Prophetic Traditions pertain to a man who is known as the Mahdi.

The first Prophetic Tradition is from Ibn Mas'ud,[1] may God be pleased with him. He reported that the Prophet (peace and blessings be upon him) said, "When there is but one day remaining for this world, God will lengthen that day until he raises up in it a man from my family whose name is the same as my name, and whose father's name is the same as my father's, who will fill the earth with equity and justice as it has been filled with tyranny and oppression." Narrated by Abu Daud. It is a sound Prophetic Tradition.

The second Prophetic Tradition is from Abu Sa'id [al-Khudri], may God be pleased with him. He reported that the Prophet (peace and blessings be upon him) said, "The Mahdi is from my family. He will have a broad forehead and a prominent nose. He will fill the earth with equity and justice as it has been filled with tyranny and oppression. He will rule for seven years." Narrated by Ahmad and Abu Daud.

The third Prophetic Tradition is from Abu Qatadah, may God be pleased with him. He said that the Prophet (peace and blessings be upon him) said, "A man will take the oath between the Corner [of the Kaabah] and the Station [of Abraham]. The House [the Grand Mosque] will not be permitted to any but its people. Once they are permitted, do not ask about the destruction of the Arabs."

(The speaker fell silent and another man began to give military orders. It is believed that it was Juhaiman al-Utaibi. He spoke in simple dialect.)

"Praise be to God, lord of the worlds, blessings and praise on the noblest of messengers.

"O Brothers, pay attention in order to calm things down.

"O Ahmad al-Luhaibi, scale the roof. Whoever you see rebelling against the declaration [of the Mahdi], open fire on him.

"O Sultan ibn Jarallah, go to the east side. Whoever you see rebelling, open fire on him. Do not let him sow confusion among you or threaten the Brothers.

"O Radan, the west side, the west side.

"Abd Allah al-Harbi,[2] to the north side, the north side

"Listen O Rakan, climb up with al-Luhaibi to the south side. Muhammad ibn Mubarak al-Kabir, who was in Medina, is up there, to the north side, the south.

"The rest of the Brothers: Shahad and Umar ibn Jarallah[3] and Sultan ibn Jarallah and Abu Hilal, stay between the Corner and the Station with a large group of Brothers, holding their positions.

"The pledge of allegiance after the declaration and after the people calm down.

"Let the truth be shown to the people. Whoever wants the truth, bring it to him. Whoever is against us, then the lord of the worlds is better than … listen and be warned."

(The speaker resumed the sermon, trying to persuade people of his call to the so-called Mahdi.)

We will finish the Traditions of the Prophet (peace and blessings be upon him) about the proclamation of the Mahdi so that you may have a clear understanding of your religion.

The next Prophetic Tradition is from Abu Qatadah, may God be pleased with him. He reported that the Prophet (peace and blessings be upon him) said, "A man will take the oath between the Corner and the Station. The House will not be permitted to any but its people. Once they are permitted, do not ask about the destruction of the Arabs. Then the Ethiopians will come and destroy it so completely that nothing will ever be built after it. They are the ones who will bring forth its treasure." Narrated by Ahmad.

The fourth Prophetic Tradition is from Abu Sa'id al-Khudri, may God be pleased with him. The Prophet (peace and blessings be upon him) said: "At the end of my community, the Mahdi will appear. God will send down rain and the earth will bring forth plants. (The sound of gunfire). He will distribute wealth in a righteous manner, livestock will multiply, and the community of believers will become mighty. He will live seven or eight years or pilgrimage seasons." Narrated by al-Hakim. It is a sound Prophetic Tradition.

The fifth Prophetic Tradition is from Umm Salamah,[4] may God be pleased with her. From the Prophet (peace and blessings be upon him): "The Mahdi will be of my family, from the descendants of Fatimah." Narrated by Abu Daud.

The sixth Prophetic Tradition: The Prophet (peace and blessings be upon him) said, "The Mahdi is from my family and God will make him right in a single night." Ahmad and Ibn Majah reported it.

The seventh Prophetic Tradition is from A'ishah, may God be pleased with her. She said that the Prophet (peace and blessings be upon him) said, "How amazing, some people of my community will be heading toward the House[5] because of a man of the Quraish who sought refuge in the House; until, when they are in the desert, they will be swallowed up."[6] Narrated by al-Bukhari and Muslim.

From that [these Prophetic Traditions] it becomes clear that:

First, the Mahdi's name is Muhammad ibn Abd Allah. Second, he is from Quraish and the Prophet's house (peace and blessings be upon him) from the sons of Fatimah, may God be pleased with her. Third, God will bring him forth in one night. Fourth, he will have a broad forehead and a prominent nose. Fifth, he will appear when the earth is filled with oppression and tyranny and he will fill it with equity and justice. Sixth, he will take the oath between the Corner and the Station. This also means that he will not seek the oath but that someone else will seek it on his behalf. Seventh, he will take refuge in the House. Eighth, a group will take refuge with him in the House because people are hunting them down everywhere. Ninth, an army will attack him while he is taking refuge at the Kaabah and God will cause this army to sink into the earth. Tenth, this army is from Muhammad's (peace and blessings be upon him) community, not the Jews or the Christians but the Muslims.

Here is the Prophetic Tradition concerning the group that is with him [the Mahdi]. Muslim narrated it in his collection of Prophetic Traditions from A'ishah, may God be pleased with her, that the Prophet (peace and blessings be upon him) said, "In this House, meaning the Kaabah, a group of people will take refuge who have no power, number, or arms. An army will be sent against them; until when they are in a desert of the earth, they will be swallowed up."[7]

This Prophetic Tradition makes it clear that this group will take refuge. According to the previously mentioned Prophetic Tradition, a man from Quraish will take refuge in the House. And when they take refuge because people everywhere are hunting them down, then they [the Mahdi and the group seeking refuge] will come together, in accordance with this portent. Likewise, it is in accordance with another portent, namely the sinking into the earth of the army pursuing both the Mahdi and the group.

If this is clear, then you must know:

O Muslims, all of these portents have been fulfilled.

This Mahdi who will take the oath in a few moments between the Corner and the Station is here with us, as is your Brother Juhaiman ibn Muhammad ibn Saif al-Utaibi. He is here with us now too. The Ikhwan were in Medina studying and giving the people sincere advice ... we printed essays and books and distributed them to people to make clear to them their religion. We came out with *Removing Confusion*, *The Three Essays*, *The Seven Essays*, *The Essay on Rulership and Monotheism*, *The Call of the Ikhwan*, and *The Balance in the Life of Man*.

As for the Mahdi, he joined the Ikhwan more than two years ago.

Today we took refuge in God's House, be He great and exalted. We found no refuge in the world except for this ancient House because we know that God defends it, as when he drove back the elephant and his people even though its inhabitants were idolaters[8] while we have committed no sin except to call people to return to the Quran and the Prophetic Tradition and to act according to them, even if that is against the government and the sheikhs and the people with salaries and official positions.

Today we are giving the oath to Muhammad ibn Abd Allah. He is from Quraish. His father is a sharif and his mother is a descendant of Husain ibn Ali, a son of Fatimah, may God be pleased with them. All of the traits described in the Prophetic Traditions are fulfilled in him. Praise be to God. Anyone who wishes to make sure of any of this, the way is clear. We are your brothers. We withhold nothing from you, we say, "That is the bounty of God, which He gives to whomever he wills, and God is the possessor of great bounty" (Surat al-Jum'ah, The Congregation 60:4).

We also give you the good news, O Muslims, that he was seen in countless dreams about the coming of the Mahdi, making clear that he is this man. Likewise, when people who did not know him previously saw him, they recognized him from their dreams about him in their sleep.

Perhaps some of it has already reached you. The Prophet (peace and blessings be upon him) said, "At the End of Time, your dreams will not be false." Narrated by al-Bukhari. He (peace and blessings be upon him) also said, "Nothing remains of revelation except for *mubashsharat*, a true dream that a believer sees or that is shown to him." Narrated by al-Bukhari and Muslim.

(The voice of Juhaiman al-Utaibi came back giving military instructions to his gang.)

"Praise be to God, lord of the world, praise and blessings on our Prophet Muhammad and his house and his companions, all of them.

(Calling out) "Id ibn Isma'il, Rudaini ...

"Listen Id ibn Isma'il and Rudaini, go with Ahmad al-Thani and take some Brothers who do not have weapons and give machine guns and arms to some of the Brothers who came in without arms and meet between the Corner and the Station.

"Id, go to the Corner and the Station.

"Rudaini, go to the Corner and the Station.

"Ahmad al-Thani, go to the Corner and the Station.

"Meet at this place. One of the Brothers whom you know will appear. Let some people give the oath. We know, we know those who came in and we know our Brothers who are being chased. The lord of the worlds said, 'O Lord, take us out of this city of oppressive people.' (Surat al-Nisa', The Women 4:75). If we understand that this is your mission, then after that …."

(Sound of gunfire)

"Fuhaid ibn Radan, Fuhaid ibn Radan, Listen! God's blessing on you. Listen Abu Hilal, O Abu Hilal to the Corner and the Station.

"Saif, to the Corner and the Station.

"Malik, to the Corner and the Station.

"Go there O …"

(An attempt to force the people to sit and be quiet.)

"Brothers, all of you, sit down, sit down. Let all the Brothers gather between the Corner and the Station.

"Ifaj ibn Jarallah, Ifaj ibn Jarallah.

"Take care to gather the Brothers between the Corner and the Station to get ready for the oath of allegiance after the declaration [of the Mahdi] and justification of the purpose of the oath. (Heads nodding). This affair includes firing off machine guns!

"This affair has what the Muslims need. Whoever keeps God's trust, God wants them to be with those fighting on the side of Jesus son of Mary. Do not fear them. Fear your own sins. Therefore, seek forgiveness and you will find mercy. Whoever rebels against you is like God, be He exalted, said, 'The retribution for an evil act is an evil one like it.' (Surat al-Shura, The Consultation 42:40). And God said, 'Whoever has assaulted you, assault him in the same way' (Surat al-Baqarah, The Cow 2:194).

"As for the government's troops, if you see one of them raise his hand against you, you have no obligation toward him. You should open fire on him because he wants to open fire on the Muslims. If ... but do not open fire until you get permission, for if you do it before the oath, it is not legitimate, and it will be like how Khalid ibn al-Walid took the oath by force.

"After the oath, the Mahdi will be in charge, but now the Mahdi is sitting, waiting, 'for us to kiss his hands.' He is arguing with one of the Ikhwan who had been wanted by the authorities. Calm down, brothers. Calm down, brothers."

(Some moments pass while Juhaiman pauses in giving instructions, then he continues):

"O Brothers from every side, the eastern side, the western side, the southern side, each side, gather together, so that you are not separated, but gather together as we mentioned before, so that you are not separated, gather together as a group, gather together from every side, to gather together as a group, as we mentioned before."

(The preacher of the corrupt band[9] resumed his sermon):

O Muslims, we give you tidings on this blessed day about the appearance of a righteous man, the Mahdi who will fill God's earth with justice and equity as it is filled with oppression and tyranny which are coming to an end.

(Voices shouting, "God is Great. There is no god but God." Then the criminal Juhaiman returned to giving instructions again):

"O Abd Allah ibn Isma'il ibn Mubayrik, get up on the roof. Get up on the roof, you and the group with you. Take telescopic rifles and machine guns up to the minarets. Go up. The oath will come later. Go up."

(The call is repeated.)

"O Brothers, take the closest way to go up ..."

(Shouts and yelling)

"O Muhammad ibn Mubarak, Muhammad ibn Mubarak, who was in Medina. Why the southern side? Take Sulaiman and go there. There is a gate that needs to be shut, Muhammad ibn Mubarak al-Kabir."

(The gang's preacher resumed yet again):

Praise be to God! O Muslims, here is the declaration of the true position. Listen, God have mercy so you may benefit. Then you will come out, God willing. A door will open for you and you will come out. The doors are locked. The doors are locked. Nobody goes out. The doors are locked. Nobody goes out. Listen, may God have mercy on you. Praise God who promised and said, "Then indeed your Lord ... to those who emigrated after they had been compelled and then fought and were patient, indeed your Lord after that is Forgiving and Merciful. On the day when every soul will come pleading for itself, and every soul will be compensated for what it did, and they will not be wronged. And God presents an example, a city which was safe and secure, its provision coming to it in abundance from all sides, but denied the favors of God. So God made it taste the garb of hunger and fear for what they had been doing."[10]

Their [Muslims who did not move from Mecca to Medina until sometime after Muhammad did so] emigration [to Medina] came after tribulations. If they had pretended to conform [to the Meccans], they would have been secure with the people of the town [Mecca] and they would have been like them. Then God made clear what they would gain [by leaving Mecca] through this next verse. He said, "God has promised those who believe and do right that He will make them succeed in the land as he made those before them succeed. And that he will establish for them their religion ... and will give them safety after their fear, worshiping me and not making anything a partner with me" (Surat al-Nur, The Light 24:55). Therefore, they had safety instead of fear, and victory instead of defeat. They could have been like the Meccans who told their companions what they feared would happen, "If we followed the Guidance with you, we would be swept from the land,"[11] so their companions would not be in fear.

And then what the Meccans feared befell them, according to the covenant of the Prophet (peace and blessings be upon him). Peace and blessings upon our messenger whose Lord told him what he sent him for without throwing him off his purpose. God told him in the sacred Prophetic Tradition, "I sent you to test you and whoever is with you." Narrated by Muslim. At the beginning, he tested him with the Meccans. They opposed him and his companions and expelled them from their homes. And in the end, God tested the Meccans with him to get rid of their idols. Whoever follows their path will experience what they did, testing at the beginning and victory and security in the end.

And now, we proceed with the declaration of the Prophet's (peace and blessings be upon him) warnings to his community about many things. They include the spread of wickedness in the earth and its issuing in the destruction of the righteous and the wicked. They are allowed to fight in the House.

(sound of gunfire)

It is the cause of the destruction of the Arabs. Likewise, God will make a cure for every disease. It is reported that the earth will be filled with tyranny and oppression, then God will send an agent to purify it, a righteous man whose traits are mentioned along with the traits of his enemies and his supporters.

And now we mention to you the Prophetic Traditions to make clear to you what has occurred. Know that we only mention what is affirmed from the Prophet (peace and blessings be upon him). Then after that we make clear to you this man's traits, his enemies' traits, and [the traits] of those who are with him. Then we mention to you the proofs after that to make it easy for you to understand and remember them.

Here is the first Prophetic Tradition: Al-Bukhari and others narrated from the Prophetic Tradition of Zainab, may God be pleased with her.[12] She said that the Prophet (peace and blessings be upon him) got up from sleep, with a flushed red face, and said, "There is no god but God. Woe to the Arabs from the evil that is approaching them. Today a gap has opened in the barrier restraining Gog and Magog." [Someone asked], "Can this happen when there are righteous ones among us?" He said, "Yes, when wickedness prevails."

O Brother, take heed. There is a difference between the righteous and the doer of right. The righteous is whoever makes only himself right. As for the doer of right, he is right in himself and makes others right. So the doer of right is not destroyed by what destroys the rest of the people. The people are not destroyed until he is separated from them. They do not triumph until they are set apart from others. The proofs from the Book and the Prophetic Tradition are many. God be He exalted said, "Your Lord did not destroy a town unjustly while its folk were doing right" (Surat Hud, 11:117). He did not say if its folk are righteous, rather he said if its folk are doers of right. About victory he said, "We supported those who believed against their enemies and they became dominant" (Surat al-Saff, The Ranks 61:14).

The second Prophetic Tradition: Ahmad reported it and it is sound. From Abu Qatadah, may God be pleased with him. He said that the Prophet (peace and blessings be upon him) said, "A man will take the oath between the Corner and the Station. The House will not be permitted to any but its people. Once they are permitted, do not ask about the destruction of the Arabs. Then the Ethiopians will come and destroy it so completely that nothing will ever be built after it. They (the sound of heavy gunfire erupts) are the ones who will bring forth its treasure."

This Prophetic Tradition attests to the permission [to enter the House] and shows that it is based on the oath. As for the government clerics who pledge allegiance to their rulers, they fight whoever opposes them and consider them to be rebels. For proof, they cite the Prophetic Tradition, "If two caliphs receive the oath, one of them will kill the other." The lawful caliph fulfills two conditions, that he is from Quraish and that he is upright in the religion of God, be He exalted. This is written in *The Essay on Rulership*.

The third Prophetic Tradition: Abu Daud cited this sound Tradition from Ibn Mas'ud, may God be pleased with him. The Prophet (peace and blessings be upon him) said,

> When there is but one day remaining for this world, God will lengthen that day until he raises up in it a man from my family whose name is the same as my name and whose father's name is the same as my father's, who will fill the earth with equity and justice as it has been filled with tyranny and oppression.

The fourth Prophetic Tradition: Ahmad and Abu Daud narrated it from Abu Sa'id [al-Khudri], who said, the Prophet (peace and blessings be upon him) said,

"The Mahdi is from my family. He will have a broad forehead and a prominent nose. He will fill the earth with equity and justice as it has been filled with tyranny and oppression, and he will rule for seven years." It is a good Prophetic Tradition.

We now explain to you first his condition, then the condition of his enemies and their traits, and the condition of the group that is with him, to make it clear.

He must have a number of traits:

First, his name will be Muhammad ibn Abd Allah, and he will have a prominent nose and a broad forehead.
Second, he will be from Quraish from the Prophet's (peace and blessings be upon him) house.
Third, he will take refuge in the House.
Fourth, his enemies will come from Muhammad's (peace and blessings be upon him) community.
Fifth, their destruction will take place in a desolate place in the desert.
Sixth, his supporters have two traits and these two traits must be evident in this man. If not for these two traits, then each group would make the same claim and would take refuge in the House and bring any member of Quraish with the same name off the street.
The first one is that they take refuge in the House and that the refuge only be from fear of one thing, namely the inability to hide him.
The second one is that their enemy will sink in the earth at a single place, at a desolate waste. The enemy of the man and of the group has the same trait.

This is understood through two Prophetic Traditions.

The first Prophetic Tradition is taken by al-Bukhari and Muslim from A'ishah, may God be pleased with her. She said that the Prophet (peace and blessings be upon him) was asleep and we said,

O Prophet, you did something in your sleep that you had not done before. He said, "How amazing, some people of my community will be heading toward the House because of a man from Quraish who sought refuge in the House; until, when they are in the desert, they will be swallowed up." Then we said, "O Prophet, the route may bring together the people." He said, "Yes, among them there will be the judicious and the constrained and the wayfarer. They will all perish in the same way but will be sent forth from different points of origin. God will raise them according to their intents."

The second Prophetic Tradition is taken by Muslim from A'ishah, may God be pleased with her, that she said the Prophet (peace and blessings be upon him) said, "In this House, meaning the Kaabah, a group of people will take refuge who have no power, number, or arms. An army will be sent against them; until when they are in a desert of the earth, they will be swallowed up."

These two traits in these two Prophetic Traditions coincide. It appears that the cause of the attack is the oath and the gathering [at the Kaabah], because if they were dispersed and not gathered together, then there would be no need to send an army. It is evident from the aforementioned Prophetic Tradition that the man will take the oath between the Yemeni Corner and the Station of Abraham.

"No one but its people may take over the House. When they take it over, do not ask about the destruction of the Arabs." It is understood from this that he will not ask for the oath but that a group will give him the oath without his asking for it.

You also have the portent of what will happen to the army and how you can be ready to learn a lesson from evil. Muslim said about the Prophetic Tradition of Hafsah,[13] that she said that she heard the Prophet (peace and blessings be upon him) say,

> Verily, an army will be heading for this House to raid it, until when they are in a desert of the earth, the one in the middle of them will be swallowed up, and the first of them will call the last. Then they will be swallowed up, and no one will be left but the fugitive who will give information about them.

Then after that, know that revelation ended [with the Prophet] and nothing remains of it except for good tidings, which are dreams. The Prophet (peace and blessings be upon him) said, "The believer's dream at the End of Time will not be false." Al-Bukhari and Muslim reported this—a dream's truth is affirmed when it is in accord with the Sunnah, as related in the Tradition of the Night of Power. The Prophet (peace and blessings be upon him) said, "I see your dreams agree with each other."

After citing the aforementioned proofs and their application to the brothers here today and to one man among them, I declare that Muslims will divide into three groups about this man. The first group does not recognize him until it is demonstrated to them through a dream that he is the Mahdi, and when they are awake and meet him, they will recognize him by clear portents in him. The second group believes that the Mahdi will soon appear. The third group sees the pledge of allegiance to him and they see him receive the pledge between the Corner and the Station. Most of them do not recognize this man. There have been twenty, indeed more than fifty dreams to this day. Three brothers have collected the dreams from those who had them. Whoever wants to be sure of that, let him ask Maras ibn Mal'at al-Ghamdi, Yusuf Akbar Al Rida and ... (sound of intense clamor and shouting, and then the criminals[14] try to calm and silence the worshippers).

(After that, an unclear voice was heard that apparently was the voice of Juhaiman al-Utaibi, the leader of the gang, calling to the people to give the oath to their so-called Mahdi. At the same time, the shouts of his band "*allahu akbar*" and "*la ilah illa allah*" mixed with the sound of intense, continuous gunfire until the recording was cut off.)

Published in *al-Riyadh* newspaper
Issue 4398, 17/1/1400 AH

Appendix III

"JUHAIMAN'S SIN:" NASIR AL-HUZAIMI: THIS IS MY STORY WITH THE EXPECTED MAHDI

The writer and researcher Nasir al-Huzaimi witnessed the rise of Juhaiman al-Utaibi. As a member of his group, he got close enough to him to learn precise details of his personality and mentality. He witnessed at first hand the early stages of the Salafi Group. He came to know the secrets of their clandestine meetings and how Juhaiman rose to become the Group's leader. Consequently, what al-Huzaimi reveals about the Group's origin, establishment, and conception of salvation is not widely known. Al-Huzaimi relates that Juhaiman avoided groups like the Muslim Brotherhood and the Tabligh Association. He also sheds light on Juhaiman's relationship with Sheikh Ibn Baz and Sheikh al-Albani, his shift from public to secret activities, and how the idea of storming the Grand Mosque arose.

Al-Majallah: How do you see the nature of society in Juhaiman's time, especially since some believe the economic situation had some effect on his emergence?

NH: That assumption is not supported by sociological studies. Juhaiman al-Utaibi grew up in a settled desert region called Sajir, which was one of the Old Ikhwan settlements that were established in the time of King Abd al-Aziz to encourage Bedouin to give up the nomadic way of life and to teach them religious sciences. Sajir eventually became embroiled in the battle against King Abd al-Aziz at Sabilah. Juhaiman grew up in a region which is considered one of the places that was harmed by the conflict. So Juhaiman grew up in this region where sedentarization was not complete. Juhaiman's father Muhammed ibn Saif had migrated from the desert to Sajir. So Juhaiman represents the first generation to follow the settlers at that place, so there was no break with tribal loyalty. Rather, the tribe remained part of Juhaiman's core identity. Sajir was just a place to live. He never forgot that he belonged to the desert. His upbringing was shaped by the desert rather than a settled place.[1]

Al-Majallah: Was there a relationship between the sedentarized desert area to which Juhaiman belonged in Sajir and the Ikhwan?

NH: I got to know this part of the desert. In the 1970s Juhaiman introduced me to many Old Ikhwan who participated in the battle of Sabilah. They were old men. In their meetings, they told us tales of the Old Ikhwan, of jihad, and of miracles they witnessed during the jihad, as if they were part of the tales of the Pious Ancestors, like the conquests and raids carried out by the Prophet's Companions. These tales were a conspicuous part of their culture and deeply rooted in their mentality. Many of them memorized these tales.

Al-Majallah: Did these tales affect their subconscious?

NH: Yes, certainly these tales had a direct effect on them. Even in Juhaiman's later acts and stances, we noticed that he took into consideration incidents that had befallen the Old Ikhwan earlier. For instance, when Juhaiman was wanted by the Saudi security forces around 1398 AH/1977 CE, or before then, he justified his flight and refusal to surrender based on his fear of meeting the same destiny that befell the Old Ikhwan, like Sultan ibn Bijad and others.[2]

Al-Majallah: Juhaiman worked in the National Guard, and joined the Islamic University in Medina. When did he start thinking of establishing the Salafi Group?

NH: He founded the Salafi Group by 1965. He was wavering between the Tablighi Association and groups of semi-nomadic people from the remnants of the Old Ikhwan. He started his activities before 1965. After that, six men got together, the most prominent of them were Nasir ibn Husain, Sulaiman ibn al-Shtaiwi, Sa'd al-Tamimi and Juhaiman al-Utaibi. They all agreed to establish the Salafi Group. Two of them had ties to the Tablighi Association. One of them, Sulaiman al-Shtaiwi, was a Salafi and a pupil of Sheikh Nasir al-Din al-Albani, and the other was Juhaiman. Juhaiman was wavering between the Salafis and the Tablighi Association. As we know, the Tablighi Association does not focus on theology. This group rather focuses its preaching on renunciation, good manners and fair exhortation without clashing with the authorities. The six men agreed [to establish the Salafi Group].

Al-Majallah: You mentioned only four of them.

NH: Because there are two whose names I do not remember. But one of them might have died before he joined the Group and the other one broke off because he was a member of the Muslim Brotherhood. He wanted to divert the group from the Salafi course of preaching to the approach of the Muslim Brotherhood. In brief, this group went to Sheikh Abd al-Aziz ibn Baz who was in Medina at that time. They met him and told him that they wanted to establish a preaching group that would follow in the footsteps of the Pious Ancestors, combat innovations in religion, and judge by the Holy Quran and the Prophetic Tradition. Sheikh Abd al-Aziz ibn Baz asked them about the name of their group and they answered him that they chose the name, Salafi Group. He told them as long as they relied in their exhortation on God, they would call their group God-Trusting Salafi Group. Thus, the group adopted that name from that time on. The name meant that the group expected to get rewarded by God alone for their actions. And so the Group was publicly launched as an Islamic preaching group. The Group's first headquarters was a house in the area of the Eastern Harrah in Medina, which Sheikh Ibn Baz rented for them. It was a large house with a courtyard for giving lectures and lessons, in addition to many other rooms. Sheikh Abd al-Aziz ibn Baz and some sheikhs from Medina attended these lessons, including Sheikh Abu Bakr al-Jaza'iri. And so the group became Salafi, devoted solely to God. Its arguments were based entirely on sound Prophetic Traditions and following the way of the Ancestors. They called to true monotheism and combated innovations in religion, veneration of tombs, and the like. The Group had its own consultative council, which would meet and discuss the Group's affairs and plans.

Al-Majallah: How did Sheikh Muhammad Nasir al-Din al-Albani influence the Group? Did he play a role in defining the Group's program?

NH: The definition of Salafism that Sheikh al-Albani set forth became an essential part of the Group's conception of it. It is a conception based on the rejection of adherence to the legal schools, the upholding of the sound Prophetic Traditions, and the purification of the true Sunnah from weak Prophetic Traditions. Thus, true Salafi doctrine and the Salafi way of understanding monotheism became the fundamental elements for the Group. For their concept of monotheism and creed, they relied on the Salafi religious scholars, particularly the books of Sheikh Muhammad ibn Abd al-Wahhab, Sheikh Ibn Taymiyyah, Sheikh Ibn al-Qayyim, and the disciples of Sheikh Muhammad ibn Abd al-Wahhab. Their rejection of adherence to the legal schools and relying on sound Prophetic Traditions were mostly taken from the writings of Sheikh Muhammed Nasir al-Din al-Albani, and the experts in Prophetic Traditions that he trained. Hence, the Group's conception of Salafism was based on a combination of the concepts of those two schools of thought.

Al-Majallah: Seeing that the Group started out as a public group, when did it turn to secret activities and recruiting followers?

NH: The Group started as a public group because its program was based on reminding people of true Islam. At that time, there was no prohibition or law that prevented the formation of any kind of Islamic groups, as long as these groups did not infringe on major points of monotheist doctrine or form a threat to national security. As a result, there were various Islamic groups, as well as preachers who were known to be affiliated with the Muslim Brotherhood and the Salafi Group. Any underground work by the group was done on a very limited scale, such as meetings of the consultative council.

Al-Majallah: How did the secret meetings evolve during the phase of recruitment, especially at the end of 1970s? And why were there were a large number of young people from various parts of the Kingdom among the Group's followers?

NH: The Group began with a small number of followers. Most of them were students at the Islamic University and religious institutes. However, the Group started to grow. Instead of having a single house in the Eastern Harrah, the Group now had a second house, the house of the Ikhwan in Mecca. Some members of the Ikhwan moved in, mostly students at the Institute of the Grand Mosque in Mecca. After that the Ikhwan house in Riyadh was founded. I remember that the justification for the establishment of the houses was that the Ikhwan had expanded. This was before 1398 AH/1977 CE. The first house for the Ikhwan in Riyadh was founded in al-Ajliyyah behind al-Khizan Street.[4] Then they established a second house in Manfuhah beside al-Ruwail mosque.[5] A third house was established in Ghubairah on al-Qanaim Street.[6] So the Ikhwan now had three houses in Riyadh, one in Jeddah, and one in Ta'if, Mecca, and in other areas. The Ikhwan continued to grow. It now had various supporters. Some of them even considered themselves as part of the Salafi Group, while others were devoted supporters, especially since by that time, 1398 AH/1977 CE, the Group was attracting "many people" from the Tablighi and other groups to join.

Al-Majallah: But when did large numbers of followers from Asir in the south start to join the Group?

NH: This happened after 1398 AH/1977 CE, following the first arrest of Group members. A false report was submitted to the authorities claiming that the Group had an arsenal of weapons. But the government confirmed that the report was false.

Al-Majallah: Was it easy to join the Group? Were there any kinds of restrictions that prevented anyone from becoming a member?

NH: The Group had none of the restrictions that you find in other groups. It did not establish a formal hierarchy. To join the Group, one only needed to be a scholar or a seeker of knowledge, and to obey its leader—Juhaiman at that time. For the most part, these were the requirements for joining. But after Juhaiman became wanted by the security forces, the Group became more careful about screening potential members. Anyone could join the Group, but few knew its many secrets, such as the ones surrounding the publications that were printed in Kuwait. Not many members knew how these publications were printed, how they were smuggled in and out. Many of them did not know how to contact Juhaiman, the intermediaries, and so on.

Al-Majallah: You said there were four founders. How was the Group organized from its establishment to the point when Juhaiman became the leader? What were his distinctive qualities?

NH: At the beginning Juhaiman was not the leader of the Group. The Group went through several phases. At first Juhaiman was on good terms with the other four founders and the Group's consultative council, such as Ahmad Hasan al-Mu'allam and Sheikh Ali al-Mazrui, and they all agreed on certain issues. But what happened was that Juhaiman became the real leader of the Group because he was the one who came and went, worked in the tents,[7] and went on pilgrimage with the Group. He was the one who would take his GMC and go to attend prayer circles [in rural areas]. This made Juhaiman very popular. As soon as it was known that he was in town, everyone would ask about Juhaiman. By contrast, no one asked about Sulaiman al-Shtaiwi or Sa'd al-Tamimi or Nasir ibn Husain. Rather, people asked about Juhaiman. After a while, Juhaiman took control. He got the Group into trouble in ways that resulted in reprimands and surveillance by preachers.

Al-Majallah: Is it possible to say that Juhaiman had a tendency from the very beginning to become the leader of the Group?

NH: Yes, of course. Juhaiman was the informal leader even if he did not call himself that, but his authority became absolute. The reason is that Juhaiman undertook the initiative, moved about a lot, and devoted all of his time to the Group, unlike the other three founders. These three were teachers and had little time to spare for preaching. Back then, Thursday was not part of the weekend. People only had a holiday on Friday and during summer vacation. This highlights the difference between a man who devoted himself to the cause during the entire year, and men who were busy with their jobs.

Al-Majallah: The first clash between the Salafi Group and security forces occurred in 1398 AH/1977 CE. What was the nature of this clash, and how did it happen?

NH: Actually, there was no clash, but a series of arrests that included the Group's prominent figures in all parts of the kingdom. After that, Juhaiman fled.

Al-Majallah: What was the cause of the arrests?

NH: It was a false report. At the time, we heard that the man who wrote it was reprimanded because he reported that the Group had large weapons caches.

Al-Majallah: Let's move on to the main idea that Juhaiman counted on for his movement, and that is the seizure of the Grand Mosque in Mecca. Who was the source of this idea?

NH: The question of invading the Grand Mosque in Mecca is originally linked to the question of the Expected Mahdi. They invaded the Mosque because they believed in a scenario after swearing allegiance to Muhammad Abd Allah al-Mahdi.[8] They adopted the scenario from the apocalyptic books of tribulations and portents of the Last Hour. The scenario states that "The man swears allegiance at the Corner of the Mosque, and this man holds fast in the Grand Mosque, and then an army comes from Tabuk only to sink in the earth. Then this man comes out of the Grand Mosque, travels to Medina and fights the Antichrist. Later on, he leaves Medina and travels to Palestine and fights the Jews there and kills them. Jesus Christ then comes back to break the cross and kill the swine. Afterwards, they will go to Syria and pray at the Umayyad

Mosque and then the Resurrection will occur."[9] This is the scenario of the Group according to the books of tribulations and portents of the Last Hour. They believed that they would remain in the Grand Mosque, then the army would sink in the earth, and then they would go out. But as it turned out, after three days, it became clear that the Mahdi was killed in the Grand Mosque. Juhaiman refused to believe that the Mahdi was killed, and refused to declare that the Mahdi was killed. He forced the Group to deny his killing. He ostracized and poured his wrath on those who said the Mahdi was killed. He also said that the Mahdi could not be killed, but was only trapped inside the Grand Mosque and would eventually come out. Of course, this was a salvationist vision that evidently occurred to them because of their obsession with the idea of salvation through the Mahdi.

Al-Majallah: Can we say that the Group was primarily obsessed, motivated, and impelled by a metaphysical or obscurantist idea of salvation?

NH: This is an accurate analysis. It is true because this Group did not have a project for an Islamic state, as we find in groups such as the Muslim Brotherhood or the [Islamic] Liberation Party. This group had nothing but the issue of the Mahdi rooted in their mentalities. They thought that the nation's salvation would come through the Mahdi, not through establishing a state or any other means.

Al-Majallah: You did not join the invasion of the Grand Mosque in Mecca even though you were with the Salafi Group?

NH: Six months[10] before the invasion of the Grand Mosque and swearing allegiance to the Mahdi, the Group split; some members were not convinced that Muhammed Abd Allah al-Qahtani was the Mahdi and did not believe in carrying arms inside the Grand Mosque. I was among the members who were not convinced of invading the Mosque.

Al-Majallah: This means that the idea emerged six months before storming the Grand Mosque?

NH: The idea of Muhammad Abd Allah al-Qahtani was discussed about a year before storming the Grand Mosque. It was based on the belief of some that Muhammad Abd Allah al-Qahtani was the Expected Mahdi, because his name was Muhammad Abd Allah al-Qahtani, which matched the portents mentioned in the religious texts that say that his name and his father's name must match those of Prophet Muhammad (peace and blessings upon him). He also had a prominent nose and a broad forehead and was a descendant of the Prophet's family. Based on these portents, it was said that Muhammad Abd Allah al-Qahtani was the Mahdi. Things continued like this until six months before they invaded the Grand Mosque, and then the schism took place. As a result, we announced that we did not believe in the Mahdi cause and taking weapons into the Grand Mosque.

Al-Majallah: You mentioned at the beginning of the interview that there was a man from the Muslim Brotherhood who withdrew from the initiative to establish the Group. What is the relationship between the Salafi Group and other Islamic movements?

NH: In his essay *Removing Confusion*, Juhaiman tried to explain his attitude towards these groups. In fact, when we look at this attitude, we find that it is relatively naïve. He opposed the Muslim Brotherhood because of their interest in politics, and blamed the Tablighi Association because of their lack of interest in preaching for monotheism. The same goes for their attitude toward other groups. They criticize the Muslim Brotherhood for their secrecy, but the truth is that their secrecy is about the same as that of the Salafi Group.

Al-Majallah: In the final analysis, was Juhaiman a rebellious personality, a religious utopian, or both?

NH: Juhaiman combined the two qualities, the rebellious and the utopian character. Juhaiman acted out of vindictiveness, influenced by what had happened to the Ikhwan at Sabilah. As a matter of fact, Juhaiman often repeated that the Ikhwan at Sabilah were wronged and killed. He considered them martyrs. This was his attitude and he often repeated it. So I believe that Juhaiman developed the rebellious and vindictive attitude early in life, but he needed a legitimate reason for the Group to accept this vengeance.

Al-Majallah: But what was Juhaiman's attitude towards the society he lived in, and towards the state? Did he accuse it of apostasy? Did he coexist with it, or did he isolate himself?

NH: Juhaiman did not reconcile with his society for several reasons: his character was originally nomadic but society in general was moving towards settled life while the nomadic character of Juhaiman rebelled against this aspect. Moreover, Juhaiman believed that this society was showing portents that the Last Hour was looming. Juhaiman believed that tribulations were afflicting all of society. Juhaiman specified evil temptations in the *Essay on Tribulations and Portents of the Last Hour*: banknotes that have images, television, etc. These evil temptations were widespread, and accordingly he developed a negative attitude towards the society and the state. In addition, Juhaiman opposed working for the government and believed a government job would prevent you from speaking the truth. He believed that as long as one took a salary from the state, one would not be able to confront it with the truth.

Al-Majallah: Is it possible to say that Juhaiman was an intellectual extension of the nomadic group of Ikhwan in Obedience to God?[11] Or did he follow a different path?

NH: Juhaiman was essentially an intellectual extension of the Old Ikhwan, with some additions. If you read the literature of the Ikhwan on questions of monotheism and doctrine, you will find it is the same as the literature of the Ikhwan in Obedience to God, but with the addition of new issues. These issues included the Sunnah, verifying and discrediting Prophetic Traditions, taking strong and weak Prophetic Traditions, and repudiating adherence to the legal schools. Some think that there is a connection between the modern takfiri and jihadist groups that have arisen recently on one hand and Juhaiman's movement on the other. They say that today's groups are the descendants of Juhaiman. In general, we cannot say that today's groups are an extension of Juhaiman's thinking for a number of reasons. The most important one is that Juhaiman's thought is based on spiritual salvation and does not have a project for establishing a state. If you look at Juhaiman's essays, you will find him talking about how the Mahdi will establish a government of justice, but where are the details? There are none, unlike current groups such as al-Qaeda: they talk about establishing a state and the stages they would go through. They create chaos to force the other side to recognize their right to establish a state. However, they do not have a plan for this state. I do not believe that the current groups, especially the jihadist or takfiri ones are completely like Juhaiman's group. I always say that Juhaiman's influence on the groups that came after him was temporary.

Al-Majallah: After the arrest and execution of Juhaiman, are there any people who still believe in the idea of salvation? Or did it end with the demise of Juhaiman?

NH: The idea of salvation in general ended as soon as the Mahdi was killed. But some people are fanatical in their belief in the Mahdi. Until now, we mock two former members of the Group who believed the Mahdi was not killed but managed to escape and lives in the mountains of Yemen. But this kind of thinking is naive, especially after the incident at the Grand Mosque.

Al-Majallah: What do you think of the attack on the Grand Mosque?

NH: There was universal consensus to condemn the attack because it happened in the most sacred place for Muslims. The attack occurred during the sacred month of Muharram, in the sacred city of Mecca, and resulted in the shedding of Muslim blood, which is forbidden. The attack was so hideous that everyone condemned it, even many of the Islamic groups. No Islamic group issued a statement to support the attack on the Grand Mosque.

Appendix IV

INTERVIEW WITH NASIR AL-HUZAIMI, BY BADR AL-RASHID

Juhaiman, the Salafi Group, and the attack on the Grand Mosque remain subjects of public interest. Indeed, the attack will not fade into history as long as many details remain hidden and researchers misunderstand so much about it, especially the connection between the attack on the Grand Mosque and the Salafi Group's ideas on one hand, and the connection to political Islamic movements and local jihadist movements that subsequently appeared on the other. In this interview, we shed light on some points that Nasir al-Huzaimi discussed in his recollections of the attack on the Grand Mosque and that we think need discussion in greater detail.

BR: What happened in the Breaking Pictures Incident in Medina, who carried it out, and what were its effects?

NH: The Breaking Pictures Incident took place in 1965. I do not have complete information about the incident but what I know is that it involved a number of students from the Islamic University who were also attending lessons at the Prophet's mosque on preaching, warning, and guiding [to Islam]. A group of these students left the Medina mosque and broke some mannequins on display in store windows and several photographs. This trouble resulted in Abd al-Rahman Abd al-Khaliq and Abd al-Rahman Abd al-Samad losing Saudi citizenship, and their expulsion to Kuwait. Others charged in the incident included Sheikh Muhammad Abd al-Wahhab al-Banna, although it later became evident that he was in Jeddah at the time. Since the sheikh was barred from residing in Medina thereafter, he settled in Jeddah.

I mention the Incident because when I later asked Juhaiman about the date of the Salafi Group's establishment, he told me that it was established after the Breaking Pictures Incident in Medina because there was no Salafi mission around which youth could rally and preach in the mosques except for the Tablighi Association, but there were some reservations about it because it did not call to doctrine and so forth. So some youths gathered for the sake of preaching the Salafi mission.

BR: Did Juhaiman harbor enmity toward the government ever since the establishment of the Group in 1965?

NH: No, Juhaiman used to work as a truck driver in the National Guard. He was still a government employee. For Juhaiman, the question of the state was inherited from the battle of Sabilah. He would repeat the phrases, "The killing of the Ikhwan at Sabilah," and "the martyrs of Sabilah." But that was not the motive for establishing the Salafi Group. Rather, when they went to Sheikh Abd al-Aziz ibn Baz, they told him that they wanted to call to the Quran, the Sunnah, and true Salafi doctrine, which the Tablighi Association and the Muslim Brotherhood neglected.

BR: Is there a relationship between the Salafi tendency in Kuwait and the Salafi Group?

NH: The Salafi Group in Kuwait avoided contact with the [Saudi] Salafi Group because the latter had taken a crude, rigid character opposed to modernization.

BR: What kind of scenario did Juhaiman follow in his preaching tours to villages and Bedouin settlements? What did he preach to their residents and how did they respond?

NH: His sermons were in the nature of warnings and guidance, adapted to the particular place he was visiting. They included innovations when he was at a place where they were found, or the issue of adhering to the Quran and the Sunnah. Usually, after prayer, there would be a session for fatwas and Juhaiman would issue fatwas to the villagers and inhabitants of Bedouin settlements, especially since he was familiar with the kinds of legal issues that the simple people in those places would raise.

BR: What was the tribal and regional composition of the Salafi Group?

NH: The Salafi Group was made up of different social elements. Members included Bedouin, city folk from Jeddah and Mecca, and individuals from the environs of Medina. In that regard, the Group was heterogeneous, but the Bedouin aspect was the most prominent element, and that of the settled Bedouin in particular. The city folk generally went along with that perspective.

BR: In your discussion of competition among the religious groups, you point to a struggle between the Qutbists, the Bannaists, and the Tablighis. Did study with the traditional Salafi ulama not have any attraction for young people?

NH: At that time, political Islam was dominant whereas scholastic books and writings were very rare.

At that time, Muslim Brotherhood books were essentially the axis of the Islamic movement. There were many writings about Muslim suffering and the enemies of Islam, especially modern groups and tendencies, such as communism, socialism, and nationalism. Books about religious law tended to deal with issues such as prayer, like Sheikh Nasir al-Din al-Albani's book, *The Prophet's Prayer*. Back then, there were not books along the lines of a Salafi perspective that dealt with contemporary issues except for some books that came out against Sufism, the legal schools, and refutations of the author al-Kawthari.¹ Those books were few and limited in scope. They did not appeal to most religious students.

The debate between the Salafis and the Muslim Brothers was over the crises and attacks afflicting the Islamic world. The Salafis wrote refutations of Sufism, Mutazilites,² Jahmites,³ and other groups that did not even exist anymore. But the Salafis replied to the Muslim Brothers that they were obsessed with politics and neglected the task of correcting doctrine and safeguarding monotheism.

BR: You indicated that there were discussions between Juhaiman and some members of the Excommunication and Emigration Group and Ansar al-Sunnah, and that they influenced his thinking. Did the toleration of the dominant group in the Ikhwan's House for pious folk from outside the Salafi Group result in their being influenced by those other groups?

NH: In the late 1970s, young people from Egypt generally followed the Islamic Group. Some of them belonged to the Excommunication and Emigration Group or the Jihad Group. The Salafi Group had a kind of flexibility and patience in dealing with them, hoping that God would favor them with guidance through dialogue. They sympathized with them and gave them places to lodge and work, based on the idea that they had a point of view and that there was an opportunity to cooperate with them.

BR: What is your understanding of the interference of traditional Hanbali Najdi legal scholars with the Zahiri legal school taught by Sheikh Badi and Sheikh al-Mazrui and with the Prophetic Tradition Folk represented by Sheikh al-Albani, and the relationship of this interference with the Salafi Group?

NH: Since their initial appearance in history until today, the Prophetic Tradition Folk and the Salafis have very similar literal discourses.⁴ All of the groups you mention depend on the surface of the text, with minor differences. The literal view is evident in Salafis from early times. It was emphasized most of all on doctrinal issues. Then it was applied to legal issues, as in the case of the Zahiri legal school for example. They [Zahiri jurists and Salafis] coexisted and coordinated efforts. The alliance between Hanbali commoners and some Zahiris like Abu Bakr Muhammad ibn Daud was unusual.⁵ Muhammad ibn Daud incited Hanbali commoners against Ibn Jarir al-Tabari because they believed in literal reading of texts.⁶ There was coexistence and implicit agreement on the premises of the Zahiri legal school with the Salafi Group and the potential for cooperation on the grounds that it was the way of the Prophetic Tradition Folk. Ibn Hazm basically called for the same thing as the Salafi Group in terms of literal reading of the text in the Quran and the Prophetic Tradition and rejecting adherence to legal schools, with minor differences over some unusual Zahiri legal positions that not all Salafis accept.

The Salafi Group is in accord with those who apply a literal reading of texts to matters of doctrine. For instance, they were in accord with Ansar al-Sunnah even though they are practically ignorant of Prophetic Tradition sciences because their emphasis is on doctrine.

BR: Arab and Western interpretations of the occupation of the Grand Mosque have multiplied. Some interpret it in terms of resistance to the marginalization of tribesmen while others interpret it in the context of the Ikhwan in Obedience to God. What do you think of these interpretations?

NH: This movement was very unusual indeed. It was called a millenarian protest in the sense that this movement bore arms and gave the oath of allegiance to the Mahdi between the Yemeni Corner and the Station of Abraham, as if we were at the end of history and the appearance of the Mahdi were inevitable—when the oath was given to him, it was inevitable that an army from Tabuk would be sent against this group and would sink in the earth en route. Then some soldiers would join the movement and together they would leave the Grand Mosque and go to Medina. Then the Antichrist would appear and they would fight him, then they would fight the Jews in Palestine, then they would go to the Damascus Mosque in Syria, and Jesus the son of Mary would come down and pray behind the Mahdi.

This vision is found in Prophetic Traditions about tribulations and apocalyptic portents. They gambled, especially Juhaiman, on this scenario. For this reason, there is nothing in Juhaiman's essays like a manifesto or plan for the Group. There was no plan to set up a state or to set up something to command good and forbid evil because they had a course of action from the Prophetic Traditions. This refutes the idea of leftist or Arab nationalist influence, or the idea that they were an extension of the Ikhwan in Obedience to God.

It is possible that the Sabilah battle was a driving force for this outcome, but the outcome and the invasion of the Grand Mosque themselves drew on the apocalyptic scenario. We must understand it in that context. What makes the influence of Sabilah likely is Juhaiman's words in the essay on *Rulership and the Oath of Allegiance* where he talked about his lack of trust in the government because it killed the Ikhwan in Obedience to God at Sabilah, and about how the Ikhwan obeyed God in truth because they wanted to wage jihad against the infidels and the idolaters in Iraq and against the Christians. They wanted to continue jihad and go to Iraq to destroy tombs and graves.

BR: Did Juhaiman have ideas about sovereignty from the beginning?

NH: Juhaiman did not have a well-developed concept about sovereignty. His idea of sovereignty was essentially messianic. I mean that Juhaiman did not address the question of excommunicating the ruler. Instead he addressed the issue of allowing rebellion against the ruler without excommunicating him.

BR: Do we see the idea of messianic sovereignty in other movements, given that most Sunnis believe in the idea of the apocalypse?

NH: I don't know that there have been movements in history that drew their agenda from the books of tribulations and apocalyptic portents except for some groups and states that were established on the basis of the call to the Mahdi, but not with this precise scenario where the Prophetic Traditions about tribulations are the basis for a sequence of steps.

BR: What issues did Juhaiman discuss with members in Mecca at the beginning of your connection with them in 1976?

NH: The most important thing was literal adherence to the Sunnah and acting according to it. I don't know of any members who were concerned with law. Their acquaintance with law was scanty, practically non-existent. I don't recall that anybody owned any important law books except for Sheikh Ali al-Mazrui who studied law and owned the major books like Ibn Hazm's book on religious law, a work on Hanbali law,[7] and some other books. As for the rest, they worked on guidance and manners and seeking to obtain Traditions of the Prophet and their proofs, to the extent that one time they were convinced that it was obligatory for a Muslim to pray in sandals in a mosque at least once in his lifetime. They went to the Grand Mosque and prayed in their sandals, which led to problems with others who frequented the Grand Mosque and condemned their behavior. They did not care about the reactions of other people, or change, or questions of general interest and religious politics.

In *Removing Confusion about the Religion of Abraham*, Juhaiman wrote that the basis of the call to Abraham's religion was to urge public declaration and confrontation with opponents, and proclaiming what you think is true. And if you believe in destroying prayer niches in mosques or wearing sandals to prayer, then you must practice it with conviction and have no shame before any who oppose you.

BR: Isn't this idea also held by agents of the Committee for Commanding Right and Forbidding Wrong and others who try to prohibit what is prohibited, not just the Salafi Group?

NH: No. In general, the approach was to be firm and balanced.[8] Many ulama adopted the principle of acting in a way that is firm and balanced. They spoke to people in a reasonable way and they took account of public welfare in many matters But the Salafi Group understood public welfare to mean what the Prophet carried out whereas we understand public welfare to mean what the Companions understood during the time of the Prophet.

BR: You wrote that you yearned to see Juhaiman because of what you had heard about him before your first meeting with him during the pilgrimage. How did this desire to see Juhaiman begin? What was your first impression of him at that time?

NH: I was not the only one to have this experience. Many parties, groups, and missions have discovered this method—they discovered how to create a symbolic figure based on reputation and how to cultivate this symbolic figure.

I was sitting with Abd Allah al-Harbi and he told me about Juhaiman as if he were a legend, as if you were going to see one of the Companions. Hamid al-Ahmadi used the same method with me. This method affects the creation of symbolic figures for young people. This way of making symbolic figures through reputation is still with us.

BR: What kinds of myths about Juhaiman did al-Harbi and al-Ahmadi try to impart to you?

NH: His manners, his conduct, his memory, his understanding. It was as if you were expecting to see one of the Companions.

BR: How did Juhaiman foster these myths when he had not finished his education and he could not speak classical Arabic?

NH: This kind of person is talented by nature because he has a unique charisma that is based entirely on his personality. It has nothing to do with any kind of diploma or material things. Juhaiman invaded the Grand Mosque with holders of doctoral and master's degrees and medical doctors. What happened to their rational capacity to distinguish true from false?

BR: How were the writings smuggled from Kuwait? Who was in charge of smuggling them?

NH: Abd al-Latif al-Dirbas is the one who smuggled the writings. He is a Kuwaiti who was angry at the [Kuwaiti] Salafis because they did not represent the true spirit of the Salafis in austere lifestyle and simplicity and so forth.

When the Ikhwan decided to print the essays, he was the one who took charge. He had torn up all of his identity papers with photographs. He would come and go from Kuwait, so he was very familiar with people on the route to Kuwait. *Removing Confusion about the Religion of Abraham* was printed in Kuwait because the Ikhwan expected they would not receive permission to print it in Saudi Arabia because publishing required a permit. They assumed that because Juhaiman's name was on it, they would not be able to have it printed. After printing *Removing Confusion*, all the essays were printed in Kuwait and Dirbas took charge of smuggling them.

BR: Do you have any idea about a meeting that reportedly took place between the Kuwaiti writer Abd Allah al-Nafisi and Juhaiman?

NH: This is according to Abd al-Latif al-Dirbas and Abd al-Aziz al-Sadhan. Sadhan was detained with al-Nafisi under the same legal proceeding [for meeting with Juhaiman]. Abd Allah al-Nafisi wanted to see Juhaiman back then. At the time, he was banned from travel and his passport withdrawn, I think for writing the book *Kuwait: An Alternative Perspective*. They rode in some pickup trucks with Abd al-Latif al-Dirbas. Apparently, they were under surveillance because this was not their first trip. Rather, it took place when stricter control was imposed on the border in response to the distribution of the essays during Ramadan and after the printing of Juhaiman's *Four Essays*. At that time, al-Nafisi was arrested and taken to al-Dammam, and then either Kuwait or his uncle's family asked for him, and he returned to Kuwait. It seems that he was permitted to travel some time later.

BR: Why did the government issue a warrant to arrest Juhaiman al-Utaibi for the first time?

NH: It seems the cause was a false report from one of the Ikhwan's enemies suggesting that the Ikhwan had arsenals of weapons and that they were training with weapons. Based on that report, the first arrest took place. Because of that arrest, Juhaiman fled.

BR: What happened when the schism took place and Juhaiman left with most of the members?

NH: When Juhaiman became the de facto leader, there was no more oversight of the direction he took. Practically everyone who could have stopped his momentum left, especially the original founders of the Group. Juhaiman became certain of his path in confronting the government and declaring his opinion on political and legal issues.

BR: Why did you go back to Riyadh after the first arrest when you were not a wanted man?

NH: The Ikwan House in Medina came under the direction of Sheikh Abu Bakr al-Jaza'iri. I was considered one of Juhaiman's followers. I had nothing left in Medina.

BR: Did the Group have an organized presence in Riyadh?

NH: Yes. They had two houses. One was close to the Ruwail Mosque, and it was the main house. That was the mosque where Muhammad ibn Abd Allah al-Qahtani would preach. The other house was near al-Ud.[9]

BR: What influence did the Salafi Group have on social life in Mecca, Medina, and Riyadh?

NH: It had no influence on social life at that time. In the Eastern Harrah in Medina, they were essentially in a state of isolation. They comprised a separate society unto themselves. The Eastern Harrah at that time was an undeveloped area—only recently did it get very basic electricity service. The Eastern Harrah at that time was on the edge of Medina.

BR: When did the issue of Muhammad al-Qahtani's mahdiship first arise and how was it discussed?

NH: I don't know who the first person was to propose it, but I know that it was early on. Most of the young men at the Ruwail Mosque were talking about al-Qahtani's mahdiship. I heard about it from his brother Sa'd. He told me in a joking manner that "the Mahdi's portents are evident in Abd Allah."[10] At the time, I did not take him seriously. This conversation was in 1978. Acting on the issue in a bigger sense took place in 1979. The first time Sa'd told me about it, he was laughing and I took it as a joke.

BR: Did Juhaiman respond to particular ulama in his essays?

NH: No. Instead, he advanced a general discourse without intending to address anyone in particular. Yet it is well known that he intended the ulama who work for the government, the sheikhs inside official institutions.

BR: What scholastic method did Juhaiman apply to religious texts?

NH: If we read Juhaiman's texts, we would see that they do not use a method. Rather his way of dealing with texts is a literalist reading of the surface of the text. It does not require any complexity. When reading Juhaiman's texts, you find them devoid of law, devoid of the opinions of experts in law other than some opinions of Ibn Taymiyyah and Ibn al-Qayyim. I do not consider any of the literalist groups to possess a method because [in their view] the text speaks for itself.

BR: Where did you see the texts of Juhaiman's essays?

NH: I was able to get the texts that Rif'at Sayyid Ahmad collected. It is a deficient book because he made a lot of mistakes in the Introduction and he ascribed to Juhaiman some pieces that he did not write. He did not describe the most important essay, *Removing Confusion*. He was confused about it.

BR: What members of the Salafi Group besides Juhaiman wrote essays?

NH: Among those who wrote essays and pamphlets and who wrote their names on them were Abd al-Muhsin al-Wahidi. Muhammad Abd Allah al-Qahtani has an essay and a poem.

BR: Did Juhaiman undergo any intellectual development during your relationship with him?

NH: There are two points that Juhaiman held from the beginning and before the first arrest.

The first is that he was attached to dreams—the idea that they are a part of prophecy and the idea that one should act in response to dreams. The second point is that he believed from the start, before I knew him even, that we were at the End of Time. This issue preoccupied Juhaiman from the start. The end of the world had to come. That is why, at times, dreams had the power of sacred scripture with the Salafi Group. As for the pivotal change in Juhaiman, it occurred when he became isolated as a result of his becoming a fugitive. It shifted his mentality to the idea of invading the Grand Mosque for salvation. He became convinced that Muhammad ibn Abd Allah al-Qahtani was the Mahdi and that it was necessary to bring about salvation.

BR: Why did Juhaiman reject the ideas of Mustafa Shukri and the Excommunication and Emigration Group?

NH: Juhaiman was afraid the [Salafi] Group would be accused of following the Kharijites because the Ikhwan in Obedience to God were accused of adopting Kharijite ideas. When some Egyptians belonging to the Excommunication and Emigration Group came to Medina, some of them were able to persuade Faisal Muhammad Faisal to adopt their idea about unbelief. Juhaiman spoke to Sheikh al-Albani about this idea, especially concerning Faisal and Isam Sheikh. Albani made Faisal aware of different degrees of unbelief and taught him that Ibn Taymiyyah held that position, and directed him to Ibn Taymiyyah's *Book of Faith*. Juhaiman and Yusuf Akbar were at this meeting. Yusuf recorded the meeting but Juhaiman destroyed the tape, fearing it might fall into the wrong hands and the Group would be accused of being Kharijites. As a result of the meeting, Isam Sheikh and Faisal Muhammad Faisal gave up these ideas.

BR: Why did the government sheikhs pay so much attention to Sheikh Ali al-Mazrui's rejection of adherence to the legal schools and opinions of the Companions on certain issues when it was Juhaiman's role that had a pivotal impact on most of the Ikhwan?

NH: Sheikh Ali al-Mazrui used to discuss these issues at the Grand Mosque. The Grand Mosque administration heard about this from someone. The Ikhwan adopted the position on rejecting adherence to the legal schools and following precedent and accepting the opinion of some Companions on legal issues and limiting reliance to the Book and the Sunnah. That all happened before Sheikh al-Mazrui. This issue was part of the debate with adherents to the legal schools.

BR: Why did Juhaiman not meet with Sheikh Abu Bakr al-Jaza'iri shortly before the schism in the Group?

NH: I attended that meeting. Ahmad al-Mu'allam and Nasir ibn Husain also attended it. They were members of the Group's consultative council. Sheikh Abu Bakr al-Jaza'iri and some other sheikhs from the Grand Mosque and the Islamic University attended as well. Juhaiman had old differences with Sheikh Abu Bakr al-Jaza'iri about several issues that Sheikh al-Jaza'iri discussed with the Group at the meeting. Juhaiman thought that the issues were settled as far as he was concerned. He knew Sheikh Abu Bakr al-Jaza'iri's views about them and felt that a conversation with him would not change anything. In addition, Juhaiman thought that the Sheikh was concerned about retaining his Saudi citizenship and did not want to cause problems for him. As a result of Juhaiman's differences with Sheikh Abu Bakr al-Jaza'iri, Ahmad al-Zamil had broken up a partnership in a bakery with the sheikh.

BR: How did Sheikh Abd al-Aziz al-Najdi explain the change that overtook his friend in religious studies Abd Allah al-Qusaimi?

NH: Sheikh Abd al-Aziz ibn Rashid thinks that the reason Abd Allah al-Qusaimi changed from a Wahhabi to someone who mocked religion was the debate that took place between him and the Azhar sheikhs. It was a sharp debate that took up matters which Sheikh Ibn Rashid thinks al-Qusaimi was not prepared to confront effectively. Ibn Rashid thinks that the Azhar sheikhs were the reason for al-Qusaimi's turn away from religion because they caused him to doubt [his religious beliefs] in a way he could not shake off.

BR: At the time that Khalid al-Yami was giving the sermon at the Grand Mosque and called for people to give the oath of allegiance to the Mahdi Muhammad ibn Abd Allah al-Qahtani, did anybody outside the Salafi Group at the Grand Mosque give the oath of allegiance?

NH: I do not know exactly. There was a group of commoners to whom Nur al-Din, the son of Sheikh Badi al-Din, was preaching in Urdu because they were Pakistanis. While he was preaching to them that he was the Mahdi, they were delirious with joy over the Mahdi. The rest of the ordinary people did not get embroiled in the issue and did not give the oath of allegiance.

BR: Was there a military leader during the occupation of the Grand Mosque other than Juhaiman?

NH: I don't think they planned anything like that. Apparently, the plan was in Juhaiman's head, especially since they did not expect the situation to last long. In their view, it would take no more than three days. They did not expect it to go on for fifteen days. Juhaiman was calling out the names of members of the Salafi Group but they did not answer. Some of them were in prison. Others were not able to be part of the invasion of the Grand Mosque. This indicates that Juhaiman did not have complete information about which members of the Group were there with him.

NOTES

Introduction to the English Edition

1 An exact figure for the rebel band has not been established. Estimates range from three hundred to five hundred.
2 "Salafi" refers to Muslims who believe that through the ages Muslims deviated from Islam in its original form and who seek its restoration.
3 That has become the standard assessment of the uprising's impact. Nabil Mouline, *The Clerics of Islam: Religious Authority and Political Power in Saudi Arabia*, translated by Ethan S. Rundell, Yale University Press, 2014, pp. 212–13. Madawi al-Rasheed, *A Most Masculine State*, Cambridge University Press, 2013, pp. 108–10. James Buchan, however, describes steps to restrict Western influence in 1978 and early 1979. "The Return of the Ikhwan," in David Holden and Richard Johns, eds., *The House of Saud: The Rise and Rule of the Most Powerful Dynasty in the Arab World*, Holt, Rinehart, and Winston, 1982 p. 519.
4 Joseph Kechichian provided the first meticulous study of Juhaiman's writings: "Islamic Revivalism and Change in Saudi Arabia: Juhayman al-'Utaybi's 'Letters' to the Saudi People," *Muslim World* 80:1 (1990), 1–16. Stephane Lacroix and Thomas Hegghammer were the first scholars to use interviews with Huzaimi and other Saudis familiar with Juhaiman's group. Their article places the Salafi Group and Juhaiman in the context of religious tendencies in Saudi Arabia by examining the Salafi Group's brief history, its members' social backgrounds, and the traces of Juhaiman's movement in Saudi Arabia's religious landscape up to the early 2000s. 'Rejectionist Islamism in Saudi Arabia: The Story of Juhayman al-'Utaybi Revisited," *International Journal of Middle East Studies* 39:1 (2007), 103–22. Yaroslav Trofimov offers the most complete account of the uprising based on interviews with Saudi government officials and Saudis familiar with the Salafi Group. *The Siege of Mecca: The Forgotten Uprising in Islam's Holiest Shrine and the Birth of Al-Qaeda*, Doubleday, 2007. Compared to other accounts, Huzaimi's memoir emphasizes religious factors more than politics in explaining tensions between Juhaiman's faction and the Saudi authorities that led to the uprising.
5 Ervand Abrahamian, *A History of Modern Iran*, Cambridge University Press, 2018, is an excellent introduction to the revolution and its historical background.
6 James Bill, *The Eagle and the Lion: The Tragedy of American-Iranian Relations*, Yale University Press, 1989, p. 233. Bill's book surveys relations between the United States and Iran from the early 1900s to the early years of the Islamic Republic.
7 William B. Quandt, *Peace Process: American Diplomacy and the Arab-Israeli Conflict since 1967*, Brookings Institution, 2005, gives an expert's first-person insights into the Camp David Accords and the Egyptian-Israeli peace treaty.
8 One difference between the Salafi Group and other Islamic groups was the former's indifference toward the Palestinian issue.
9 Trofimov's *The Siege of Mecca* provides the most detailed account of the uprising.

10 Trofimov, *The Siege of Mecca*, pp. 104–16, 142–4, 202–6.
11 Toby Craig Jones, "Rebellion on the Saudi Periphery: Modernity, Marginalization, and the Shi'a Uprising of 1979," *International Journal of Middle East Studies* 38:2 (2006), 213–33.
12 Some details about the precise role of the French advisers remain unclear, particularly whether they directed the assault from a nearby town outside the zone forbidden to non-Muslims or undertook a nominal conversion to Islam and entered Mecca.
13 Trofimov, *The Siege of Mecca*, pp. 224–5. Some estimates of the death count run to a thousand or more. About 170 militants surrendered.
14 Steve Coll, *Ghost Wars: The Secret History of the CIA, Afghanistan, and Bin Laden, from the Soviet Invasion to September 10, 2001*, Penguin, 2004.
15 Two introductory texts on Islam that discuss the topics in this section are Frederick Denny, *An Introduction to Islam*, 4th ed., Pearson Hall, 2011, and Jonathan P. Berkey, *The Formation of Islam: Religion and Society in the Near East, 600 to 1800*, Cambridge University Press, 2003.
16 Medina is short for *Madinat al-Nabi*, the City of the Prophet.
17 The common English translation for jihad is holy war.
18 The Quran, Surat al-Hijr, al-Hijr 15:1.
19 The Quran, Surat al-Zukhruf, Ornaments of Gold, 43:2–3.
20 On the early history of hadith literature and hadith scholars, J. Robson, "Hadith," *Encyclopaedia of Islam*, 2nd ed., Brill, 2006.
21 Technically, a hadith may originate with someone who knew the Prophet and not the Prophet himself.
22 Wilferd Madelung, "'Abd Allah B. Al-Zubayr and the Mahdi," *Journal of Near Eastern Studies* 40:4, Arabic and Islamic Studies in Honor of Nabia Abbott: Part Two (October 1981), 291–305; hadith cited from p. 294.
23 J. Robson, "al-Bukhari, Muhammad b. Isma'il," *Encyclopaedia of Islam*, 2nd ed., Brill, 2006; G. H. A. Juynboll, "Muslim b. al-Hadjdjadj," *Encyclopaedia of Islam*, 2nd ed., Brill, 2006; A. J. Wensinck, "al-Nasa'i," *Encyclopaedia of Islam*, 2nd ed., Brill, 2006; J. Robson, "Abu Da'ud al-Sidjistani," *Encyclopaedia of Islam*, 2nd ed., Brill, 2006; G. H. A. Juynboll, "al-Tirmidhi," *Encyclopaedia of Islam*, 2nd ed., Brill, 2006; J. W. Fück, "Ibn Madja," *Encyclopaedia of Islam*, 2nd ed., Brill, 2006.
24 For an overview of apocalyptic thought and Mahdist movements in Islam from early times to the present, Jean-Pierre Filiu, *Apocalypse in Islam*, University of California Press, 2011.
25 Vernon O. Egger, *A History of the Muslim World to 1750: The Making of a Civilization*, 2nd ed., Routledge, 2017, pp. 65–71. The word "Shiism" comes from the Arabic phrase *Shi'at Ali*, or partisans of Ali.
26 On the second civil war, Egger, *A History of the Muslim World to 1750*, pp. 73–4; Filiu, *Apocalypse in Islam*, pp. 8–10.
27 Madelung, "'Abd Allah B. Al-Zubayr and the Mahdi;" Filiu, *Apocalypse in Islam*, pp. 9–10, 12, 21–2.
28 The grandson's name was Muhammad ibn al-Hanafiyyah.
29 F. E. Peters, *Mecca: A Literary History of the Muslim Holy Land*, Princeton University Press, 1994, pp. 98–101.
30 Abu Daud, *Kitab al-sunan*, Book 31, Number 4272.
31 Filiu, *Apocalypse in Islam*, pp. 12–13, 45, 64, 69; W. Madelung, "al-Mahdi," *Encyclopaedia of Islam*, 2nd ed., Brill, 2006.
32 W. Madelung, "Karmati," *Encyclopaedia of Islam*, 2nd ed., Brill, 2006.

33 For a general history of the Wahhabi mission, David Commins, *The Mission and the Kingdom: Wahhabi Power behind the Saudi Throne*, rev. paperback ed., I.B. Tauris, 2016. For a study of its founder, Michael Crawford, *Ibn Abd al-Wahhab*, One World, 2014.
34 For a comprehensive history of Saudi Arabia, Alexei Vassiliev, *The History of Saudi Arabia*, New York University Press, 2000. For a concise work, Madawi al-Rasheed, *A History of Saudi Arabia*, 2nd ed., Cambridge University Press, 2010.
35 Sunni opponents included scholars from the same Hanbali legal tradition that Ibn Abd al-Wahhab followed.
36 Abdulaziz Al-Fahad, "From Exclusivism to Accommodation: Doctrinal and Legal Evolution of Wahhabism," *New York University Law Review* 79:2 (2004), 485–519.
37 John S. Habib, *Ibn Sa'ud's Warriors of Islam: The Ikhwan of Najd and Their Role in the Creation of the Sa'udi Kingdom, 1910–1930*, Brill, 1978.
38 *Salaf* refers to early generations of Muslims. *Salafi* refers to a Muslim seeking to follow the early generations. The best introduction to Salafism is Bernard Haykel, "On the Nature of Salafi Thought and Action," in Roel Meijer, ed., *Global Salafism: Islam's New Religious Movement*, Columbia University Press, 2009, pp. 33–57.
39 David Commins, "Modernism," in John Esposito, ed., *The Oxford Encyclopedia of the Modern Islamic World. Oxford Islamic Studies Online*, http://www.oxfordislamicstudies.com/article/opr/t236MIW/e0539 (accessed June 28, 2020).
40 J. Robson, "Bid'a," *Encyclopaedia of Islam*, 2nd ed., Brill, 2006.
41 For discussion of grassroots religious movements and their differences with Wahhabism, Commins, *The Mission and the Kingdom*, pp. 130–45.
42 Vassiliev, *The History of Saudi Arabia*, p. 425.
43 Stephen D. Hayes, "Riyadh on the Move," *Aramco World* (July/August 1980), 26–33.
44 James Larocco Interview, "Rich and Eager to Buy—Saudi Arabia in the Oil Boom '70s," Moments in US Diplomatic History. Online: https://adst.org/2016/04/smelly-rich-and-eager-to-buy-saudi-arabia-in-the-oil-boom-70s/ (accessed June 26, 2020).
45 Thomas Ferris, "Riding the Saudi Boom," *New York Times*, March 25, 1979.
46 Holden and Johns, *The House of Saud*, p. 169.
47 See discussion of the Committees in the following section.
48 Holden and Johns, *The House of Saud*, pp. 260–2.
49 Holden and Johns, *The House of Saud*, pp. 170, 260–2. On clandestine cinemas, Ferris, "Riding the Saudi Boom."
50 Robert Lacey, *The Kingdom: Arabia and the House of Saud*, Avon, 1983, pp. 369–71.
51 For overviews of religious scholars and Islamic law, Denny, *An Introduction to Islam*; Berkey, *The Formation of Islam*; N. Calder, "Shari'a," *Encyclopaedia of Islam*, 2nd ed., Brill, 2006; I. Goldziher and J. Schacht, "Fikh," *Encyclopaedia of Islam*, 2nd ed., Brill, 2006; Cl. Gilliot, "'Ulama," *Encyclopaedia of Islam*, 2nd ed., Brill, 2006.
52 Burak, G. "Madhhab," *The Oxford Encyclopedia of Islam and Law*, Oxford Islamic Studies. Online: http://www.oxfordislamicstudies.com/article/opr/t349/e0094.
53 The Arabic term for consensus is *ijma'*. M. Bernand, "Idjma," *Encyclopaedia of Islam*, 2nd ed., Brill, 2006.
54 One qualified to undertake ijtihad is a *mujtahid*. J. Schacht and D. B. MacDonald, "Idjtihad," *Encyclopaedia of Islam*, 2nd ed., Brill, 2006.
55 Jonathan Brown, "Is Islam Easy to Understand or Not?: Salafis, the Democratization of Interpretation, and the Need for the Ulama," *Journal of Islamic Studies* 26:2 (2015), 127. The Arabic term for following or imitating a legal scholar is *taqlid*. N. Calder, "Taklid," *Encyclopaedia of Islam*, 2nd ed., Brill, 2006.

56 Brown, "Is Islam Easy to Understand or Not?" 133–8; Sh. Inayatullah, "Ahl-i Hadith," *Encyclopaedia of Islam*, 2nd ed., Brill, 2006; Barbara Daly Metcalf, *Islamic Revival in British India: Deoband, 1860–1900*, Princeton University Press, 1982, pp. 264–96.
57 David Commins, *Islamic Reform: Politics and Social Change in Late Ottoman Damascus*, Oxford University Press, 1990, pp. 69–72.
58 A. Merad, "Islah," *Encyclopaedia of Islam*, 2nd ed., Brill, 2006.
59 Brown, "Is Islam Easy to Understand or Not?" 117.
60 There is a common mistaken idea about him that he was a reformer in the area of Islamic law, but in fact, he generally followed the Hanbali legal school. Crawford, *Ibn Abd al-Wahhab*, pp. 52–4.
61 W. Ende, "Mudjawir," *Encyclopaedia of Islam*, 2nd ed., Brill, 2006.
62 Michael Farquhar, *Circuits of Faith: Migration, Education, and the Wahhabi Mission*, Stanford University Press, pp. 26–8.
63 Crawford, *Ibn Abd al-Wahhab*, p. 121; William Ochsenwald, "The Annexation of the Hijaz," in Mohammed Ayoob and Hasan Kosebalaban, eds., *Religion and Politics in Saudi Arabia*, Lynne Rienner, 2009, pp. 75–89; see pp. 77–9 on Ibn Saud's desire for international approval.
64 Farquhar, *Circuits of Faith*, pp. 55–6, 62–5.
65 Mouline, *The Clerics of Islam*, pp. 137–8.
66 For background on this influential figure in the religious establishment, see Muhammad Al Atawneh, *Wahhabi Islam Facing the Challenges of Modernity: Dar al-Ifta in the Modern Saudi State*, Brill, 2010, pp. 31–4.
67 Chanfi Ahmed, "For the Saudi's Kingdom or for the Umma? Global 'Ulama' and in the Dar al-Hadith in Medina," *Journal for Islamic Studies* 32 (2012), 72–6.
68 Farquhar, *Circuits of Faith*, pp. 39–40.
69 Ahmed, "For the Saudi's Kingdom or for the Umma?" 75. Abd al-Zahir Abu Samah was a leader in an Egyptian religious movement called "Helpers of the Prophetic Tradition" that was close to the Hadith Folk and the Wahhabi mission. See the discussion of Ansar al-Sunnah al-Muhammadiyyah in the section on Islamic groups.
70 On the founding of the Islamic University of Medina, Farquhar, *Circuits of Faith*, pp. 67–77.
71 On Albani's life and thought, Stephane Lacroix, "Between Revolution and Apoliticism: Nasir al-Din al-Albani and His Impact on the Shaping of Contemporary Salafism," in Roel Meijer, ed., *Global Salafism: Islam's New Religious Movement*, Columbia University Press, 2009, pp. 58–80.
72 Kamaruddin Amin, "Nasiruddin al-Albani on Muslim's *Sahih*: A Critical Study of His Method," *Islamic Law and Society* 11:2 (2004), 149–76.
73 The memoir describes a Tunisian follower who caused an uproar at the Mosque of the Prophet by wearing sandals to prayer.
74 Stephane Lacroix, *Awakening Islam: The Politics of Religious Dissent in Contemporary Saudi Arabia*, Harvard University Press, 2011, p. 85.
75 See the section on Islamic groups for discussion of controversy over excommunication.
76 Farquhar, *Circuits of Faith*, pp. 52–3, 137–43.
77 Lacroix, *Awakening Islam*, pp. 89–90.
78 Michael Cook, "Vices and Virtues," in Jane Dammen McAuliffe, ed., *Encyclopedia of the Qur'an*, Brill, 2006, vol. 5, pp. 436–43.
79 Michael Cook, *Commanding Right and Forbidding Wrong in Islamic Thought*, Cambridge University Press, 2010, p. 33.

80 Michael Cook, *Forbidding Wrong in Islam: An Introduction*, Cambridge University Press, 2012, pp. 13–21.
81 Cook, *Forbidding Wrong*, p. 17.
82 Cl. Cahen, M. Talbi, R. Mantran, A. K. S. Lambton, and A. S. Bazmee Ansari, "Hisba," *Encyclopaedia of Islam*, 2nd ed., Brill, 2006.
83 Mouline, *The Clerics of Islam*, pp. 82–4.
84 Mouline, *The Clerics of Islam*, pp. 207–9.
85 Mouline, *The Clerics of Islam*, pp. 210–11.
86 *Al-Jama'ah al-Salafiyyah al-Muhtasibah* is the group's full name.
87 Alexander Thurston, *Salafism in Nigeria*, Cambridge University Press, 2016, pp. 1–2, 12, 17, 35–63.
88 Farquhar, *Circuits of Faith*, p. 47.
89 Abdel-Magid Turki, "Zahiriyya," *Encyclopaedia of Islam*, 2nd ed., Brill, 2006.
90 The recommended book was Ibn Kathir's exegesis.
91 Nasir al-Huzaimi, Arabic edition, p. 37; English edition, p. 81.
92 On Tablighi Jama'at, Jan A. Ali, "Tabligh Jama'at: A Transnational Movement of Islamic faith regeneration," *European Journal of Economic and Political Studies* 3 (2010), 103–31; M. M. Qurashi, "The Tabligh Movement: Some Observations," *Islamic Studies* 28:3 (1989), 237–48.
93 There is no study of the group in English. For an account in Arabic, Aziz Dawud, *al-Jam'iyyat al-islamiyyah fi misr wa dawruha fi nashr al-da'wah al-islamiyyah* (The Islamic Groups in Egypt and Their Role in Spreading the Islamic Call), Al-Zahra li'l-i'lam al-'Arabi, 1992. A separate Sudanese organization inspired by the Egyptian group took the same name.
94 The Egyptian group and the Wahhabis shared a preoccupation with the doctrine of God's attributes, an issue that was the cause of sharp controversy in early Islamic times because of verses in the Quran that describe God as possessing physical traits and senses.
95 Mouline, *The Clerics of Islam*, p. 208.
96 On Ansar al-Sunnah's activities in Saudi Arabia, Farquhar, *Circuits of Faith*, pp. 56, 93, 97–8.
97 On the history of the Muslim Brotherhood, Richard P. Mitchell, *The Society of the Muslim Brothers*, Oxford University Press, 1993.
98 John Calvert, *Sayyid Qutb and the Origins of Islamic Radicalism*, Oxford University Press, 2014.
99 See discussion of the Society of Muslims below.
100 On the Muslim Brotherhood's activities in Saudi Arabia, Lacroix, *Awakening Islam*.
101 Lacroix, "Between Revolution and Apoliticism," p. 69.
102 Lacroix, "Between Revolution and Apoliticism," p. 71.
103 *Al-Takfir wa al-Hijrah*.
104 On the Society of Muslims, Saad Eddin Ibrahim, "Anatomy of Egypt's Militant Islamic Groups: Methodological Note and Preliminary Findings," *International Journal of Middle East Studies* 12:4 (1980), 423–53.
105 On comparisons between the Islamic State and the Wahhabi mission, Cole Bunzel, *The Kingdom and the Caliphate: Duel of the Islamic States*, Carnegie Endowment for International Peace, 2016, pp. 3–10. On takfir in the Algerian civil war of the 1990s, Quintan Wiktorowicz, "The New Global Threat: Transnational Salafis and Jihad," *Middle East Policy* 8:1 (2001), 18–38.
106 Crawford, *Ibn Abd al-Wahhab*, pp. 61–7.

107 Ibrahim, "Anatomy of Egypt's Militant Islamic Groups," 434.
108 Habib, *Ibn Sa'ud's Warriors of Islam* is the major work on the subject.
109 Monera Nahedh, "The Sedentarization of a Bedouin Community in Saudi Arabia," doctoral dissertation, University of Leeds, 1989, p. 148.
110 Habib, *Ibn Sa'ud's Warriors of Islam*, p. 153.
111 Donald Cole, "Where Have the Bedouin Gone?" *Anthropological Quarterly* 76:2 (2003), 237.
112 Cited in Marcel Kurpershoek, *Arabia of the Bedouins*, Saqi, 2002, p. 26.
113 Abdulaziz Al-Fahad, "Raiders and Traders: A Poet's Lament on the End of the Bedouin Heroic Age," in Bernard Haykel, Stephane Lacroix, and Thomas Hegghammer, eds., *Saudi Arabia in Transition*, Princeton University Press, 2015, p. 232.
114 P. M. Kurpershoek, *Oral Poetry and Narratives from Central Arabia: A Saudi Tribal History: Honour and Faith in the Traditions of the Dawasir*, Brill, 2002, p. 113.
115 Abdulaziz Al-Fahad, "The 'imama vs. the 'iqal: Hadari-Bedouin Conflict and the Formation of the Saudi State," in Madawi Al-Rasheed and Robert Vitalis, eds., *Counter-Narratives: History, Contemporary Society, and Politics in Saudi Arabia and Yemen*, Palgrave Macmillan, 2004, pp. 35–75.
116 Crawford, *Ibn Abd al-Wahhab*, pp. 76–82.
117 Fahad, "Raiders and Traders," p. 233.
118 Ugo Fabietti, "State Policies and Bedouin Adaptations in Saudi Arabia, 1900–1980," in Martha Mundy and Basim Musallam, eds., *The Transformation of Nomadic Society in the Arab East*, Cambridge University Press, 2000, pp. 84–5.
119 Cole, "Where Have the Bedouin Gone?" 239.
120 Cole, "Where Have the Bedouin Gone?" 241.
121 Fabietti, "State Policies and Bedouin Adaptations," p. 85; Cole, "Where Have the Bedouin Gone?" 242–9.
122 Cole, "Where Have the Bedouin Gone?" 237.
123 Najd is the Arabic name for central Arabia.
124 Kurpershoek, *Oral Poetry*, pp. 615–17.
125 Motoko Katakura, *Bedouin Village: A Study of a Saudi Arabian People in Transition*, University of Tokyo Press, 1977, pp. 111–12; Cole, "Where Have the Bedouin Gone?" 248.
126 Al-Fahad, "Raiders and Traders," pp. 232–7.
127 David Cook, *Studies in Muslim Apocalyptic*, Darwin Press, 2002, pp. 248–9.
128 Crawford, *Ibn Abd al-Wahhab*, pp. 73–5, 85.
129 *The Clarification and Explanation of What Befalls the Majority Who Imitate the Polytheists*.
130 According to Huzaimi's memoir, Juhaiman was one of the Salafi Group's founders. Arabic edition, 42–3; English edition pp. 83–4. Lacroix and Hegghammer write that he joined the group sometime after leaving the National Guard around 1973. "Rejectionist Islamism," 109.
131 Most accounts emphasize Juhaiman's criticism of the Saudi rulers for permitting Western influences as the cause for rupture.
132 See the discussion of the prayer niche, or *mihrab*, in the section "Withdrawal from Society."
133 According to Lacroix and Hegghammer, Juhaiman was present and argued with the clerics. They cite interviews with men who attended, including Huzaimi. "Rejectionist Islamism," 108, 120 note 33.

134 Lacroix and Hegghammer report the incident as falling in December 1977. "Rejectionist Islamism," 110. Trofimov has it occurring in late spring 1978. *The Siege of Mecca*, p. 40.
135 Rodney Stark and William S ms Bainbridge, "Of Churches, Sects and Cults: Preliminary Concepts for a Theory of Religious Movements," *Journal for the Scientific Study of Religion* 18:2 (1979), 123.
136 Stark and Bainbridge, "Of Churches, Sects and Cults," 125.
137 Rodney Stark and William S ms Bainbridge, citing Russell Dynes, "Church-sect Typology and Socio-Economic Status," *American Sociological Review* 20 (1955) in "Sectarian Tension," *Review of Religious Research* 22:2 (December 1980), 106.
138 On the sectarian traits of the early Wahhabi mission, Crawford, *Ibn Abd al-Wahhab*, p. 60.
139

> Muawiyah b. Abi Sufyan stood among us and said, 'Beware! The Messenger of God stood among us and said: Beware! The People of the Book [Jews and Christians] before us were split up into seventy-two sects, and this community will be split up into seventy-three. Seventy-two of them will be in the Fire and one will be in the Garden.

Abu Daud, *Sunan Abi Dawud*, Book of Model Behavior of the Prophet (*Kitab al-sunnah*), Number 1677. Sunnah.com. Online: https://sunnah.com/abudawud/42/2.
140 A. J. Wensinck and T. Fahd, "Sura," *Encyclopaedia of Islam*, 2nd ed., Brill, 2006.
141 L. M. Landau, "Taswir," *Encyclopaedia of Islam*, 2nd ed., Brill, 2006.
142 Farquhar, *Circuits of Faith*, pp. 61–2.
143 On the Buraidah Ikhwan, Lacroix, *Awakening Islam*, pp. 104–9.
144 M. S. Makki, *Medina, Saudi Arabia: A Geographical Analysis of the City and Region*, Avebury, 1982, pp. 21, 101.
145 Makki, *Medina*, p. 140.
146 G. Fehervari, "Mihrab," *Encyclopaedia of Islam*, 2nd ed., Brill, 2006.
147 Richard Gauvain, *Salafi Ritual Purity: In the Presence of God*, Routledge, 2013, p. 10.
148 Justin Jeffcoat Schedtler and Kelly J. Murphy, "Introduction: From before the Bible to Beyond the Bible," in Schedlter and Murphy, eds., *Apocalypses in Context: Apocalyptic Currents throughout History*, Augsburg Fortress, 2016, pp. 5–8; Filiu, *Apocalypse in Islam*, p. 4.
149 Christopher B. Hayes, "'Proto-Apocalyptic' Constellations in the Bible and the Ancient Near East," in Justin Jeffcoat Schedtler and Kelly J. Murphy, eds., *Apocalypses in Context*, Augsburg Fortress, 2016, pp. 48–53.
150 Hayes, "'Proto-Apocalyptic' Constellations in the Bible and the Ancient Near East," 39–43.
151 Filiu, *Apocalypse in Islam*, pp. 4–6; Isaac Hasson, "Last Judgment," in Jane Dammen McAuliffe, ed., *Encyclopaedia of the Qur'an*, Brill, 2006; Frederik Leemhuis, "Apocalypse," Jane Dammen McAuliffe, ed., *Encyclopaedia of the Qur'an*, Brill, 2006.
152 Huzaimi, Arabic edition, pp. 125–6.
153 Hayes, "'Proto-Apocalyptic' Constellations in the Bible and the Ancient Near East," pp. 38–47; Elizabeth Sirriyeh, *Dreams and Visions in the World of Islam*, I.B. Tauris, 2015, pp. 48–57.
154 According to Lacroix and Hegghammer, Juhaiman became convinced that Qahtani was the Mahdi in late 1978. "Rejectionist Islamism in Saudi Arabia," 112.
155 The hadiths cited in Huzaimi, Arabic edition, pp. 135, 146–7.
156 Shortly before the invasion of the mosque, Juhaiman married Qahtani's sister.

The Memoir

1. A dervish or Sufi belongs to the ascetic, mystical tradition in Islam. A dervish or Sufi lodge is a gathering place for religious celebrations in Islam's mystical tradition. Lodges are also sites of spiritual retreat from the distractions of everyday life and sometimes provide material relief to the poor.
2. Movement between Kuwait and southern Iraq seems to have been easy and common at the time.
3. He died in November 1965.
4. From *Caravan* (*Qawafil Magazine*), number 23, November 2007.
5. Probably his 1958 book, *The Disaster of Palestine* (*Karithat Filastin*) about the 1948 war.
6. A popular Iraqi singer in the 1940s and 1950s.
7. A popular Jewish Iraqi singer, married to al-Ghazzali.
8. A well-known professional wrestler in the United States, where he spent much of his life.
9. Abu Tubar, "the axe man," was a fictitious figure invented by the Iraqi government to deflect blame for killings of dissidents in the early 1970s. Wafaa Bilal, *Shoot an Iraqi: Life, Art, and Resistance under the Gun*, City Lights, 2008, pp. 34–5.
10. This is the end of the material about al-Huzaimi's childhood that is not in the Arabic edition.
11. Footnote 1 in al-Huzaimi: I ask the reader's forgiveness for I am writing from memory a quarter century after the storming of the Grand Mosque and eighteen years after my release from prison, which I entered on 15 Muharram 1400 and left on 26 Ramadan 1406, that is, from November 15, 1979 to April 26, 1986. [NB: There is an error in either the Hijri or Common Era dates. 15 Muharram 1400 corresponds to December 5, 1979, and 26 Ramadan 1406 corresponds to June 4, 1986].
12. That is to say, a good choice for conservative regimes.
13. Footnote 2 in al-Huzaimi: Al-Sheikh Abd al-Hamid Kishk was a partially blind preacher who went to prison in 1966 and was released in 1968. From that time, he resumed his sermons and lessons until around 1982. He died in 1996. [N.B. See Johannes J. G. Jansen, "Kishk, Abd al-Hamid," in John L. Esposito, *Oxford Encyclopedia of the Modern Islamic World*. Oxford Islamic Studies Online, http://www.oxfordislamicstudies.com/article/opr/t236MIW/e0465 (accessed June 28, 2020).]
14. The Muslim Brotherhood is the largest modern Islamist movement, founded in Egypt in 1928 by a young schoolteacher named Hasan al-Banna. The Brotherhood established branches in other Arab countries. The Saudi authorities refused to allow the formation of a branch in the kingdom, but hundreds of members spent many years there and their views became popular with young Saudis because they gave more attention to political matters than the local Wahhabi tradition or the Salafis.
15. The Egyptian thinker Sayyid Qutb (1906–1966) is a major influence in contemporary Muslim political activism. He wrote for Muslim Brotherhood publications in the 1950s and spent most of the last twelve years of his life in prison after he clashed with the Arab nationalist regime of Gamal Abd al-Nasir. The Egyptian government executed him for sedition in 1966. *Milestones* is notable for inspiring Islamists to regard the rulers of Muslim countries as apostates.
16. Sayyid Sabiq was a graduate of Egypt's Al-Azhar seminary and a member of the Muslim Brotherhood. His work on Islamic law became widely popular in Islamist

circles. Ahmed El Shamsy, "Fiqh al-Sunnah," in John L. Esposito, *Oxford Encyclopedia of the Islamic World. Oxford Islamic Studies Online.* http://www.oxfordislamicstudies.com/article/opr/t236/e0937 (accessed June 28, 2020). Sunnah is the Arabic term for the Prophet's custom—his words and actions that are exemplars for believers. The Sunnah consists of thousands of Prophetic Traditions, or *hadith*s.

17 Muhammad Nasir al-Din al-Albani was a self-taught expert in Prophetic Traditions. He was the most influential religious scholar in the contemporary Salafi movement outside Saudi Arabia.

18 One of the hallmarks of Salafis is their preoccupation with ranking the reliability of Prophetic Traditions and with basing their beliefs and practices on them.

19 More precisely, the Kuwaiti Salafi Group. It was distinct from the Salafi Group created in Saudi Arabia, as described below.

20 Important figures in the Kuwait Salafi movement. Abd al-Rahman Abd al-Khaliq in particular became famous and influential. Born in Egypt and educated at the Islamic University of Medina in Saudi Arabia, he settled in Kuwait in the 1960s. He belonged to the Salafi tendency endorsing involvement in political activity. Zoltan Pall, *Salafism in Lebanon: Local and Transnational Movements*, Cambridge University Press, 2018, pp. 40–56.

21 In the Sunni historical tradition, there were many approaches to religious law in the early centuries. Four of them took shape as *madhhab*'s, usually referred to as legal schools or schools of law. They represent different approaches to interpreting the Quran and the Sunnah in order to elaborate religious law. The modern Salafi tendency does not recognize the authority of the legal schools to be binding and claims that Muslims should examine the Quran and the Sunnah without bowing to the historical authority of the legal schools

22 A South Asian association established in the 1920s devoted to calling on Muslims to regular observance of religious duties and morality.

23 An offshoot of the Muslim Brotherhood formed in Palestine in the early 1950s distinctive for its emphasis on reestablishing the caliphate.

24 The apolitical "Jamis" get their name from the Ethiopian Muslim scholar Muhammad Aman al-Jami, a specialist in Prophetic Traditions at the Islamic University of Medina. Stephane Lacroix, *Awakening Islam: The Politics of Religious Dissent in Contemporary Saudi Arabia*, Harvard University Press, 2011, pp. 212–14. The political "Sururis" get their name from Muhammad Surur Zain al-Abidin, a Syrian Muslim Brother who found asylum in Saudi Arabia and propagated an activist version of Salafism. Lacroix, *Awakening Islam*, pp. 69–71.

25 Footnote 3 in al-Huzaimi: "*al-'Izbah*" refers to a residence for bachelors.

26 At this point, I have changed the order of the text in order to place discussion of the author's description of Riyadh in one section.

27 A neighborhood in the older section of Riyadh.

28 *Mukhtasar sahih Muslim* by Abd al-Azim al-Mundhiri (1185–1258), a Shafi'i expert in Prophetic Traditions and compiler of an abridgement of Muslim's canonical collection of Prophetic Traditions. See "Biography of al-Hafiz al-Mundhiri," in *The Translation of the Meanings of Summarized Sahih Muslim: Arabic-English*, compiled by al-Hafiz Zakiuddin Abdul-Azim al-Mundhiri, Darussalam Publishers and Distributors, 2000.

29 *Sifat salat al-nabi* by Nasir al-Din al-Albani is a collection of Prophetic Traditions about the prayers of the Prophet Muhammad.

30 *Adab al-zafaf fi al-sunnah al-mutahharah* by Nasir al-Din al-Albani.

31 *Ulama* are Muslim religious scholars.

32 *Hijab al-mar'ah wa libsuha fi al-salah.* The book stirred controversy because Albani denied that Muslim women were obliged to cover their faces. See "Between Revolution and Apoliticism: Nasir al-Din al-Albani and His Impact on the Shaping of Contemporary Salafism," in Roel Meijer, ed., *Global Salafism: Islam's New Religious Movement*, Columbia University Press, 2009, pp. 66–7.
33 Sindi taught at the Islamic University of Medina. Michael Farquhar, *Circuits of Faith: Migration, Education and the Wahhabi Mission*, Stanford University Press, 2016, p. 220 n.56. Sindi's book is *Lifting the Shield in Front of the Muslim Woman's Cloak in the Quran and the Prophetic Tradition (Raf' al-junnah amam jilbab al-mar'ah al-muslimah fi al-kitab wa al-sunnah)*. Isma'il ibn Muhammad Ansari, a deputy to the leading Saudi cleric Abd al-Aziz ibn Baz, was the author of the second book. Stephane Lacroix, *Awakening Islam*, p. 84.
34 The debate centered on defining the term *al-'awra'*, which has the general sense of private parts or genitals. Hanbalism is one of the four classical legal schools and the official legal school in Saudi Arabia. H. Laoust, "Hanabila," *Encyclopaedia of Islam*, 2nd ed., Brill, 2006. Hanbalism is named after Ahmad ibn Hanbal (780–855), a Baghdad teacher who emphasized literal interpretation of religious texts and scrupulous imitation of the Prophet. One of the major collections of Prophetic Traditions is attributed to him. H. Laoust, "Ahmad b. Hanbal," *Encyclopedia of Islam*, 2nd ed., Brill, 2006.
35 A *fatwa* is the opinion or ruling of an expert in Islamic law.
36 The Companions refers to the men and women who embraced Islam and personally knew the Prophet Muhammad. Sunnis consider them an authoritative source for religious knowledge. See the section on Islamic Scriptures in the introduction.
37 The classical legal schools adopted nontextual methods to arrive at rulings on issues that are not covered in the Quran and the Sunnah.
38 Often referred to in the West as the religious police. The Committees represent the commitment to perform a duty mentioned in the Quran to take action in order to promote good acts and to prohibit bad acts: commanding right and forbidding wrong. See the section on Commanding Right and Forbidding Wrong in the introduction. Michael Cook, *Commanding Right and Forbidding Wrong in Islamic Thought*, Cambridge University Press, 2010.
39 Established in the 1920s, the Committees saw their influence grow in the 1980s as part of the rulers' reaction to the Mecca uprising by giving new emphasis to the religious basis of their right to rule. Nabil Mouline, *The Clerics of Islam: Religious Authority and Political Power in Saudi Arabia*, Yale University Press, 2014, pp. 203–34.
40 A reference to the words in Surat al-Nahl, The Bee 16:125: "Call unto the way of your Lord, with wisdom and fair exhortation."
41 At this point, the text returns to earlier pages in the memoir.
42 Sunni Muslims consider six collections of Prophetic Traditions to contain the most carefully selected, and therefore the most reliable, sources for knowing the Sunnah. The standard names for the six collections are the *Sahih* of al-Bukhari, the *Sahih* of Muslim, the *Sunan* of Abu Daud, the *Jami'* or *Sunan* of al-Tirmidhi, the *Sunan* of al-Nasa'i, and the *Kitab al-Sunan* of Ibn Majah.
43 The Science of Prophetic Traditions includes study of the men and women who memorized and passed on Prophetic Traditions through oral and written means, the "chain" or list of transmitters that validate a particular Tradition, and variations in wording between different versions of the same Prophetic Tradition.

44 *The Book of God's Unity* (*Kitab al-tawhid*) was the first treatise composed by the founder of the Wahhabi tradition, in 1740.
45 Footnote 4 in al-Huzaimi: The group was known by this name in reference to a house called "The Abode of Knowledge" (*Dar al-Ilm*) it had in the Dukhnah neighborhood in downtown Riyadh. A number of sheikhs attended its meetings, including Sheikh Ibrahim al-Ghaith, the former head of the Committee for Commanding Right and Forbidding Wrong, the Grand Mufti Sheikh Abd al-Aziz Al al-Sheikh, and the famous mufti Sheikh Abd Allah ibn Jibrin (may God have mercy on him).
46 Hasan al-Banna (1906–1949) was born in a provincial town in Egypt. He founded the Muslim Brotherhood in 1928, when he was a young schoolteacher. Under his leadership, the Brotherhood became a powerful religious movement with branches throughout Egypt and in other Arab countries. In the 1960s, the Muslim Brotherhood divided between wings that emphasized the teachings of Banna and of Sayyid Qutb, respectively. The Banna wing is known for relying on preaching and education to revive Islam whereas the Qutb wing is known for endorsing political action to overthrow "apostate" regimes.
47 The Social Reform Society was the charitable wing of the Muslim Brotherhood in Kuwait.
48 Muslims may perform the lesser pilgrimage to Mecca, or *umrah*, at any time of year whereas the major pilgrimage, or *hajj*, takes place toward the end of the Muslim lunar calendar. R. Paret and E. Chaumont, "'Umra," *Encyclopaedia of Islam*, 2nd ed., Brill, 2006. Ramadan is the ninth month in the Muslim lunar calendar. Observing a daytime fast during Ramadan is one of the fundamental religious duties for Muslims.
49 Dar al-Hadith is a center for teaching Prophetic Traditions established in 1931 by Ahmad Dihlawi, an Indian religious scholar who came to Saudi Arabia from Delhi in 1926. Chanfi Ahmed, *West African 'Ulama and Salafism in Mecca and Medina*, Brill, 2015, p. 83.
50 Perhaps six weeks after he went to Mecca to perform the lesser pilgrimage, around September 1976. Dhu al-Qa'dah is the eleventh month in the Muslim lunar calendar.
51 Footnote 5 in al-Huzaimi: Members of the Salafi Group were known as Ikhwan, or Brethren.
52 The Haram is the Grand Mosque.
53 The Arabic word *ikhwan* means "brethren" or "brotherhood." Various Muslim groups adopt the term to indicate close bonds among their members. In the 1910s and 1920s, the "Ikhwan in Obedience to God" were Arabian Bedouin gathered in agricultural colonies where they received religious instruction from Wahhabi sheikhs. See section "Overview of the Wahhabi Mission" in the introduction. Juhaiman's group referred to itself as the Ikhwan. In the memoir, Ikhwan usually refers to the members of the Salafi Group, but it sometimes refers to the older group. Furthermore, the Muslim Brotherhood's Arabic name, *jama'at al-ikhwan al-muslimin*, is sometimes abbreviated to Ikhwan. For the sake of clarity, the translation uses "Ikhwan" to refer to the Salafi Group, "Old Ikhwan" or "Ikhwan in Obedience to God" to refer to the early-twentieth-century movement, and the "Muslim Brotherhood" to refer to the modern transnational movement.
54 In this context, "sheikhs" refers to religious scholars teaching in Mecca.
55 The pilgrimage rites take place at several locations in and near Mecca. The Kaabah is the cube-like structure at the center of the Grand Mosque toward which Muslims face when they pray. Al-Safa and al-Marwah are two elevations, now enclosed in the enlarged Grand Mosque, between which pilgrims rush seven times.

56 Footnote 1 in al-Huzaimi [NB: The footnotes in the memoir are numbered for each chapter]: The basement of the Grand Mosque has many small rooms. The Meccan Ikhwan were very familiar with them and the passages between them, something that provided an advantage for Juhaiman during the storming of the Grand Mosque.
57 Mina is a small valley outside Mecca where pilgrims gather on their way to Mt. Arafat, the location for the Day of Standing, the essential phase of the ritual.
58 Dhu al-Hijjah is the twelfth month in the Muslim lunar calendar.
59 Muqbil al-Wadi'i was from Yemen. The Saudi government deported him to Yemen shortly after the Mecca uprising. He became a leading thinker and activist in Yemen's Salafi movement until his death in 2001. See Laurent Bonnefoy, *Salafism in Yemen: Transnationalism and Religious Identity*, Oxford University Press, 2012.
60 Sajir was a *hijrah* or agricultural settlement for the early twentieth-century Ikhwan movement. Juhaiman grew up there.
61 Ha'il is a town in northern Najd. In the late 1800s and early 1900s, it was the capital of the Rashidi emirate.
62 Ansar al-Sunnah is a Salafi association that was founded in Egypt in 1926.
63 Ta'if is a town located near Mecca.
64 Kunafah is a pastry.
65 Abd al-Rahman ibn Nasir al-Sa'di was an early-twentieth-century Saudi scholar. Isma'il ibn Kathir (c. 1300–1373) was an important religious figure in Damascus. His major works are in history, Prophetic Traditions, and exegesis of the Quran. See H. Laoust, "Ibn Kathir," *Encyclopaedia of Islam*, 2nd ed., Brill, 2006. Al-Husain al-Baghawi (d. 1122) was an eleventh-/twelfth-century Persian scholar known for his works on the Prophetic Traditions and his exegesis of the Quran. See James Robson, "Al-Baghawi," *Encyclopaedia of Islam*, 2nd ed., Brill, 2006.
66 *Gift to the Community on Tribulations, Battles and Portents of the Last Hour* (*Ithaf al-jama'ah bi ma ja'a fi fitan wa al-malahim wa ashrat al-sa'ah*) by Hammud al-Tuwaijiri (1916–1992), an ultraconservative Saudi religious scholar. Lacroix, *Awakening Islam*, pp. 103–8.
67 Muhammad al-Shawkani (1759–1834) was a major religious scholar in Yemen whose writings are an important source for Salafis. *The Attainment of Objectives* (*Nayl al-awtar*) is a commentary on the legal content of Prophetic Traditions. See Bernard Haykel, *Revival and Reform in Islam: The Legacy of Muhammad Al-Shawkani*, Cambridge University Press, 2003.
68 Muhammad ibn Isma'il al-San'ani Ibn al-Amir (1687–1769) was a major eighteenth-century religious scholar in Yemen. Haykel, *Revival and Reform in Islam*, pp. 63–5, 128–9. His *Paths to Peace* (*Subul al-salam*) is a commentary on a famous collection of Prophetic Traditions by Ibn Hajar al-Asqalani (1372–1449), an Egyptian and one of the most influential scholars in the study of Prophetic Traditions. See Franz Rosenthal, "Ibn Hadjar al-Askalani," *Encyclopaedia of Islam*, 2nd ed., Brill, 2006.
69 *Majmu'at al-tawhid* is a collection of early Wahhabi writings edited by Rashid Rida.
70 Ahmad Taqi al-Din ibn Taymiyyah (1263–1328) and his pupil Ibn Qayyim al-Jawziyyah (1292–1350) are the two most influential medieval thinkers among Salafis. See H. Laoust, "Ibn Taymiyya" and "Ibn Kayyim al-Djawziyya," *Encyclopaedia of Islam*, 2nd ed., Brill, 2006.
71 Ahmad al-Tahawi (c. 850–933) was renowned for his brief exposition of Islamic creed and for his expertise in religious law according to the Hanafi legal school. See N. Calder, "al-Tahawi," *Encyclopaedia of Islam*, 2nd ed., Brill, 2006. The *Commentary on al-Tahawi's Creed* (*Sharh al-aqidah al-tahawiyyah*) is a classic statement of Sunni

belief composed by Muhammad ibn Abi al-Izz al-Hanafi (1331–1390), a fourteenth-century Damascus scholar.
72 In this sense, *haram* does not refer to the Grand Mosque but to a larger, sacred area from which non-Muslims are excluded.
73 Pious Ancestors or Forefathers is a common translation for *al-salaf al-salih*, the early Muslims, commonly defined as the first three generations of Muslims. See Overview of the Wahhabi Mission in the introduction.
74 Forbidding wrong is part of the ethical duty to "command right and forbid wrong."
75 *Victory of the Creator (Fath al-bari sharh sahih al-Bukhari)* is a famous commentary on al-Bukhari's canonical collection of Prophetic Traditions composed by the fifteenth-century Egyptian scholar Ibn Hajar al-Asqalani. Bulaq Press was the first printing press in Egypt, dating to 1822, so its editions are rare and valuable.
76 A Hadrami is somebody from the Hadramaut region of South Yemen.
77 From 1967 to 1990, South Yemen was the People's Democratic Republic of Yemen, a Marxist republic.
78 Indian-born religious scholar (d. 2002) who settled and taught in Saudi Arabia.
79 Al-Huzaimi mentions two works by Ibn Hajar al-Asqalani: *God's Help on the Commentary on Abu Daud's Collection (Kitab awn al-ma'bud fi sharh sunan Abi Daud)* is a commentary on the canonical collection of Abu Daud. *The Cream of Thought on the Technical Terms of Tradition Folk (Kitab nukhbat al-fikr fi mustalah ahl al-athar)* is a treatise on technical terms in the study of Prophetic Traditions.
80 Ibn Kathir's *Abridgement (al-Mukhtasar)* is an abbreviated version of his exegesis of the Quran.
81 For some details on peer learning in religious education in Morocco, see Dale Eickelman, "The Art of Memory and Its Social Reproduction," *Comparative Studies in Society and History* 20:4 (1973), 485–516; on peer learning, pp. 503–4.
82 A religious movement that arose in the mid-1800s during the British colonial period, the Ahl-i Hadith, or "the folk of the Prophetic Tradition," are close to the Wahhabis and Salafis in theology and literal method of interpreting the Quran and the Sunnah.
83 Ibn Hazm was an eleventh-century religious scholar in Muslim Spain. R. Arnaldez, "Ibn Hazm," *Encyclopaedia of Islam*, 2nd ed., Brill, 2006. His work on Islamic law, *al-Muhalla (The Sweetened or The Ordained)*, is controversial for its adherence to the extinct "Zahiri" Legal School. On the Zahiri Legal School, see Abdel-Magid Turki, "Zahiriyya," *Encyclopaedia of Islam*, 2nd ed., Brill, 2006.
84 Students from the Central Asian city of Bukhara.
85 The Arabic word here is a crude pun on Hanafi.
86 Mecca and Medina.
87 *The Ring of the Dove (Tawq al-hamamah)*.
88 The verse refers to Jesus.
89 *The Ornamented Ladder to the Science of Logic (Sullam al-murawniq fi i'lm al-mantiq)* by Abd al-Rahman al-Akhdari, c. 1512–1576. J. Schacht, "Abd al-Rahman al-Akhdari," *Encyclopaedia of Islam*, 2nd ed., Brill, 2006.
90 *Ulama al-salaf*: religious scholars among the pious ancestors, in other words, authorities whose views modern Salafis consider authoritative.
91 The Arabic term for illegitimate innovation in ritual is *bid'ah*. Eliminating these kinds of innovation is an important goal for Salafis because they consider innovations to harbor overtones of polytheism. See Overview of the Wahhabi Mission in introduction.

92 A Saudi writer who became a Marxist critic of Saudi Arabia in the 1960s. Ralph M. Coury, *Sceptics of Islam: Revisionist Religion, Agnosticism, and Disbelief in the Modern Arab World*, I.B. Tauris, 2018.
93 A Saudi writer on local history.
94 The major center for religious learning in Egypt, founded in the tenth century.
95 An Egyptian educator and author of works on religious pedagogy.
96 A reference to the words in Surat al-Qasas, The Story 28:20. "Moses, the council is conspiring against you to kill you."
97 Footnote 2 in al-Huzaimi: Al-Sheikh Muhammad Amin al-Misri (may God have mercy on him) died in 1397 AH/1977 CE.
98 The reference is to the first time that the Saudi authorities arrested members of the Salafi Group, in December 1977.
99 A Saudi sheikh responsible for teaching appointments at the Grand Mosque. Mouline, *The Clerics of Islam*, pp. 172–3.
100 A Saudi religious scholar who followed the Maliki legal school instead of the official Hanbali legal school that Wahhabis follow.
101 The inference is that he suffered in Egypt for teaching Salafi beliefs and may have expected more considerate treatment in Saudi Arabia.
102 The Arabic term is *Wahhabi khamisiyyah*.
103 Al-Huzaimi is using the term "Islamic State" in a generic sense. He is not referring to the Islamic State in the Levant and Iraq, the al-Qaeda offshoot that briefly controlled territory in Syria and Iraq between 2013 and 2019.
104 The practice prohibited in Islamic law where two guardians agree to marriage between minors without payment of dowry to the bride. Islamic law requires at least a nominal payment to the bride.
105 Islamic law requires men and women to wait three months before remarrying.
106 A more literal translation: the official did not greet him with proper humility or modesty.
107 See Note 53, p. 163.
108 Footnote 3 in al-Huzaimi: It is believed that Sajir was founded in 1333 AH at the direction of King Abd al-Aziz (may God have mercy on him).
109 Sultan ibn Bijad was a powerful leader of Ikhwan forces who rebelled against Abd al-Aziz.
110 The nickname, The Sultan of Religion, was a play on words referring to his first name and his commitment to upholding Islam.
111 At the battle of Sabilah in March 1929, Abd al-Aziz inflicted a decisive defeat on rebellious Ikhwan tribal leaders. In its aftermath, the government created a new military formation for loyal tribesmen that evolved into the Saudi National Guard.
112 Footnote 4 in al-Huzaimi: Sunaitan al-Utaibi was in prison with me and told me that he used to smuggle cigarettes from Kuwait with Juhaiman. Cigarettes were not banned but were subject to high taxes, and there was intense surveillance of the central province to catch smugglers, in contrast to the western and eastern provinces. He mostly smuggled cigarettes for some merchants who provided red Ford cars. This is clear from a lot of popular poetry.
113 Footnote 5 in al-Huzaimi: Muhammad ibn Yusuf al-Dann al-Utaibi, Juhaiman's father, died in the early 1970s in a traffic accident on the Medina Road with Juhaiman in his company. His grandfather Saif was killed as a young man some time before Sabilah in one of the skirmishes that used to arise from tribal disputes. It is not true that he was killed at Sabilah, as claimed in Rif'at Sayyid Ahmad's book.

[Rif'at Sayyid Ahmad is the Egyptian author of a work in Arabic about Juhaiman and the Ikhwan, *The Essays of Juhaiman al-Utaibi, Leader of the Storming of the Grand Mosque in Mecca*, Madbuli, 1988 (*Rasa'il Juhaiman al-Utaibi, qa'id al-muqtahimin li'l Masjid al-Haram bi-Makka*)].

114 Footnote 6 in al-Huzaimi: As he wrote in *The Essay on Rulership, the Oath of Allegiance, and the Ruling on Deception by Rulers of Religious Students and the Public* (*Risalat al-imarah wa'l bay'ah wa hukm talbis al-hukkam ala talabat al-ilm wa al-ammah*):

> The closest and clearest examples are the founder of their state, King Abd al-Aziz, and the religious sheikhs who sided with him … they either supported him and backed him up on whatever he wished, or they kept silent about his dishonesty, or they were confused about things. The Ikhwan [of the early 1900s], God bless them, emigrated to various villages for the sake of God, may He be exalted, and he [King Abd al-Aziz] called on them to swear allegiance to him on the Quran and the Prophetic Tradition. They fought and conquered lands. They sent him the ruler's one-fifth share of booty, revenue from conquered lands, and similar things as though he were the legitimate ruler of the Muslims. Then when his power stabilized and he attained his goal, he developed ties with Christians and forbade continuing jihad outside Arabia. So when they went to fight the polytheists in Iraq who worshipped Ali, Fatimah, and Hasan alongside God, the king and his sheikhs called them ignorant and called them a hateful term, Kharijites.
>
> [Kharijites were an early Muslim group at war with other Muslims over questions of political leadership and doctrine.]

115 Established in 1961. Part of its purpose was to spread Wahhabi doctrine to other Muslim countries by opening its doors to non-Saudi Muslim students. See Farquhar, *Circuits of Faith*.
116 Al-Huzaimi's account of Juhaiman's role as a founder differs from other accounts that have him joining the Salafi Group in the early 1970s. Thomas Hegghammer and Stephane Lacroix, "Rejectionist Islamism in Saudi Arabia: The Story of Juhayman al-'Utaybi Revisited," *International Journal of Middle East Studies* 39 (2007), 109. Robert Lacey, *Inside the Kingdom: Kings, Clerics, Modernists, Terrorists, and the Struggle for Saudi Arabia*, Viking, 2009, p. 9.
117 One of the most prominent Saudi religious scholars from the early 1970s until his death in 1999. Muhammad Al Atawneh, *Wahhabi Islam Facing the Challenges of Modernity: Dar al-Ifta in the Modern Saudi State*, Brill, 2010, pp. 31–4.
118 Later in the memoir, al-Huzaimi discusses the Prophetic Traditions about the millennium and the role of the Antichrist, in Arabic, *al-Dajjal*.
119 Al-Jaza'iri served as the contact person between Ibn Baz and the Ikhwan.
120 The Ikhwan considered both tobacco and television to be prohibited in religious law.
121 The beginning of 1399 AH was in December 1978.
122 Al-Huzaimi mentions two works by the fifteenth-century scholar Ibn Hajar al-Asqalani: *Enhancement and Perfection in the Science of Prophetic Traditions* (*al-Raf' wa al-takmil fi al-jarh wa al-ta'dil*) is about the method of analyzing Prophetic Traditions; *Attaining the Goal* (*Bulugh al-maram*) is a collection of Prophetic Traditions pertaining to law.
123 *Kitab al-iman*.
124 *Takfir* is Arabic for excommunication. Here it refers to the tendency among some Muslims to regard other Muslims as infidels.

125 Sometimes referred to by its Arabic name, *al-Takfir wa'l-Hijrah*, and also known as the Islamic Group, one of the early militant bands of Islamists that became active in Egypt in the 1970s.
126 The allusion to sovereignty comes from a debate over Sayyid Qutb's concept of divine sovereignty, wherein political authority stems from adherence to divine law and deviation from divine law forfeits political authority.
127 The Kharijites were an early Muslim sect that had a bad reputation for extremism. See the section on Early Islamic History in the introduction.
128 Footnote 1 in al-Huzaimi: The Salafi Ikhwan used to call Faisal Muhammad Faisal "The Little Ibn Taimiyyah" for having memorized his fatwas and opinions.
129 Footnote 2 in al-Huzaimi: Ahmad ibn Hasan al-Mu'allam, a preacher and poet from the Hadramaut region of Yemen, born in 1373 AH/1953 CE, holds a master's degree in doctrinal studies and has held a number of educational and proselytizing positions in Yemen.
130 Footnote 3 in al-Huzaimi: I asked Ahmad if he was related to Hasan al-Banna. He said the names are similar but there was no relation to Hasan al-Banna, founder of the Muslim Brotherhood. His family and Hasan al-Banna's family were from different villages. He mentioned his home province in Egypt but I have forgotten it. His father Sheikh Muhammad Abd al-Wahhab al-Banna belonged to the Ansar al-Sunnah al-Muhammadiyyah Group and moved to Medina and became a Saudi citizen. He was banished from Medina after the incident of breaking pictures and he moved to Jeddah.
131 The *Ummah* is the community of Muslim believers.
132 The Salafi Group came to view him as the Mahdi.
133 The idea of occultation is part of millennial belief in both Sunni and Shiite Islam. According to it, the Mahdi is in hiding until God will bring him back to lead forces of righteousness to triumph over tyranny and injustice.
134 The Jihad Group is a militant group that formed in Egypt in the 1970s.
135 A mujtahid is someone possessing a high level of knowledge and expertise in Islamic law. Here, the term refers to someone who strives to reach correct understanding of religious questions that do not have an obvious answer.
136 Footnote 4 in al-Huzaimi: After graduating from the Islamic University, Id al-Shabihi bought a compressor and started working in excavation. He had good business in those days and some of his workers were antigovernment Egyptians coming for the lesser pilgrimage or the regular pilgrimage.
137 Al-Huzaimi mentions Ibn Hajar al-Asqalani's *Attaining the Goal* and *The Expansion on the Science of Inheritance* (*Al-Rahbiyyah fi 'ilm al-fara'id*), which is a work on Islamic law of inheritance by Muhammad al-Mutafannanah, a twelfth-century jurist in the Shafi'i school.
138 Al-Dir'iyyah was the capital of the first Saudi state destroyed in the Egyptian conquest in 1818. It is located near Riyadh.
139 Al-Tuwaijiri's book attacks modern astronomy for contradicting a literal understanding of the Quran and the Prophetic Traditions: *The Intense Thunderbolts against Modern Astronomy* (*al-Sawa'iq al-shadidah ala a'da' al-hai'ah al-jadidah*).
140 Literally, *ijtihad* (independent legal reasoning) and *taqlid* (following previous rulings).
141 Footnote 5 in al-Huzaimi: Usually *Addition to the Seeker of Contentment* (*Zad al-mustaqni'*). [NB: This work is a condensed treatment of law according to the

142 Hanbali legal school by the sixteenth-century scholar Musa al-Hujawi. H. Laoust, "Hanabila," *Encyclopaedia of Islam*, 2nd ed., Brill, 2006].
142 A sound Prophetic Tradition is considered reliable and a weak Prophetic Tradition is considered unreliable.
143 A mufti is an expert in religious law who issues a legal opinion in unprecedented cases.
144 Al-Huzaimi again mentions al-Hujawi's *Addition to the Seeker of Contentment*.
145 The Awakening Movement (*al-Sahwah*) in Saudi Arabia came about as a result of contacts between Saudis and Islamists from other Muslim countries from the 1960s onward. Its combination of Wahhabi theology with Islamist political and social activism gained influence in the 1980s and became a protest movement in the early 1990s. Stephane Lacroix, *Awakening Islam*.
146 Footnote 6 in al-Huzaimi: This is known as *al-tathwib*.
147 See Challenges to Clerical Authority in the introduction.
148 Footnote 7 in al-Huzaimi: Munir al-Tunisi came to lead prayer for the group at the Ikhwan mosque at the sunset prayer. He recited Surat Al Imran, The Family of Imran, to them. He went on at length until we approached the evening prayer. When he did *sallam* there arose a clamor of objections and a tumult happened at the mosque. Sa'd al-Tamimi was a founder [of the Salafi Group] and he was present. They kicked Tunisi out of the mosque and threatened him if he ever tried to lead prayer in the Ikhwan mosque again or the like. Thus this provocative character left, cursing the Salafi doctrine of the Ikhwan and their attachment to Prophetic Tradition.
149 The Salafi Group's religious guide, Abd al-Aziz ibn Baz, had left Medina and did not attend the meeting. Hegghammer and Lacroix, "Rejectionist Islamism in Saudi Arabia," p. 108.
150 The implication is that Juhaman's itinerant preaching made him the best-known figure in the Group throughout the country.
151 This incident occurred in December 1977.
152 Footnote 8 in al-Huzaimi: Meaning the man is from his tribe.
153 The *dabb* lizard.
154 A region located in central Najd, north of Riyadh. Its two major cities are Buraidah and Unaizah.
155 Members of the Muslim Brotherhood were subject to persecution in Egypt and Syria in particular. Other Islamists admired them for courageously standing up to secular Arab nationalist governments.
156 The reference is to men who volunteered for the anti-communist war in Afghanistan during the 1980s. In the Muslim world, the war was considered a jihad, or holy struggle, to defend Islam.
157 The former Ikhwan fighters were enlisted in a military force that eventually became the National Guard.
158 *The Book of Additions and Revisions* (*al-Ilzamat wa al-tatabbu'*) is a collection of Sound Traditions that are not found in the canonical collections of al-Bukhari and Muslim. The compiler, Ali ibn Umar al-Daraqutni (918–995), was a religious scholar widely known for his expertise in Prophetic Traditions. See J. Robson, "al-Daraqutni," *Encylopaedia of Islam*, 2nd ed., Brill, 2006.
159 The ninth-century scholar al-Tirmidhi compiled one of the six canonical collections of Prophetic Traditions.
160 *Raf' al-iltibas an millat Ibrahim alayhi salam* is one of Juhaiman's works. Al-Huzaimi cites passages later in the memoir.

161 Footnote 1 in al-Huzaimi: In Rif'at Sayyid Ahmad's book *The Essays of Juhaiman al-Utaibi, Leader of the Storming of the Grand Mosque*, he attributes some essays to Juhaiman that he did not write. I do not know why Ahmad insisted on that. He was not certain about the authorship of *Removing Confusion*. Likewise, he overlooked an important essay because he did know about it: *Call of the Ikhwan: How It Began and Where It Is Going* (*Da'wat al-ikhwan kayfa bada'at wa ila ayna tasir*). The essays that Rif'at Sayyid Ahmad misattributed to Juhaiman include: *The Explanation of Idolatry and Its Perils* (*Bayan al-shirk was khatrihi*) by a Yemeni religious student, Muhammad al-Saghir. *The Strongest Bond Is Love for God's Sake and Enmity for God's Sake* (*Awthaq ura al-iman al-hubb fi allah wa al-bughd fi allah*) by Hasan ibn Muhsin al-Wahidi, a Yemeni national. *Satan's Ways to Corrupt Hearts* (*Madakhil al-shaitan li-ifsad al-qulub*) by a Yemeni religious student, Muhammad al-Saghir. *The Explanation and Detail on the Obligation to Know the Legal Proof* (*Al-Bayan wa al-tafsil fi wujub ma'rifat al-dalil*) by Muhammad Abd Allah al-Qahtani, the so-called Mahdi.
162 Abd al-Aziz ibn Baz was blind.
163 The night of 27 Ramadan has special religious meaning. It is called the Night of Power and is associated with the first revelation to the Prophet. In the Common Era calendar, that would have been August 31, 1978.
164 A reference to the essay *Removing Confusion about the Religion of Abraham*.
165 A daily newspaper published in Mecca.
166 Mount Tamiah is a prominent peak on the route from Riyadh to Medina.
167 References to verses in the Quran, Prophetic Traditions, and classical works.
168 Footnote 2 in al-Huzaimi: Juhaiman ibn Saif al-Utaibi, *The Tribulations, Reports of the Mahdi, the Descent of Jesus, and Portents of the Last Hour* (*Risalat al-fitan wa akhbar al-mahdi wa nuzul 'Isa alaihi al-salam wa ashrat al-sa'ah*), in *The Collection of Seven Essays* (*Majmu' al-saba' rasa'il*), p. 3.
169 Footnote 3 in al-Huzaimi: From the previous citation, p. 3.
170 Quraish is the tribe of the Prophet Muhammad. Hasan and Husain were the Prophet's grandsons, offspring of his daughter Fatimah and her husband Ali.
171 A sharif is someone claiming descent from the Prophet Muhammad. Muhammad Ali Pasha, the Ottoman governor of Egypt, ordered an invasion of Arabia in 1811 to expel the Saudis from Hijaz. The invasion and ensuing war lasted until 1818, when the invading forces destroyed the first Saudi emirate and its capital, al-Dir'iyyah. The Saudis were able to regain power in the early 1820s and established their capital at Riyadh, a few miles from the ruins of al-Dir'iyyah.
172 That would have been early November 1979.
173 Coinciding with November 20, 1979.
174 The Yemeni Corner is the southern corner of the Kaabah. S. Nomanul Haq, "Rukn," *Encyclopaedia of Islam*, 2nd ed., Brill, 2006. Abraham's Station is a stone near the Kaabah that according to Muslim belief bears the footprints of the Prophet Abraham that he left when he built the Kaabah. It is presently enclosed by a small glass and metal structure. M. J. Kister, "Makam Ibrahim," *Encyclopaedia of Islam*, 2nd ed., Brill, 2006.
175 Bearing arms in the Grand Mosque is permitted in Islamic law under certain conditions but not to stage an uprising.
176 Footnote 4 in al-Huzaimi: There was a group of Ikhwan that rejected the idea that the Expected Mahdi Muhammad Abd Allah al-Qahtani was killed or had died, even after the Grand Mosque uprising, and the idea that the Mahdi had failed even

though his two brothers Sa'id and Sa'd and his nephew were later able to identify him among the corpses. Some of them, like Abd al-Rahman Hamudah, a Palestinian, and Yusuf Akbar, swear that he did not die.

177 A town in northern Saudi Arabia.
178 Muharram is the first month in the Muslim lunar calendar.
179 Pronouncing *Allahu Akbar* in the call to prayer.
180 Qusayy was an ancestor of the Prophet Muhammad. According to Muslim tradition, Qusayy restored the Kaabah as a shrine for the pre-Islamic Arabs.
181 Muhammad al-Subayyil was a prayer leader at the Grand Mosque. He died in 2013.
182 Footnote 5 in al-Huzaimi: He was the father of Muhammad Abd Allah al-Qahtani's wife and the father of the wife of Sa'id, the Mahdi's brother, but I do not recall his name, only that he was from Asir.
183 Al-Mas'ah is a covered concourse that connects two small hills, al-Safa and al-Marwah, near the Grand Mosque.
184 Zamzam is a well inside the Grand Mosque.
185 Footnote 6 in al-Huzaimi: These materials were available in the Grand Mosque. The clay Zamzam bottles were commonly used to give water to people. Zamzam water and gasoline were stored in the two tanks that had been used to bring dates and weapons into the Grand Mosque. As for the cloth, it was abundant.
186 Footnote 7 in al-Huzaimi: Except, of course, his own group, the Salafi Group, in which he represented the main proselytizer and a founder of the Group on which he forcibly imposed his ideas.
187 Here, Islamic mission work (*al-'amal al-da'wi al-islami*) refers to calling Muslims to correct religious practice and not to proselytizing among non-Muslims.
188 Footnote 8 in al-Huzaimi: Some say that Sajir was set up in 1333 AH, or about 1914 CE, at his majesty King Abd al-Aziz's order, God have mercy on him.
189 The implication is that if the Pious Ancestors did not know about these fields of knowledge, then later Muslims did not need to know them either.
190 *Al-Bayan wa al-tafsil fi wujub ma'rifat al-dalil.*
191 Literally, an Arab, but the sense here is a Bedouin.
192 Talhah was one of the Prophet's Companions and an early convert to Islam. W. Madelung, "Talha," *Encyclopaedia of Islam*, 2nd ed., Brill, 2006.
193 Footnote 9 in al-Huzaimi: *The Essays*, p. 374. References henceforth are to *Juhaiman's Essays* edited by Rif'at Sayyid Ahmad.
194 Ijtihad is independent reasoning about unprecedented legal questions. The "conditions of ijtihad" refer to the qualifications one is supposed to possess in order to undertake ijtihad.
195 The Quran.
196 The canonical collections of al-Bukhari and Muslim.
197 Footnote 10 in al-Huzaimi: Same source, p. 377.
198 Abu Umar Yusuf ibn Abd Allah ibn Abd al-Barr was an eleventh-century scholar of Prophetic Traditions and Islamic law from Cordoba. See Ch. Pellat, "Ibn Abd al-Barr," *Encyclopaedia of Islam*, 2nd ed., Brill, 2006.
199 *Jami' bayan al-ilm wa fadluhu.*
200 Footnote 11 in al-Huzaimi: Same source, p. 378.
201 Literally, blocking means to a prohibited act, a principle in Islamic law that is invoked to prohibit something that is permitted but might result in a prohibited act.
202 Sunni scholars propose different lists of the canonical collections of Prophetic Traditions.

203 He lists the following works here: Muhammad al-San'ani's *Paths to Peace* (*Subul al-salam*); Ibn Hajar al-Asqalani's *Victory of the Creator* (*Fath al-bari sharh Sahih al-Bukhari*); and Muhammad al-Shawkani's *The Attainment of Objectives* (*Nayl al-awtar*).

204 He lists the following works here: Three works by Ibn Hajar al-Asqalani: His biographical dictionary of men who transmitted Prophetic Traditions, *Refinement of the Refinement* (*Tahdhib al-tahdhib*); an abridgement of that biographical dictionary, *Clarification of the Refinement* (*Taqrib al-tahdhib*); and another biographical dictionary of transmitters of Prophetic Traditions, *The Eloquence of the Scales* (*Lisan al-mizan*). Three works by Muhammad al-Dhahabi: His biographical dictionary of transmitters of Prophetic Traditions, *The Scales of Moderation* (*Mizan al-i'tidal*); a biographical dictionary of transmitters in the six canonical collections of Prophetic Traditions, *The Uncovering* (*al-Kashif*); and a biographical dictionary of unreliable transmitters, *The Unreliable Ones* (*al-Du'afa*). Muhammad al-Dhahabi (1274–1348) was a Damascus scholar and specialist in Prophetic Traditions and Shafi'i law, and author of a major historical work. See Moh. Ben Cheneb and J. de Somogyi, "al-Dhahabi," *Encylopaedia of Islam*, 2nd ed., Brill, 2006.

205 In reporting a Prophetic Tradition, Muslims list the "chain" of individuals who transmitted it, going back to the Prophet or to one of his Companions. Specialists in Prophetic Traditions consider the chain of transmitters the basis for determining their authenticity.

206 Literally, blameworthy imitation.

207 Footnote 12 in al-Huzaimi: *The Explanation and Detail on the Obligation to Know the Legal Proof* (*Risalat al-bayan wa al-tafsil fi wujub ma'rifat al-dalil*), p. 402, from *Juhaiman's Essays*. Rif'at Sayyid Ahmad mistakenly attributed this essay to Juhaiman, when in fact it is by Muhammad Abd Allah al-Qahtani. Likewise, this essay is attributed to Juhaiman in *Monotheism and Jihad* (*al-Tawhid wa al-jihad*) by Abu Muhammad al-Maqdisi. [Al-Maqdisi is a major contemporary Salafi authority living in Jordan. See Joas Wagemakers, *A Quietist Jihadi: The Ideology and Influence of Abu Muhammad al-Maqdisi*, Cambridge University Press, 2012.]

208 Footnote 13 in al-Huzaimi: This poem had not been attributed to Muhammad Abd Allah al-Qahtani (the Mahdi) because he had not publicly declared his hostility toward the government at the time so he was not wanted [by the government] and therefore at the time of the first arrest of Ikhwan members he was set free for lack of evidence.

209 God's guidance revealed in the Quran and the Prophetic Tradition.

210 In the pejorative sense of someone who introduces ideas and habits contrary to religion.

211 *Al-Idah wa al-tabyin li-ma waqa'a fi-hi al-aktharun min mushabahat al-mushrikin.*

212 Abd Allah ibn Umar was a prominent early Muslim: the son of the second caliph Umar and the transmitter of many Prophetic Traditions. L. Veccia Vaglieri, "Abd Allah b. 'Umar b. al-Khattab," *Encyclopaedia of Islam*, 2nd ed., Brill, 2006.

213 Imam Ahmad refers to Ahmad ibn Hanbal. Abu Daud al-Sijistani was a ninth-century compiler of one of the canonical collections of Prophetic Traditions. J. Robson, "Abu Da'ud al-Sidjistani," *Encyclopaedia of Islam*, 2nd ed., Brill, 2006.

214 Abu Bakr Muhammad ibn Hibban was a tenth-century expert in Prophetic Traditions from eastern Iran. J.W. Fück, "Ibn Hibban," *Encyclopaedia of Islam*, 2nd ed., Brill, 2006.

215 Abd Allah ibn Amr was a prominent early Muslim, the son of the conqueror of Egypt, 'Amr ibn al-'As. See Martin Lings, *Muhammad: His Life based on the Earliest Sources*, Inner Traditions International, 1983, p. 285.

216 This and similar Prophetic Traditions warning Muslims against adopting the customs of Jews and Christians are a staple of Salafi doctrine.

217 Abu Ya'la Muhammad ibn al-Farra' (990–1066) was scholar of Prophetic Traditions from Baghdad and a major figure in the historical development of Hanbali law and theology. See H. Laoust, "Ibn al-Farra," *Encyclopaedia of Islam*, 2nd ed., Brill, 2006. Al-Tabarani (873–971) was a specialist in Prophetic Traditions born in Syria. He spent most of his life in Isfahan, Iran. See Maribel Fierro, "al-Tabarani," *Encyclopaedia of Islam*, 2nd ed., Brill, 2006. Al-Tuwaijiri cites al-Tabarani's work on Prophetic Traditions, *The Middle Collection* (*Mu'jam al-awsat*). Ahmad al-Baihaqi (994–1066) was a scholar of Prophetic Traditions and specialist in Shafi'i law from Iran. His *Branches of Faith* (*Shu'ab al-iman*) is a multivolume work on belief. Said Naficy, "Ahmad al-Baihaki," *Encyclopaedia of Islam*, 2nd ed., Brill, 2006. Jabir ibn Abd Allah was an early convert to Islam and a major transmitter of Prophetic Traditions. M. J. Kister, "Djābir b. Abd Allah," *Encyclopaedia of Islam*, 2nd ed., Brill, 2006. Ali ibn Abu Bakr al-Haithami (1335–1404) was an Egyptian scholar of Prophetic Traditions.

218 Al-Nasa'i (830–915) was a compiler of one of the canonical collections, *al-Sunan*.

219 Al-Bukhari and Muslim, the collectors of canonical Prophetic Traditions.

220 Al-Hakim Muhammad al-Naysapuri (933–1014) was a specialist in Prophetic Traditions and author of *The Supplement to the Two Sound Collections* (*al-Mustadrak 'ala al-sahihain*) on the two canonical collections of al-Bukhari and Muslim. See J. Robson, "al-Hakim al-Naysapuri," *Encyclopaedia of Islam*, 2nd ed., Brill, 2006. Ibn Juraij (699–767) was a collector and transmitter of Prophetic Traditions, from Mecca. See Ch. Pellat, "Ibn Djuraydj," *Encyclopaedia of Islam*, 2nd ed., Brill, 2006. Muhammad ibn Qais ibn Makhramah (c. 704–767), known as Ibn Ishaq, collected Prophetic Traditions that formed the core of the first biography of the Prophet Muhammad. See J. M. B. Jones, "Ibn Ishak," *Encyclopaedia of Islam*, 2nd ed., Brill, 2006. Al-Miswar ibn Makhramah was a Companion of the Prophet Muhammad and transmitter of Prophetic Traditions. Muhammad al-Dhahabi, *The Abridgement of the Supplement* (*Talkhis al-mustadrak*) is a work that assesses the reliability of Prophetic Traditions in al-Naysapuri's collection.

221 *Musnad al-Shafi'i* is a compilation of Prophetic Traditions that lists traditions according to the first person who transmitted them from the Prophet.

222 A *mursal* Prophetic Tradition has a chain of transmitters that includes one unknown person and is therefore not completely reliable.

223 Abu Hurairah (d. c. 678) was a Companion of the Prophet and the source of a large number of Prophetic Traditions. See J. Robson, "Abu Hurayrah," *Encyclopaedia of Islam*, 2nd ed., Brill, 2006.

224 Sa'id ibn Jubair was an important late-seventh/early-eighth-century scholar in Kufa, an early Muslim settlement in Iraq. H. Motzki, "Sa'id b. Djubayr," *Encyclopaedia of Islam*, 2nd ed., Brill, 2006. Al-Hasan al-Basri was an influential late-seventh/early-eighth-century figure renowned for his piety. H. Ritter, "Hasan al-Basri," *Encyclopaedia of Islam*, 2nd ed., Brill, 2006. Qatadah ibn Nu'man was a Companion of the Prophet and one of the helpers of Medina. Ibn Shihab al-Zuhri was an important figure in the collection of Prophetic Traditions during the late seventh and

eighth centuries. M. Lecker, "Ibn Shihab al-Zuhri," *Encyclopaedia of Islam*, 2nd ed., Brill, 2006.
225 *Jami'* of al-Tirmidhi.
226 Abu Tamimah al-Hujaimi, Tarif ibn Mujalid (d. 713) was an early transmitter of Prophetic Traditions. Lyall Armstrong, *The Qussas of Early Islam*, Brill, 2017, p. 294.
227 Ibn Majah (824–887) is the compiler of one of the six canonical collections of Prophetic Traditions, *Kitab al-Sunan*. See J. W. Fück, "Ibn Madja," *Encyclopaedia of Islam*, 2nd ed., Brill, 2006.
228 Abd al-Rahman ibn Abi Hatim al-Razi (854–938) composed an influential exegesis of the Quran and was an important scholar in the development of the study of Prophetic Traditions. See Eerik Dickinson, *The Development of Early Sunnite Hadith Criticism: The Taqdima of Ibn Abi Hatim al-Razi*, Brill, 2001.
229 *Kitab al-tawsiyah*.
230 *Raf' al-iltibas an millat Ibrahim*.
231 Surat al-Nahl, The Bee 16:123.
232 Surat al-An'am, The Cattle 6:161.
233 He divided the people between believers and unbelievers.
234 Abu Sai'd al-Khudri (d. c. 690) was one of the "helpers" in Medina and a frequently cited source of Prophetic Traditions. W. Montgomery Watt, *Muhammad at Medina*, Clarendon Press, 1956, p. 167.
235 Salafis consider popular practices at the tombs of respected pious men and women to constitute idolatry.
236 Footnote 14 in al-Huzaimi: Ansar al-Sunnah was established by Sheikh Muhammad Hamid al-Fiqi in 1926 in Cairo. Its main goals are calling to pure monotheism and fighting innovations and signs of polytheism. It had followers in Sudan and elsewhere. Juhaiman knew them well, especially some Sudanese members.
237 A battle in 629 fought between Muslims and Jews at the oasis of Khaibar, north of Medina.
238 *Al-Hakimiyyah al-malhamiyyah*: In Arabic, *hakimiyyah* denotes sovereignty and has the connotation of a system of rule or government. In Arabic, *malhami* denotes a fierce battle and it has the connotation of battles that will take place when God sends the Mahdi. "Millenarian" captures the sense common to other religions of a rupture in time when God will intervene to rid the world of injustice and corruption to install a reign of justice.
239 The essay is in Rif'at Sayyid Ahmad, *Rasa'il Juhaiman al-Utaibi, qa'id al-muqtahimin li'l Masjid al-Haram bi-Makkah*, Madbuli, 1988, pp. 57–99.
240 Literally, realization of the text about fierce battles.
241 *Fasl al-khilafah allati ala minhaj al-nubuwwah wa al-mulk al-jabri*.
242 Nu'man ibn Bashir was a later Companion of the Prophet from Medina. See K. V. Zettersteen, "Al-Nu'man b. Bashir," *Encyclopaedia of Islam*, 2nd ed., Brill, 2006.
243 Ahmad ibn Hanbal.
244 Sunni doctrine holds that descent from the Prophet's tribe of Quraish is a necessary qualification for the caliphate.
245 Juhaiman uses a derogatory term for Shiites—*Rawafid*—meaning rejectors, for their rejection of the first three caliphs on the grounds that Ali should have followed Muhammad as leader of the Ummah.
246 Namely, allowing other religions in the country.
247 Namely, the Shiites.
248 This refers to popular veneration of holy men whose graves were turned into shrines.

249　The original Ikhwan of the early twentieth century.
250　In other words, their physical emigration to agricultural colonies was at the same time a spiritual relocation or emigration from idolatry to monotheism.
251　In other words, Shiites in Iraq, despised by Salafis for what they deem excessive veneration of Ali and his family. Ali ibn Abi Talib was the cousin and son-in-law of the Prophet. Shiites consider him and his descendants the legitimate successors to the Prophet as leader, or imam, of the Muslims. Fatimah was the Prophet's daughter, Ali's wife, and mother of the main lie of Shiite imams, including his sons Hasan and Husain.

Appendix I

1　Footnote 1 in al-Huzaimi: Salah al-Din Khalil Aybak al-Safadi, *al-Wafi bi al-wafiyat*, vol. 15, p. 175. [Al-Safadi (1297–1363) was a prolific writer in a number of literary fields and is famous for his biographical dictionary, *al-Wafi*. See F. Rosenthal, "al-Safadi," *Encyclopaedia of Islam*, 2nd ed., Brill, 2006.]
2　Footnote 2 in al-Huzaimi: These pages are from *The Dream and Its Role in the Making of the Incident*.
3　Urwah ibn al-Zubair (c. 643–712) was the son of one of the Prophet's eminent Companions. He was an early transmitter of Prophetic Traditions, an adviser to caliphs on legal matters, and a compiler of reports that formed the core of accounts of early Muslim history. See G. Schoeler, "Urwa ibn al-Zubayr," *Encyclopaedia of Islam*, 2nd ed., Brill, 2006.
4　One of the Prophet's wives and a source of many Prophetic Traditions. See W. Montgomery Watt, "A'ishah bint Abi Bakr," *Encyclopaedia of Islam*, 2nd ed., Brill, 2006.
5　Footnote 3 in al-Huzaimi: *Fath al-bari sharh Sahih al-Bukhari*, Part 1, p. 8 [*Victory of the Creator: Commentary on al-Bukhari*, by Ibn Hajar al-Asqalani].
6　Abu Qatadah al-Ansari (d. c 661) was one of the helpers of Medina and a source of many Prophetic Traditions. *The History of al-Tabari: An Annotated Translation*, vol. VII, *The Foundation of the Community*, translated by M. V. McDonald and annotated by W. Montgomery Watt, State University of New York Press, 1987, pp. 101–3.
7　Footnote 4 in al-Huzaimi: *Fath al-bari*, Part 12, p. 368.
8　Footnote 5 in al-Huzaimi: *Fath al-bari*, Part 12, p. 369.
9　Ubadah ibn al-Samit was one of the helpers of Medina, one of the first to embrace Islam. He died during the caliphate of Uthman. Watt, *Muhammad at Medina*, pp. 179–82.
10　Footnote 6 in al-Huzaimi: *Fath al-bari*, Part 12, p. 373.
11　Footnote 7 in al-Huzaimi: *Fath al-bari*, Part 12, p. 373.
12　Footnote 8 in al-Huzaimi: *Fath al-bari*, Part 12, p. 373.
13　Footnote 9 in al-Huzaimi: *Fath al-bari*, Part 12, p. 375.
14　Footnote 10 in al-Huzaimi: This was especially the case for those who did not use reason to arrive at legal positions and instead stopped at a literal understanding of the Quran and the Prophetic Tradition, which is the case for Salafism in general and for the Awakening in particular. [NB: See Note 145, p. 169 on the Awakening Movement].
15　Footnote 11 in al-Huzaimi: Muhammad ibn al-Husain ibn Abi Ya'la al-Farra', *Tabaqat al-Hanabila*, volume 1, p. 24, in the biography of Ahmad ibn Ja'far ibn Ya'qub ibn Abd Allah Abu al-Abbas al-Farisi al-Istakhri. [N.B. *Tabaqat al-hanabilah* (*The*

Ranks of Hanbali Scholars) is a "biographical dictionary," that is, a compilation of biographies of scholars in the Hanbali legal school].

16 The *ahl al-athar* emerged in the eighth century and claimed to follow the Traditions of the Prophet and his Companions in figuring out the rules of Islamic law as opposed to the *ahl al-ra'y*, or jurists who used reasoning. They are more commonly referred to as *ahl al-hadith*. See J. Schacht, "Ahl al-Hadith," *Encyclopaedia of Islam*, 2nd ed., Brill, 2006.

17 Footnote 12 in al-Huzaimi: In his exegesis of Surat Yusuf (Joseph), al-Qurtubi wrote,

> In general, the good dream is from God, it is truth, and it has a sound interpretation. Some might do without the interpretation. As a divine miracle and blessing, it increases the believer in his belief. The people of religion and truth, the people of opinion (*ra'y*), and the people of tradition (*athar*) do not dispute this matter. Only atheists and a few Mu'tazilites deny it.

[N.B. Abu Abd Allah al-Qurtubi (1214–1273) is the author of an important exegesis of the Quran. See R. Arnaldez, "al-Kurtubi," *Encyclopaedia of Islam*, 2nd ed., Brill, 2006; Mustansir Mir, "Tafsir," *The Oxford Encyclopedia of the Islamic World*]. Ibn Hajar al-Haitami wrote in *Al-Fatawa al-Hadithiyyah*, p. 4,

> He, may God be pleased with him, was once asked, "What is the truth about dreams?" He answered, may God give benefit with his knowledge, "The truth about dreams according to most Sunnis is that God, be he exalted, creates them in the heart or the senses of someone while asleep, just as he creates awakening. He does what he wills, and nothing impedes him, neither sleep [a person's being asleep] or anything else. The dream may occur during wakefulness [as a vision] or in sleep; the dream may be a token of matters that He will create later or that He already created and took place."

[N.B. Ibn Hajar al-Haitami (1504–1567) was an Egyptian scholar in the Shafi'i school. See C. van Arendonk and J. Schacht, "Ibn Hadjar al-Haytami," *Encyclopaedia of Islam*, 2nd ed., Brill, 2006.]

18 Footnote 13 in al-Huzaimi: So it is wrong to be surprised that fundamentalist groups do not have a plan for the future. In general, they believe we are near the End of Time. What they think is necessary, according to the texts they rely upon, is represented by decline in every possible way, then will come the appearance of the Mahdi and the Antichrist, so why worry about the future?

19 Muhammad ibn Sirin (654–728) was a renowned interpreter of dreams. See Toufic Fahd, "Ibn Sirin," *Encyclopaedia of Islam*, 2nd ed., Brill, 2006.

20 Footnote 14 in al-Huzaimi: *Fath al-bari sharh Sahih al-Bukhari*, Book of the Beginning of Revelation, vol. 12, p. 404.

21 Footnote 15 in al-Huzaimi: According to the Science of Prophetic Traditions, there is not a single proof that the Mahdi will appear at the End of Time or any other time.

22 Footnote 16 in al-Huzaimi: Juhaiman thought he had special insight into people and affairs, which is the most important qualification for interpreting dreams. Such confidence made him push the issue of Muhammad Abd Allah al-Qahtani as the Expected Mahdi. He treated the issue as a personal matter due to his certainty and belief in his insight.

23 *Kitab ithaf al-jama'ah bi-ma ja'a fi fitan wa al-malahim wa ashrat al-sa'ah*.

24 Footnote 17 in al-Huzaimi: *Risalat al-fitan wa akhbar al-Mahdi*, in *Rasa'il Juhaiman*, p. 209.

25 Footnote 18 in al-Huzaimi: Before he recorded it in *Risalat al-fitan wa akhbar al-mahdi wa nuzul Isa wa ashrat al-sa'ah*.

26 A Companion of the Prophet and transmitter of Prophetic Traditions.
27 Footnote 19 in al-Huzaimi: They were from Jizan and they were nicknamed al-Turki because they came with the Turks.
28 Footnote 20 in al-Huzaimi: It is well known that the Turks were accompanied by sharifs on their military expeditions, like a good luck charm for the invasion.
29 Prophetic Traditions foretell the Mahdi will have the same name as the Prophet.

Appendix II

This account was published in *al-Riyadh* newspaper, number 4397, 17 Muharram 1400 AH/December 7, 1979 CE.

1 Abd Allah ibn Mas'ud (c. 594–653) was one of the Prophet's earliest and closest Companions and an important source of Prophetic Traditions. See J.-C. Vadet, "Ibn Mas'ud," *Encyclopaedia of Islam*, 2nd ed., Brill, 2006.
2 Footnote 1 in al-Huzaimi: Abd Allah al-Harbi did not storm the Grand Mosque. He was killed far away from there. It seems that Juhaiman did not know which Ikhwan had gone in with him because he had been in hiding, in flight, and isolated from them for a long time.
3 Footnote 2 in al-Huzaimi: Umar ibn Jarallah did not storm the Grand Mosque because he was in prison for distributing the pamphlets.
4 Hind bint Abu Umayyah "Umm Salamah" was one of the Prophet's wives. Ruth Roded, "Umm Salama Hind," *Encyclopaedia of Islam*, 2nd ed., Brill, 2006.
5 The Kaabah.
6 Translation from Wilferd Madelung, "Abd Allah B. Al-Zubayr and the Mahdi," *Journal of Near Eastern Studies* 40 (1981), 295.
7 Translation from Madelung, "Abd Allah B. Al-Zubayr and the Mahdi," pp. 294–5.
8 A reference to the Quran, Surat al-Fil, The Elephant, where God wards off an attack on Mecca by an army with fighters mounted on elephants.
9 This account is from an official Saudi newspaper.
10 Surat al-Nahl, The Bee 16:110–112.
11 Surat al-Qasas, The Story 28:57.
12 Zainab bint Jahsh (c. 591–641) was one of the Prophet's wives. See C. E. Bosworth, "Zaynab bt. Djahsh," *Encyclopaedia of Islam*, 2nd ed. Brill, 2006.
13 Hafsah bint Umar (c. 605–665) was one of the Prophet's wives and the daughter of Umar, the second caliph. See L. Veccia Vaglieri, "Hafsa," *Encyclopaedia of Islam*, 2nd ed., Brill, 2006.
14 The newspaper account adopted the government's view of Juhaiman's group as criminals.

Appendix III

Interview with *Electronic al-Majallah* magazine published on Saturday, November 21, 2009: the thirtieth anniversary of the uprising. "Juhayman's Sins." *Majalla*. https://eng.majalla.com/2009/11/article55110940/juhayman%E2%80%99s-sins. Accessed July 31, 2019. I have modified the translation in the online article.

1 Al-Huzaimi is drawing on a contrast in Saudi culture between nomadic folk in the desert and settled folk in oasis settlements.

2 Sultan ibn Bijad and other leaders died in detention after their surrender.
3 Al-Huzaimi is distinguishing between Albani and Saudi clerics.
4 These streets are located in al-Batha, the old city center.
5 Manfuhah was once a separate town south of Riyadh. It is now a neighborhood in the city's south end.
6 Ghubairah is a district in the south end of Riyadh, near Manfuhah.
7 In other words, Juhaiman would travel out of town to the desert and spend time with desert dwellers in their tents while other leaders tended to stay in the cities.
8 Muhammad Abd Allah al-Qahtani.
9 The Umayyad Mosque is in Damascus.
10 Around May 1979.
11 That is the Old Ikhwan.

Appendix IV

1 Muhammad Zahid al-Kawthari (1879–1951) was a prolific writer of theological works critical of the Hanbali–Salafi tradition. Mustafa Macit Karagozolgu, "Contested Avenues in Post-Classical Sunni Hadith Criticism: A Reading through the Lens of *al-Mughni 'an al-Hifz wa-l-kitab*," *Journal of Islamic Studies* 29:2 (2018), 176.
2 The Mutazilites adopted rationalistic interpretations of theological issues. The Hanbali–Salafi tradition considers their positions to be heretical. Racha El Omari, "Mu'tazilah," *The Oxford Encyclopedia of the Islamic World. Oxford Islamic Studies Online*, http://www.oxfordislamicstudies.com/article/opr/t236/e1073 (accessed June 30, 2020).
3 The Jahmites were a theological tendency associated with the doctrine that the Quran was not eternal but created. Salafis consider that doctrine to be heretical. See W. Montgomery Watt, "Djahmiyya," *Encyclopaedia of Islam*, 2nd ed., Brill, 2006.
4 Al-Huzaimi is referring to the Prophetic Tradition Folk and Salafis during the early Muslim centuries.
5 Muhammad ibn Daud al-Zahiri (868–909) developed his father Daud ibn Khalaf's literalist legal method that is the foundation for the Zahiri legal school. J.-C Vadet, "Ibn Dawud," *Encyclopaedia of Islam*, 2nd ed., Brill, 2006.
6 Muhammad ibn Jarir al-Tabari (839–923) is best known for his vast history of early Islam. He also composed an influential exegesis of the Quran. See C. E. Bosworth, "al-Tabari," *Encyclopaedia of Islam*, 2nd ed., Brill, 2006.
7 *Al-Mughni (The Enricher)* is a major work on Hanbali law by Muwaffaq al-Din Ibn Qudamah (1147–1223) who was born near Jerusalem and spent most of his life in Damascus. See G. Makdisi, "Ibn Qudama," *Encyclopaedia of Islam*, 2nd ed., Brill, 2006.
8 A reference to the phrase *yusaddid wa yuqarib*.
9 Al-Ud is an old neighborhood in Riyadh.
10 Al-Qahtani was sometimes referred to by his middle name, Abd Allah.

FURTHER READING AND WORKS CITED

The Mecca Uprising

Al-'Utaibi, Juhaiman. *Rasa'il Juhaiman al-'Utaybi: Qa'id al-muqtahimin li al-masjid al-haram bi-Makkah (Juhaiman al-'Utaibi's Essays: Leader of the Invaders of the Haram Mosque in Mecca)*. Rif'at Sayyid Ahmad, ed. Madbuli, 1988.

Buchan, James. "The Return of the Ikhwan," in David Holden and Richard Johns, eds., *The House of Saud: The Rise and Rule of the Most Powerful Dynasty in the Arab World*. Holt, Rinehart, and Winston, 1982, pp. 511–26.

Kechichian, Joseph A. "Islamic Revivalism and Change in Saudi Arabia: Juhayman al-'Utaybi's 'Letters' to the Saudi People." *Muslim World* 80:1 (1990), 1–16.

Lacroix, Stephane, and Thomas Hegghammer. "Rejectionist Islamism in Saudi Arabia: The Story of Juhayman al-'Utaybi Revisited." *International Journal of Middle East Studies* 39:1 (2007), 103–22.

Trofimov, Yaroslav. *The Siege of Mecca: The Forgotten Uprising in Islam's Holiest Shrine and the Birth of Al-Qaeda*. Doubleday, 2007.

Saudi Arabia

Al-Rasheed, Madawi. *A History of Saudi Arabia*, 2nd ed. Cambridge University Press, 2010.

Lacey, Robert. *Inside the Kingdom: Kings, Clerics, Modernists, Terrorists, and the Struggle for Saudi Arabia*. Viking, 2009.

Lacey, Robert. *The Kingdom: Arabia and the House of Saud*. Avon, 1983.

Vasiliev, Alexei. *The History of Saudi Arabia*. New York University Press, 2000.

Wahhabism

Al-Fahad, Abdulaziz. "From Exclusivism to Accommodation: Doctrinal and Legal Evolution of Wahhabism." *New York University Law Review* 79:2 (2004), 485–519.

Commins, David. *The Mission and the Kingdom: Wahhabi Power behind the Saudi Throne*, rev. paperback ed. I.B. Tauris, 2016.

Crawford, Michael. *Ibn Abd al-Wahhab*. One World, 2014.

Habib, John S. *Ibn Sa'ud's Warriors of Islam: The Ikhwan of Najd and Their Role in the Creation of the Sa'udi Kingdom, 1910–1930*. Brill, 1978.

Lacroix, Stephane. *Awakening Islam: The Politics of Religious Dissent in Contemporary Saudi Arabia*. Harvard University Press, 2011.

Religious Authority in Saudi Arabia

Farquhar, Michael. *Circuits of Faith: Migration, Education, and the Wahhabi Mission*. Stanford University Press, 2016.

Mouline, Nabil. *The Clerics of Islam: Religious Authority and Political Power in Saudi Arabia*. Ethan S. Rundell, trans. Yale University Press, 2014.

Bedouin

Al-Fahad, Abdulaziz. "The 'imama vs. the 'iqal: Hadari-Bedouin Conflict and the Formation of the Saudi State," in Madawi Al-Rasheed and Robert Vitalis, eds., *Counter-Narratives: History, Contemporary Society, and Politics in Saudi Arabia and Yemen*. Palgrave Macmillan, 2004, pp. 35–75.

Al-Fahad, Abdulaziz. "Raiders and Traders: A Poet's Lament on the End of the Bedouin Heroic Age," in Bernard Haykel, Stephane Lacroix, and Thomas Hegghammer, eds., *Saudi Arabia in Transition*. Princeton University Press, 2015, pp. 231–62.

Cole, Donald. "Where Have the Bedouin Gone?" *Anthropological Quarterly* 76:2 (2003), 235–67.

Kurpershoek, Marcel. *Arabia of the Bedouins*. Saqi, 2002.

Islam and Early Muslim History

Berkey, Jonathan P. *The Formation of Islam: Religion and Society in the Near East, 600 to 1800*. Cambridge University Press, 2003.

Cook, Michael. *Commanding Right and Forbidding Wrong in Islamic Thought*. Cambridge University Press, 2010.

Denny, Frederick. *An Introduction to Islam*, 4th ed. Pearson Prentice Hall, 2011.

Egger, Vernon O. *A History of the Muslim World to 1750: The Making of a Civilization*, 2nd ed. Routledge, 2017.

Encyclopaedia of Islam, 2nd ed. P. Bearman, Th. Bianquis, C. E. Bosworth, E. van Donzel, and W. P. Heinrichs, eds. Brill, 2006.

Encyclopaedia of the Qur'an. Jane Dammen McAuliffe, ed. Brill, 2006.

Salafism

Haykel, Bernard. "On the Nature of Salafi Thought and Action," in Roel Meijer, ed., *Global Salafism: Islam's New Religious Movement*. Columbia University Press, 2009, pp. 33–57.

Lacroix, Stephane. "Between Revolution and Apoliticism: Nasir al-Din al-Albani and His Impact on the Shaping of Contemporary Salafism," in Roel Meijer, ed., *Global Salafism: Islam's New Religious Movement*. Columbia University Press, 2009, pp. 58–80.

Thurston, Alexander. *Salafism in Nigeria*. Cambridge University Press, 2016.

Wiktorowicz, Quintan. "The New Global Threat: Transnational Salafis and Jihad." *Middle East Policy* 8:1 (2001), 18–38.

Apocalypse, Mahdi, and Dreams

Filiu, Jean-Pierre. *Apocalypse in Islam*. University of California Press, 2011.
Schedtler, Justin Jeffcoat, and Kelly J. Murphy, eds. *Apocalypses in Context: Apocalyptic Currents throughout History*. Augsburg Fortress, 2016.
Sirriyeh, Elizabeth. *Dreams and Visions in the World of Islam*. I.B. Tauris, 2015.

Theory of Sects

Stark, Rodney, and William Sims Bainbridge. "Of Churches, Sects and Cults: Preliminary Concepts for a Theory of Religious Movements." *Journal for the Scientific Study of Religion* 18:2 (1979), 117–33.

Islamic Movements

Egyptian

Calvert, John. *Sayyid Qutb and the Origins of Islamic Radicalism*. Oxford University Press, 2014.
Ibrahim, Saad Eddin. "Anatomy of Egypt's Militant Islamic Groups: Methodological Note and Preliminary Findings." *International Journal of Middle East Studies* 12:4 (1980), 423–53.
Mitchell, Richard P. *The Society of the Muslim Brothers*. Oxford University Press, 1993.

South Asian

Ali, Jan A. "Tabligh Jama'at: A Transnational Movement of Islamic Faith Regeneration." *European Journal of Economic and Political Studies* 3 (2010), 103–31.
Metcalf, Barbara. *Islamic Revivalism in British India: Deoband, 1860–1900*. Princeton University Press, 1982.
Qurashi, M. M. "The Tabligh Movement: Some Observations." *Islamic Studies* 28:3 (1989), 237–48.

Works Cited

Abrahamian, Ervand. *A History of Modern Iran*, 2nd ed. Cambridge University Press, 2018.
Abu Daud. *Sunan Abi Dawud*, Book of Model Behavior of the Prophet (*Kitab al-sunnah*), Number 1677. *Sunnah.com*. https://sunnah.com/abudawud/42/2.
Ahmed, Chanfi. "For the Saudi's Kingdom or for the Umma? Global 'Ulama in the Dar al-Hadith in Medina." *Journal for Islamic Studies* 32 (2012), 70–90.
Ahmed, Chanfi. *West African 'Ulama and Salafism in Mecca and Medina*. Brill, 2015.
Al-Atawneh, Muhammad. *Wahhabi Islam Facing the Challenges of Modernity: Dar al-Ifta in the Modern Saudi State*. Brill, 2010.

Al-Fahad, Abdulaziz. "From Exclusivism to Accommodation: Doctrinal and Legal Evolution of Wahhabism." *New York University Law Review* 79:2 (2004), 485–519.

Al-Fahad, Abdulaziz. "The 'imama vs. the 'iqal: Hadari-Bedouin Conflict and the Formation of the Saudi State," in Madawi Al-Rasheed and Robert Vitalis, eds., *Counter-Narratives: History, Contemporary Society, and Politics in Saudi Arabia and Yemen*. Palgrave Macmillan, 2004, pp. 35–75.

Al-Fahad, Abdulaziz. "Raiders and Traders: A Poet's Lament on the End of the Bedouin Heroic Age," in Bernard Haykel, Stephane Lacroix, and Thomas Hegghammer, eds., *Saudi Arabia in Transition*. Princeton University Press, 2015, pp. 231–62.

Al-Mundhiri, Abdul-Azim. *The Translation of the Meanings of Summarized Sahih Muslim, Arabic-English*, 2 vols. Darussalam, 2000.

Al-Rasheed, Madawi. *A History of Saudi Arabia*, 2nd ed. Cambridge University Press, 2010.

Al-Rasheed, Madawi. *A Most Masculine State*. Cambridge University Press, 2013.

Ali, Jan A. "Tabligh Jama'at: A Transnational Movement of Islamic Faith Regeneration." *European Journal of Economic and Political Studies* 3 (2010), 103–31.

Al-Tabari. *The History of al-Tabari: An Annotated Translation*, vol. VII, *The Foundation of the Community*. Translated by M. V. McDonald and annotated by W. Montgomery Watt. State University of New York Press, 1987.

Amin, Kamaruddin. "Nasiruddin al-Albani on Muslim's *Sahih*: A Critical Study of His Method." *Islamic Law and Society* 11:2 (2004), 149–76.

Arendonk, C. van, and J. Schacht. "Ibn Hadjar al-Haytami," *Encyclopaedia of Islam*, 2nd ed. Brill, 2006.

Armstrong, Lyall. *The Qussas of Early Islam*. Brill, 2017.

Arnaldez, R. "al-Kurtubi," *Encyclopaedia of Islam*, 2nd ed. Brill, 2006.

Arnaldez, R. "Ibn Hazm," *Encyclopaedia of Islam*, 2nd ed. Brill, 2006.

Ben Cheneb, Moh, and J. de Somogyi. "al-Dhahabi," *Encylopaedia of Islam*, 2nd ed. Brill, 2006.

Berkey, Jonathan P. *The Formation of Islam: Religion and Society in the Near East, 600 to 1800*. Cambridge University Press, 2003.

Bernand, M. "Idjma'," *Encyclopaedia of Islam*, 2nd ed. Brill, 2006.

Bilal, Wafaa. *Shoot an Iraqi: Life, Art, and Resistance under the Gun*. City Lights, 2008.

Bill, James. *The Eagle and the Lion: The Tragedy of American-Iranian Relations*. Yale University Press, 1989.

Bonnefoy, Laurent. *Salafism in Yemen: Transnationalism and Religious Identity*. Oxford University Press, 2012.

Bosworth, C. E. "al-Tabari," *Encyclopaedia of Islam*, 2nd ed. Brill, 2006.

Bosworth, C. E. "Zaynab bt. Djahsh," *Encyclopaedia of Islam*, 2nd ed. Brill, 2006.

Brown, Jonathan A. C. "Is Islam Easy to Understand or Not?: Salafis, the Democratization of Interpretation, and the Need for the Ulama." *Journal of Islamic Studies* 26:2 (2015), 117–44.

Buchan, James. "The Return of the Ikhwan," in David Holden and Richard Johns, eds., *The House of Saud: The Rise and Rule of the Most Powerful Dynasty in the Arab World*. Holt, Rinehart, and Winston, 1982.

Bunzel, Cole. *The Kingdom and the Caliphate: Duel of the Islamic States*. Carnegie Endowment for International Peace, 2016.

Burak, G. "Madhhab," *Oxford Encyclopedia of Islam and Law*. Oxford Islamic Studies. Online: http://www.oxfordislamicstudies.com/article/opr/t349/e0094 (accessed June 28, 2020).

Cahen, Cl, Talbi, M., Mantran, R., Lambton, A. K. S., and Bazmee Ansari, A. S. "Hisba," *Encyclopaedia of Islam*, 2nd ed. Brill, 2006.
Calder, N. "al-Tahawi," *Encyclopaedia of Islam*, 2nd ed. Brill, 2006.
Calder, N. "Shari'a," *Encyclopaedia of Islam*, 2nd ed. Brill, 2006.
Calder, N. "Taklid," *Encyclopaedia of Islam*, 2nd ed. Brill, 2006.
Calvert, John. *Sayyid Qutb and the Origins of Islamic Radicalism*. Oxford University Press, 2014.
Cole, Donald. "Where Have the Bedouin Gone?" *Anthropological Quarterly* 76:2 (2003), 235–67.
Coll, Steve. *Ghost Wars: The Secret History of the CIA, Afghanistan, and Bin Laden, from the Soviet Invasion to September 10, 2001*. Penguin, 2004.
Commins, David. *Islamic Reform: Politics and Social Change in Late Ottoman Damascus*. Oxford University Press, 1990.
Commins, David. *The Mission and the Kingdom: Wahhabi Power behind the Saudi Throne*, rev. paperback ed. I.B. Tauris, 2016.
Commins, David. "Modernism," in John L. Esposito, ed., *The Oxford Encyclopedia of the Modern Islamic World*. Oxford Islamic Studies Online, http://www.oxfordislamicstudies.com/article/opr/t236MIW/e0539 (accessed June 28, 2020).
Cook, David. *Studies in Muslim Apocalyptic*. Darwin Press, 2002.
Cook, Michael. *Commanding Right and Forbidding Wrong in Islamic Thought*. Cambridge University Press, 2010.
Cook, Michael. *Forbidding Wrong in Islam: An Introduction*. Cambridge University Press, 2012.
Cook, Michael. "Vices and Virtues," in Jane Dammen McAuliffe, ed., *Encyclopedia of the Qur'an*. Brill, 2006, vol. 5, pp. 436–43.
Coury, Ralph M. *Sceptics of Islam: Revisionist Religion, Agnosticism, and Disbelief in the Modern Arab World*. I.B. Tauris, 2018.
Crawford, Michael. *Ibn Abd al-Wahhab*. One World, 2014.
Dawud, Aziz. *al-Jam'iyyat al-islamiyyah fi misr wa dawruha fi nashr al-da'wah al-islamiyyah* (The Islamic Groups in Egypt and their role in spreading the Islamic call). Al-Zahra li'l-i'lam al-'Arabi, 1992.
Denny, Frederick. *An Introduction to Islam*, 4th ed. Pearson Hall, 2011.
Dickinson, Eerik. *The Development of Early Sunnite Hadith Criticism: The Taqdima of Ibn Abi Hatim al-Razi*. Brill, 2001
Egger, Vernon O. *A History of the Muslim World to 1750: The Making of a Civilization*, 2nd ed. Routledge, 2017.
Eickelman, Dale. "The Art of Memory and Its Social Reproduction." *Comparative Studies in Society and History* 20:4 (1978), 485–516.
El Omari, Rachel. "Mu'tazilah," in John Esposito, ed., *The Oxford Encyclopedia of the Islamic World*. Oxford Islamic Studies Online, http://www.oxfordislamicstudies.com/article/opr/t236/e1073 (accessed June 30, 2020).
El Shamsy, Ahmed. "Fiqh al-Sunnah," in John Esposito, ed., *The Oxford Encyclopedia of the Islamic World*. Oxford Islamic Studies Online, http://www.oxfordislamicstudies.com/article/opr/t236/e0937 (accessed June 28, 2020).
Encyclopaedia of Islam, 2nd ed., P Bearman, Th. Bianquis, C. E. Bosworth, E. van Donzel, and W. P. Heinrichs, eds. Brill, 2006.
Encyclopedia of the Qur'an, Jane Dammen McAuliffe, ed. Brill, 2006.
Ende, W. "Mudjawir," *Encyclopaedia of Islam*, 2nd ed. Brill, 2006.

Fabietti, Ugo. "State Policies and Bedouin Adaptations in Saudi Arabia, 1900–1980," in Martha Mundy and Basim Musallam, eds., *The Transformation of Nomadic Society in the Arab East*, Cambridge University Press, 2000, pp. 82–9.

Farquhar, Michael. *Circuits of Faith: Migration, Education, and the Wahhabi Mission*. Stanford University Press, 2016.

Fehervari, G. "Mihrab," *Encyclopaedia of Islam*, 2nd ed. Brill, 2006.

Ferris, Thomas. "Riding the Saudi Boom," *New York Times*, March 25, 1979.

Fierro, Maribel. "al-Tabarani," *Encyclopaedia of Islam*, 2nd ed. Brill, 2006.

Filiu, Jean-Pierre. *Apocalypse in Islam*. University of California Press, 2011.

Fück, J. W. "Ibn Hibban," *Encyclopaedia of Islam*, 2nd ed. Brill, 2006.

Fück, J. W. "Ibn Madja," *Encyclopaedia of Islam*, 2nd ed. Brill, 2006.

Gauvain, Richard. *Salafi Ritual Purity: In the Presence of God*. Routledge, 2013.

Gilliot, Cl. "'Ulama," *Encyclopaedia of Islam*, 2nd ed. Brill, 2006.

Goldziher, I., and J. Schacht, "Fikh," *Encyclopaedia of Islam*, 2nd ed. Brill, 2006.

Habib, John S. *Ibn Sa'ud's Warriors of Islam: The Ikhwan of Najd and Their Role in the Creation of the Sa'udi Kingdom, 1910–1930*. Brill, 1978.

Haq, S. Nomanul. "Rukn," *Encyclopaedia of Islam*, 2nd ed. Brill, 2006.

Hasson, Isaac. "Last Judgment," in Jane Dammen McAuliffe, ed., *Encyclopedia of the Qur'an*. Brill, 2006, vol. 3, 136–45.

Hayes, Stephen D. "Riyadh on the Move," *Aramco World* 31:4 (July/August 1980), 26–32.

Haykel, Bernard. "On the Nature of Salafi Thought and Action," in Roel Meijer, ed. *Global Salafism: Islam's New Religious Movement*. Columbia University Press, 2009, pp. 33–57.

Haykel, Bernard. *Revival and Reform in Islam: The Legacy of Muhammad Al-Shawkani*. Cambridge University Press, 2003.

Hays, Christopher B. "'Proto-Apocalyptic Constellations in the Bible and the Ancient Near East," in Justin Jeffcoat Schedtler and Kelly J. Murphy, eds., *Apocalypses in Context: Apocalyptic Currents throughout History*. Augsburg Fortress, 2016, pp. 37–59.

Holden, David, and Richard Johns. *The House of Saud: The Rise and Rule of the Most Powerful Dynasty in the Arab World*. Holt, Rinehart, and Winston, 1982.

Ibrahim, Saad Eddin. "Anatomy of Egypt's Militant Islamic Groups: Methodological Note and Preliminary Findings." *International Journal of Middle East Studies* 12:4 (1980), 423–53.

Inayatullah, Sh. "Ahl-i Hadith," *Encyclopaedia of Islam*, 2nd ed. Brill, 2006.

Jansen, Johannes J. G. "Kishk, Abd al-Hamid," in John L. Esposito, *Oxford Encyclopedia of the Modern Islamic World*. Oxford Islamic Studies Online, http://www.oxfordislamicstudies.com/article/opr/t236MIW/e0465 (accessed 28-Jun-2020).

Jones, J. M. B. "Ibn Ishak," *Encylopaedia of Islam*, 2nd ed. Brill, 2006.

Jones, Toby Craig. "Rebellion on the Saudi Periphery: Modernity, Marginalization, and the Shi'a Uprising of 1979." *International Journal of Middle East Studies* 38:2 (2006), 213–33.

Juynboll, G. H. A. "al-Tirmidhi," *Encyclopaedia of Islam*, 2nd ed. Brill, 2006.

Juynboll, G. H. A. "Muslim b. al-Hadjdjadj," *Encyclopaedia of Islam*, 2nd ed. Brill, 2006.

Karagozoglu, Mustafa Macit. "Contested Avenues in Post-Classical Sunni Hadith Criticism: A Reading through the Lens of *al-Mughni 'an al-Hifz wa-l-kitab*." *Journal of Islamic Studies* 29:2 (2018), 149–80.

Katakura, Motoko. *Bedouin Village: A Study of a Saudi Arabian People in Transition*. University of Tokyo Press, 1977.

Kechichian, Joseph. "Islamic Revivalism and Change in Saudi Arabia: Juhayman al-'Utaybi's 'Letters' to the Saudi People." *Muslim World* 80:1 (1990), 1–16.

Kister, M. J. "Djabir ibn Abd Allah," *Encyclopaedia of Islam*, 2nd ed. Brill, 2006.
Kister, M. J. "Makam Ibrahim," *Encyclopaedia of Islam*, 2nd ed. Brill, 2006.
Kurpershoek, Marcel. *Arabia of the Bedouins*. Saqi, 2002.
Kurpershoek, P. M. *A Saudi Tribal History: Honour and Faith in the Traditions of the Dawasir*. Brill, 2002
Lacey, Robert. *Inside the Kingdom: Kings, Clerics, Modernists, Terrorists, and the Struggle for Saudi Arabia*. Viking, 2009.
Lacey, Robert. *The Kingdom: Arabia and the House of Saud*. Avon, 1983.
Lacroix, Stephane. *Awakening Islam: The Politics of Religious Dissent in Contemporary Saudi Arabia*. Harvard University Press, 2011.
Lacroix, Stephane. "Between Revolution and Apoliticism: Nasir al-Din al-Albani and His Impact on the Shaping of Contemporary Salafism," in Roel Meijer, ed., *Global Salafism: Islam's New Religious Movement*. Columbia University Press, 2009, pp. 58–80.
Lacroix, Stephane, and Thomas Hegghammer. "Rejectionist Islamism in Saudi Arabia: The Story of Juhayman al-'Utaybi Revisited." *International Journal of Middle East Studies* 39:1 (2007), 103–22.
Landau, L. M. "Taswir," *Encyclopaedia of Islam*, 2nd ed. Brill, 2006.
Laoust, H. "Ahmad b. Hanbal," *Encyclopedia of Islam*, 2nd ed., Brill, 2006.
Laoust, H. "Hanabila," *Encyclopaedia of Islam*, 2nd ed. Brill, 2006.
Laoust, H. "Ibn al-Farra," *Encyclopaedia of Islam*, 2nd ed. Brill, 2006.
Laoust, H. "Ibn Kathir," *Encyclopaedia of Islam*, 2nd ed. Brill, 2006.
Laoust, H. "Ibn Kayyim al-Djawzyya," *Encyclopaedia of Islam*, 2nd ed. Brill, 2006.
Laoust, H. "Ibn Taymiyya," *Encyclopaedia of Islam*, 2nd ed. Brill, 2006.
Larocco, James. Interview, "Rich and Eager to Buy–Saudi Arabia in the Oil Boom '70s," Moments in US Diplomatic History. Online: https://adst.org/2016/04/smelly-rich-and-eager-to-buy-saudi-arabia-in-the-oil-boom-70s/ (accessed June 30, 2020).
Lecker, M. "Ibn Shihab al-Zuhri," *Encyclopaedia of Islam*, 2nd ed. Brill, 2006.
Leemhuis, Frederik. "Apocalypse," in Jane Dammen McAuliffe, ed., *Encyclopedia of the Qur'an*. Brill, 2006, vol. 1, pp. 11–14.
Lings, Martin. *Muhammad: His Life Based on the Earliest Sources*. Inner Traditions International, 1983.
Madelung, Wilferd. "'Abd Allah B. Al-Zubayr and the Mahdi." *Journal of Near Eastern Studies*, 40:4, Arabic and Islamic Studies in Honor of Nabia Abbott: Part Two (October 1981), 291–305.
Madelung, Wilferd. "al-Mahdi," *Encyclopaedia of Islam*, 2nd ed. Brill, 2006.
Madelung, Wilferd. "Karmati," *Encyclopaedia of Islam*, 2nd ed. Brill, 2006.
Madelung, Wilferd. "Talha," *Encyclopaedia of Islam*, 2nd ed. Brill, 2006.
Makdisi, G. "Ibn Kudama," *Encyclopaedia of Islam*, 2nd ed. Brill, 2006.
Makki, M. S. *Medina, Saudi Arabia: A Geographical Analysis of the City and Region*. Avebury, 1982.
Merad, A. "Islah," *Encyclopaedia of Islam*, 2nd ed. Brill, 2006.
Metcalf, Barbara. *Islamic Revivalism in British India: Deoband, 1860–1900*. Princeton University Press, 1982.
Mir, Mustansir. "Tafsir," in John L. Esposito, ed., *The Oxford Encyclopedia of the Islamic World*. Oxford Islamic Studies Online, http://www.oxfordislamicstudies.com/article/opr/t236MIW/e0775 (accessed June 30, 2020).
Mitchell, Richard P. *The Society of Muslim Brothers*. Oxford University Press, 1993.
Motzki, H. "Sa'id b. Dubayr," *Encyclopaedia of Islam*, 2nd ed. Brill, 2006.

Mouline, Nabil. *The Clerics of Islam: Religious Authority and Political Power in Saudi Arabia*, Ethan S. Rundell, trans. Yale University Press, 2014.
Naficy, Said. "Ahmad al-Baihaki," *Encyclopaedia of Islam*, 2nd ed. Brill, 2006.
Nahedh, Monera. "The Sedentarization of a Bedouin Community in Saudi Arabia," doctoral dissertation, University of Leeds, 1989.
Ochsenwald, William. "The Annexation of the Hijaz," in Mohammed Ayoob and Hasan Kosebalaban, eds., *Religion and Politics in Saudi Arabia*. Lynne Rienner, 2009, pp. 75–89.
Pall, Zoltan. *Salafism in Lebanon: Local and Transnational Movements*. Cambridge University Press, 2018.
Paret, R., and E. Chaumont. "'Umra," *Encyclopaedia of Islam*, 2nd ed. Brill, 2006.
Pellat, Ch. "Ibn Abd al-Barr," *Encyclopaedia of Islam*, 2nd ed. Brill, 2006.
Pellat, Ch. "Ibn Djuraydj," *Encylopaedia of Islam*, 2nd ed. Brill, 2006.
Peters, F. E. *Mecca: A Literary History of the Muslim Holy Land*. Princeton University Press, 1994.
Quandt, William B. *Peace Process: American Diplomacy and the Arab-Israeli Conflict since 1967*, 3rd ed. Brookings Institution, 2005.
Qurashi, M. M. "The Tabligh Movement: Some Observations." *Islamic Studies* 28:3 (1989), 237–48.
Ritter, H. "Hasan al-Basri," *Encyclopaedia of Islam*, 2nd ed. Brill, 2006.
Robson, J. "Abu Da'ud al-Sidjistani," *Encyclopaedia of Islam*, 2nd ed. Brill, 2006.
Robson, J. "Abu Hurayrah," *Encyclopaedia of Islam*, 2nd ed. Brill, 2006.
Robson, J. "al-Baghawi," *Encyclopaedia of Islam*, 2nd ed. Brill, 2006.
Robson, J. "Bid'a," *Encyclopaedia of Islam*, 2nd ed. Brill, 2006.
Robson, J. "al-Bukhari, Muhammad b. Isma'il," *Encyclopaedia of Islam*, 2nd ed. Brill, 2006.
Robson, J. "al-Daraqutni," *Encylopaedia of Islam*, 2nd ed. Brill, 2006.
Robson, J. "Hadith," *Encyclopaedia of Islam*, 2nd ed. Brill, 2006.
Robson, J. "al-Hakim al-Naysapuri," *Encylopaedia of Islam*, 2nd ed. Brill, 2006.
Roded, Ruth. "Umm Salama Hind," *Encyclopaedia of Islam*, 2nd ed. Brill, 2006.
Rosenthal, F. "al-Safadi," *Encyclopaedia of Islam*, 2nd ed. Brill, 2006.
Rosenthal, F. "Ibn Hadjar al-Askalani," *Encyclopaedia of Islam*, 2nd ed. Brill, 2006.
Schacht, J. "Abd al-Rahman al-Akhdari," *Encyclopaedia of Islam*, 2nd ed. Brill, 2006.
Schacht, J. "Ahl al-Hadith," *Encyclopaedia of Islam*, 2nd ed. Brill, 2006.
Schacht, J., and D. B. MacDonald. "Idjtihad," *Encyclopaedia of Islam*, 2nd ed. Brill, 2006.
Schedtler, Justin Jeffcoat, and Kelly J. Murphy, "Introduction: From before the Bible to Beyond the Bible," in Schedlter and Murphy, eds., *Apocalypses in Context: Apocalyptic Currents throughout History*. Augsburg Fortress, 2016, pp. 3–17.
Schoeler, G. "Urwa ibn al-Zubayr," *Encyclopaedia of Islam*, 2nd ed. Brill, 2006.
Sirriyeh, Elizabeth. *Dreams and Visions in the World of Islam*. I.B. Tauris, 2015.
Stark, Rodney, and William Sims Bainbridge. "Of Churches, Sects and Cults: Preliminary Concepts for a Theory of Religious Movements." *Journal for the Scientific Study of Religion* 18:2 (1979), 117–33.
Stark, Rodney, and William Sims Bainbridge. "Sectarian Tension." *Review of Religious Research* 22:2 (December 1980), 105–24.
Thurston, Alexander. *Salafism in Nigeria*. Cambridge University Press, 2016.
Toufic, Fahd. "Ibn Sirin," *Encyclopaedia of Islam*, 2nd ed. Brill, 2006.
Trofimov, Yaroslav. *The Siege of Mecca: The Forgotten Uprising in Islam's Holiest Shrine and the Birth of Al-Qaeda*. Doubleday, 2007.
Turki, Abdel-Magid. "Zahiriyya," *Encyclopaedia of Islam*, 2nd ed. Brill, 2006.

Vadet, J.-C. "Ibn Dawud," *Encyclopaedia of Islam*, 2nd ed. Brill, 2006.
Vadet, J.-C. "Ibn Mas'ud," *Encyclopaedia of Islam*, 2nd ed. Brill, 2006.
Vaglieri, L. Veccia. "'Abd Allah b. 'Umar b. al-Khattab," *Encyclopaedia of Islam*, 2nd ed. Brill, 2006.
Vaglieri, L. Veccia. "Hafsa," *Encyclopaedia of Islam*, 2nd ed. Brill, 2006.
Vasiliev, Alexei. *The History of Saudi Arabia*. New York University Press, 2000.
Wagemakers, Joas. *A Quietist Jihadi: The Ideology and Influence of Abu Muhammad al-Maqdisi*. Cambridge University Press, 2012.
Watt, W. Montgomery. "A'ishah Bint Abi Bakr," *Encyclopaedia of Islam*, 2nd ed. Brill, 2006.
Watt, W. Montgomery. "Djahmiyya," *Encyclopaedia of Islam*, 2nd ed. Brill, 2006.
Watt, W. Montgomery. *Muhammad at Medina*. Clarendon Press, 1956.
Wensinck, A. J. "al-Nasa'i," *Encyclopaedia of Islam*, 2nd ed. Brill, 2006.
Wensinck, A. J., and T. Fahd, "Sura," *Encyclopaedia of Islam*, 2nd ed. Brill, 2006.
Wensinck, A. J., Jomier, J., and Lewis, B. "Hadjdj," *Encyclopaedia of Islam*, 2nd ed. Brill, 2006.
Wiktorowicz, Quintan, "The New Global Threat: Transnational Salafis and Jihad." *Middle East Policy* 8:1 (2001), 18–38.
Zettersteen, K. V. "Al-Nu'man b. Bashir," *Encyclopaedia of Islam*, 2nd ed. Brill, 2006.

GLOSSARY

Companions: Men and women who embraced Islam and personally knew the Prophet Muhammad. Sunnis consider them an authoritative source for religious knowledge.

Dar al-Hadith: A school for teaching Prophetic Traditions established in 1931 by Ahmad Dihlawi, an Indian religious scholar who came to Saudi Arabia from Delhi in 1926.

Dervish: An adherent of the ascetic, mystical tradition in Islam known as Sufism.

Dhu al-Hijjah: The twelfth month in the Muslim lunar calendar.

Dhu al-Qa'dah: The eleventh month in the Muslim lunar calendar.

Fatwa: The opinion or ruling of an expert in Islamic law.

Hadith: A Prophetic Tradition that reports the Prophet's words or actions.

Hajj: The annual pilgrimage to Mecca.

Hanafi: One of the four legal schools in Sunni Islam.

Hanbali: One of the four legal schools in Sunni Islam and the official legal school in Saudi Arabia.

Haram: The Grand Mosque in Mecca, the holiest site in Islam.

Hijrah: A colony for settling nomads during the 1910s and 1920s. SEE Ikhwan.

Ijtihad: Independent reasoning to arrive at a ruling on a legal question without precedent.

Ikhwan: The "old" Ikhwan, or Brethren, were former nomadic tribesmen who settled in agricultural colonies during the 1910s and 1920s and comprised part of the military forces backing the revival of Saudi power. Members of the Salafi Group in the 1960s and 1970s adopted the name Ikhwan as well.

Imam: A leader of congregational prayer.

Jahmites: A classical Muslim theological tendency associated with the doctrine that the Quran is created, not the eternal word of God. Salafis consider that doctrine to be heretical.

Jami: Followers of Muhammad Aman al-Jami, a teacher at the Islamic University of Medina, known for refraining from engagement in political activity.

Kaabah: The cube-like structure at the center of the Grand Mosque toward which Muslims face when they pray.

Kharijite: An early Muslim group at war with other Muslims over questions of political leadership and doctrine.

Madhhab: A legal school in the sense of a method for deciding matters of religious law (shari'ah) on the basis of the Quran and the Sunnah.

Mahdi:	"The rightly guided one" is a messianic figure who will establish the reign of justice.
Maliki:	One of the four legal schools in Sunni Islam.
Mihrab:	A niche in the wall of a mosque to indicate the direction of Mecca toward which Muslims face during prayer.
Mufti:	An expert in Islamic law authorized to issue a legal opinion or ruling.
Muharram:	The first month in the Muslim lunar calendar.
Mujtahid:	An expert in Islamic law qualified to undertake independent reasoning on legal issues without precedent.
Mu'tazilites:	A classical Muslim theological tendency that adopted rationalistic interpretations of theological issues. The Hanbali–Salafi tradition considers their positions to be heretical.
Quraish:	The tribe of the Prophet Muhammad. Sunni doctrine holds that descent from the Prophet's tribe of Quraish is a necessary qualification for the caliphate.
Ramadan:	The ninth month in the Muslim lunar calendar. Observing a daytime fast is one of the fundamental religious duties for Muslims.
Sahwah:	The "Awakening" is a Saudi religious movement that arose in the 1980s and that blended Wahhabi theology with political activism along the lines of the Muslim Brotherhood.
Al-Salaf al-Salih:	The Pious Ancestors are the first three generations of Muslims. For Sunni Muslims, they represent Islam in its pristine form.
Shafi'i:	One of the four legal schools in Sunni Islam.
Shari'ah:	Islamic law.
Sharif:	Someone claiming descent from the Prophet Muhammad.
Sunnah:	The Prophet's custom—his words and actions—that sets a normative example for believers. The Sunnah consists of thousands of Prophetic Traditions, known as hadiths.
Sururi:	An activist version of Salafism named for Muhammad Surur Zain al-Abidin, a Syrian Muslim Brother who found asylum in Saudi Arabia.
Takbirah/takbir:	Pronouncing *Allahu Akbar* in the call to prayer.
Takfir:	Excommunication; declaring another Muslim to be an infidel.
Ulama:	Muslim religious scholars.
Ummah:	The community of believers encompassing all Muslims.
Umrah:	The "lesser pilgrimage" to Mecca may be performed at any time of year, in contrast to the major pilgrimage, or hajj, that is performed during the first ten days of Dhu'l Hijjah.
Zahiri:	An early legal school known for strictly following the literal meaning of the Quran and the Sunnah.

INDEX

Abd al-Khaliq, Abd al-Rahman 71–2, 143, 161 n.20
Akbar, Yusuf 86–7, 133, 151, 171 n.176
Albani, Muhammad Nasir al-Din al- 74, 135, 145
  background 30
  controversial legal opinions 31, 59
  excommunication doctrine 43, 86, 150
  friction with Muslim Brotherhood 41
  friction with Saudi clerics 96
  Islamic University of Medina 31
  Juhaiman's criticism of 32, 114
  Salafi Group, influence on 31–2, 34, 76–7, 107, 119, 136–7
  scholastic method 30
  writings 71–3, 144
Ansar al-Sunnah 37, 39, 43, 76, 114, 117, 145–6, 174 n.236

Banna, Hasan al- 39–40, 73–4
Buraidah Ikhwan 58, 87–8

Committee for Commanding Right and Forbidding Wrong 22, 33, 39, 73, 147

Dar al-Hadith 29, 74, 97, 104
Dirbas, Abd al-Latif al- 94, 148

Excommunication and Emigration Group 42–4, 85–7, 145, 150
  see also Society of Muslims

Faisal, Faisal Muhammad 90
  excommunication doctrine 85–6, 150–1
  Mecca uprising, account of 99–104, 124
  withdrawal from society 114–15

Haidari, Muhammad al- 72, 92–3
Hanafi legal school 25, 35, 73, 79, 81
Hanbali legal school
  history of 25, 27
  Salafi dissent 31, 36, 73
  Saudi clerics 35–6, 55, 73, 81, 88, 145
Haram Institute 31, 75, 77–9
Harbi, Abd Allah al- 85, 126
  death at checkpoint 100

Mahdi, doubts about 99–100
  Salafi Group, role in 74–6, 79–81, 148

Ibn Abd al-Wahhab, Muhammad 48, 73, 122
  career 14–15, 51
  excommunication doctrine 42
  Salafi Group, influence on 34, 137
  teachings 14, 24, 27, 55
Ibn Baz, Abd al-Aziz 113, 144
  Albani's suspicion of 32, 96
  Huzaimi's studies with 93, 96, 98
  Juhaiman's essays 95
  Juhaiman's opposition to 60, 96
  Salafi Group, supervisor of 29, 56, 84, 135–7, 144
Ibn Bijad, Sultan 44, 46–7, 83, 136
Ibn Hazm, Ali ibn Ahmad 35, 79–81, 145, 147
Ibn Qayyim al-Jawziyyah, Muhammad 34, 39, 77, 86, 137, 150
Ibn Sahl, Mutlaq 76, 92, 94–5
Ibn Saud, Abd al-Aziz 16, 51
  annexation of holy cities 27–9, 35
  clash with Old Ikhwan 17, 44–6, 83, 135
  Juhaiman's attitude toward 44, 46–7, 83, 117–18, 122, 167 n.114
  policies toward Bedouin 48
  relations with outside world 55, 57
Ibn Shtaiwi, Sulaiman 76, 84, 89, 92, 96, 119, 136, 139
Ibn Subayyil, Muhammad 35, 79, 101–2
Ibn Taymiyyah, Ahmad Taqi al-Din 34, 43, 77, 86, 89, 137, 150
Ikhwan in Obedience to God (the Old Ikhwan)
  history of 17, 44
  Juhaiman, influence on 46–7, 50–1, 83, 135–6, 141, 144, 146
  Juhaiman's writings, in 117–18, 167 n.114
  rebellion 45–6
Islamic University of Medina 97, 136, 151
  Ansar al-Sunnah 39
  foreign students 87, 89
  history of 29–30, 34
  Salafi Group, influence on 31–2, 138, 143
  Salafi Group members 84, 86, 93
Society of Muslims 43, 85

Jaza'iri, Abu Bakr Jabir al- 53, 84, 90, 137, 149, 151

Kharijites
  comparison to Wahhabi mission 42, 55
  excommunication doctrine 43, 86, 150–1
  history of 11–12
Kuwaiti Salafis 56, 59, 71, 76, 81, 144

Mahdi
  apocalyptical beliefs about 60, 62–4, 139–40, 146
  dreams about 119–24
  hadiths about 11–13, 62–3, 125–7, 130–3
  history of 11–13
  Juhaiman's belief in 19, 43–4, 97–8, 116–17, 142
  Mecca uprising 5, 99–104, 151–2
  see also Qahtani, Muhammad Abd Allah al-
Mazrui, Ali al- 75, 84, 138
  arrested 92
  banned from teaching 88
  controversial legal opinions 36, 88, 151
  Mahdi, doubts about 99, 124
  personal library 77, 147
  teaching at Dar al-Hadith 31, 74, 85
  Zahiri legal school 145
Mu'allam, Ahmad Hasan al- 76
  fugitive 92–3, 96
  Juhaiman's essays 86, 97
  Salafi Group leadership 86, 90, 93, 138, 151
Muslim Brotherhood 83, 140, 144
  history of 18, 37–43
  Juhaiman's views on 114, 117, 141
  Kuwait 71
  Saudi Arabia 72–4, 92, 110, 135–7
Mustafa, Shukri 42–3, 85–6, 150

Nafi'i, A'id ibn Duraimeeh al- 74–6, 92
Najdi, Abd al-Aziz ibn Rashid al- 79–81, 151

Qahtani, Muhammad Abd Allah al-
  arrested 92
  dreams about 62–3
  Juhaiman's essays 86, 97, 150
  Mahdi 98–9, 124, 140, 149
  Mecca uprising 63, 87, 100, 102–3, 128, 151
  rejection of public schools 107–10
Qutb, Sayyid 40, 42, 71, 73–4, 87

Rashidi, Badi al Din ibn Ihsanallah Shah al- 78–80, 92, 95, 102, 145

Rashidi, Nur al-Din ibn Badi al Din al- 75, 80, 102, 152

Sabilah 46–8, 83, 135, 141, 144, 146, 166 n.113
Sadhan, Abd al-Aziz al- 93–4, 108, 148
Sajir
  history of 44
  Juhaiman's hometown 44, 50, 83, 104, 135
  Juhaiman as fugitive 53, 92, 94
  opposition to Saudi rulers 46, 83
  Salafi Group members 76, 100, 107
Salafism 145
  alignment with Wahhabism 28
  canonical writings 33–4
  challenge to legal schools 26
  definition of 17–18
  dreams, belief in 120–1
  see also Albani, Muhammad Nasir al-Din al-
Sheikh, Isam 85–6, 90, 115, 150–1
Shiites 24, 36
  history of 11–13
  Juhaiman's views on 47, 117–18, 122
  1979 uprising 2–3, 6
  Wahhabi doctrine on 14–15, 45
Shuraimi, Khalid al- 87, 93, 96, 98
Society of Muslims 37, 40, 42–3, 85
  see also Excommunication and Emigration Group

Tablighi Association 117, 138
  history of 37–8
  Juhaiman's views on 135, 141, 143–4
  Kuwait 71
  Salafi Group, influence on 38, 43, 83, 110, 136
  Saudi Arabia 41, 73–5, 81
Tamimi, Sa'd al- 76, 84, 89–90, 136, 139
Tuwaijiri, Hammud al- 51, 77, 88, 110–13, 121–2

Utaibi, Juhaiman al-
  background 17, 43–4, 46–50, 83, 104, 135
  dreams, belief in 61–3, 121, 150
  education 50, 97, 104
  excommunication doctrine 43, 85–6, 145, 150–1
  dissident faction 24, 52–3, 59–60, 90, 149
  fugitive 53–4, 59, 91–5
  Islamic movements, views on 38, 41, 110, 114, 136, 140–1
  Mahdi, belief in 19, 60–3, 97–8, 124, 139–41
  Mecca uprising 1, 5–7, 63–4, 99–104, 124–33
  Old Ikhwan, influence of 44, 46–7, 135–6, 141, 146

personality 2, 52, 141
preaching 51, 82, 90, 139, 144
rejection of clerical authority 27, 37 44, 50–1, 53, 57–8, 89–90, 105–6
rejection of public schools 107–8
rejection of Saudi rulers 23, 32, 47, 17–18

Wadi'i Muqbil al- 76–7, 81, 85, 92–3
Wahhabism
  comparison to Islamic movements 8

cooperation with foreign Muslims 28, 32
excommunication doctrine 42
history of 14–17, 27, 44–5, 55–6
rejection of Western culture 21–2, 51–2
Saudi government agencies 28–9

Yami, Khalid al- 102, 125, 151

Zahiri legal school 35, 79–81, 145
Zamil, Ahmad al- 85, 90, 92, 96, 115, 151